The Epistemology of Belief

Also by Hamid Vahid

EPISTEMIC JUSTIFICATION AND THE SKEPTICAL CHALLENGE

The Epistemology of Belief

Hamid Vahid
Institute for Fundamental Sciences (IPM)

palgrave
macmillan

First published 2009 by
PALGRAVE MACMILLAN

Palgrave Macmillan in the UK is an imprint of Macmillan Publishers Limited, registered in England, company number 785998, of Houndmills, Basingstoke, Hampshire RG21 6XS.

Palgrave Macmillan in the US is a division of St Martin's Press LLC, 175 Fifth Avenue, New York, NY 10010.

Palgrave Macmillan is the global academic imprint of the above companies and has companies and representatives throughout the world.

Palgrave® and Macmillan® are registered trademarks in the United States, the United Kingdom, Europe and other countries.

ISBN-13: 978–0–230–20146–0 hardback
ISBN-10: 0–230–20146–6 hardback

This book is printed on paper suitable for recycling and made from fully managed and sustained forest sources. Logging, pulping and manufacturing processes are expected to conform to the environmental regulations of the country of origin.

A catalogue record for this book is available from the British Library.

Library of Congress Cataloging-in-Publication Data
Vahid, Hamid, 1959–
   The epistemology of belief / Hamid Vahid.
      p.   cm.
   Includes bibliographical references (p.   ) and index.
   ISBN 978–0–230–20146–0 (alk. paper)
   1. Knowledge, Theory of (Religion)   2. Belief and doubt.   I. Title.
   BL51.V325 2008
   212′.6—dc22   2008027564

10   9   8   7   6   5   4   3   2   1
18   17   16   15   14   13   12   11   10   09

Printed and bound in Great Britain by
CPI Antony Rowe, Chippenham and Eastbourne

Contents

Acknowledgements

Epistemology today is a thriving subject influencing every area of philosophy. The epistemological issues involving the nature of belief make it one of the central topics in the history of epistemology. My goal in this book is to provide an in-depth analysis of certain distinctive epistemological features of belief and their consequences against the background of some widely held views in philosophy.

In writing this book, I have been fortunate to receive help and assistance from many colleagues, friends and students. I am particularly indebted to those who gave me feedback on close ancestors of various parts of this book: Jonathan Adler, Keith Korcz, Peter Markie, Brian McLaughlin, Ernest Sosa, Jonathan Vogel, John Williams and Tim Williamson. Special thanks are due to my generous friend Muhammad Legenhausen with whom I discussed the issues raised in this book on many occasions. Thanks are also due to the Institute for Fundamental Sciences (IPM) for providing me with support while I worked on this project. In addition, I would like to thank the students in my epistemology and philosophy of language classes at IPM for their useful feedback on earlier drafts. I also owe a debt of gratitude to my family who cheerfully put up with me while I was engaged in writing.

Finally, I would like to thank the editors and publishers of *Philosophy and Phenomenological Research*, *Philosophical Studies* and *Metaphilosophy* for permission to reuse and rework material from my papers in those journals.

Introduction

This book is primarily concerned with delineating certain salient epistemological features of belief. Beliefs are generally distinguished from other cognitive states by possessing certain epistemic traits. When we ascribe beliefs and desires to a certain creature, we are, in effect, trying to make rational sense of its doings. Rationality and coherence are thus of the essence of belief. It has, however, been claimed that these epistemic characteristics of belief are not only threatened by internal incoherence but also by certain widely shared views in recent philosophical thought. This book aims at challenging such claims by providing an in-depth analysis of some of these distinctive features of belief and their consequences. My principle objective is to provide a re-examination of the epistemic features of belief and show how they can be consistent with some of the widely held views in philosophy, yielding, in the end, a unified and coherent picture of the epistemology of belief.

Belief is generally thought to be the primary cognitive state representing the world as being in a certain way, regulating our behavior and guiding us around the world. It functions, in Ramsey's word, like a map by which we steer. It has a representational content that is deemed correct or true in case its content matches what it is intended to represent. In addition to having a particular propositional content, beliefs stand in various psychological relations to an agent's other beliefs, to his non-doxastic psychological states and to actions he imitates. There are, however, certain salient epistemic features of belief that render it a distinctive cognitive state. These include, first and foremost, its commitment to the truth of the proposition that constitutes its content. Unless one has grasped that truth bears this constitutive relation to belief, they will not have grasped the meaning of "belief."

Beliefs are also distinguished by the fact that they are sensitive to evidence. The reasonableness or warrant of belief, thus, hinges on

1

its possession of adequate grounds. Of particular importance is the rationality of perceptual beliefs that are governed by evidential norms in the sense that a rational perceptual belief is one that is supported by sensory evidence. The immediate question is how, as in certain epistemological theories, one can appeal to sensory experiences to give an account of the justification of perceptual beliefs. Another pertinent question concerns the nature of the relation which justified that beliefs stand in with their justification-conferring grounds. This is the problem of the basing relation where the existing attempts at explicating what it is for justified beliefs to be based on their grounds have all been unsatisfying for some reason or another.

Assuming that perceptual experiences are able to justify the beliefs they cause, on a prominent theory of the structure of justification, the ensuing justified beliefs, called "basic" beliefs, are then standardly taken to constitute the foundation of an agent's belief system. Given certain plausible assumptions, these basic beliefs give rise to the idea that has come to be known as the basic knowledge thesis. It has been argued recently that such a position falls victim to the so-called problem of easy knowledge, the idea that, on such theories, certain inferences, involving closure and bootstrapping, allow us far too easily to acquire knowledge (justification) that seems unlikely under the envisaged circumstances. It has further been claimed that certain closure inferences involving basic knowledge are actually instances of the failure of transmission of warrant across entailment. What has added to the interest in these problems is the claim (made by some philosophers) that answering these questions would enable us to explain our felt dissatisfaction with Moore's famous "proof" of the external world and arguments that purportedly share a similar structure.

Basic beliefs are also said to be fallible in that holding a belief attitude towards a relevant proposition does not entail that the proposition in question is true. There is also the fact that we seem to be good at finding out about our beliefs. Such knowledge seems to be direct and immediate in the sense that there is no other thing that one needs to know or observe from which one can infer that one is holding the beliefs in question. There is, of course, a question mark hanging over the extent to which knowledge of our beliefs is direct and immediate or our ordinary practices of ascribing beliefs are fallible – especially in the light of the recent externalist theories of content.

To tackle these issues, I begin by looking at the thesis that, unlike other cognitive states, beliefs are constitutively linked with the truth of their contents. This feature of belief has been famously captured in the thesis that believing is a purposive state aiming at truth. It has however proved to be notoriously difficult to explain what the thesis really involves. The first three chapters deal with the truth-directedness or truth-sensitivity of belief, its consequences and the problems it gives rise to. The first chapter critically examines a number of recent attempts to unpack the metaphor that beliefs aim at truth. I shall highlight an important distinction between, what I call, the doxastic and epistemic goals and then proceed to illustrate how some of the recent accounts of the aim-of-belief thesis have failed to respect this distinction. Finally, I shall propose my own story of what the thesis involves while emphasizing its deflationary nature. The bulk of the second chapter is taken up with seeing how the truth-directed nature of belief gives rise to the so-called Moore's paradoxes. Despite differing over details, all the attempted resolutions of Moore's paradox tend to see the absurdity of Moorean sentences as eventually stemming, one way or another, from the violation of the law of non-contradiction.

While some philosophers construe the problem with such sentences as involving some sort of pragmatic contradiction arising from their assertion, others seek to locate the source of paradox in the alleged fact that such sentences cannot consistently be believed. Still others seem to think that what gives rise to the paradox is the violation of certain necessary conditions of epistemic justification. In this chapter I shall try to uncover a common pattern among all this diversity, and show how these disparate approaches to the paradox appeal to analogous strategies to resolve it. They are subsequently criticized by calling into question the principles they help themselves with to tackle the problem. Finally, I shall propose my own solution of the paradox according to which Moorean sentences are defective not because of some associated logical impropriety but because their assertion violates a certain interpretive constraint, namely the principle of charity, on an adequate theory of meaning. What these findings indicate about the nature of belief is that when we ascribe beliefs and desires to a certain creature, we are, in effect, trying to make rational sense of its doings. These results square nicely with the account developed in Chapter 1.

Next, to develop further the theses propounded with regard to the truth-directed character of belief, I turn (in Chapter 3) to two competing requirements for knowledge, namely sensitivity and safety. Both requirements have been subjected to a variety of Gettier-type examples for and against them. While focusing mostly on safety, I shall try to evaluate these criticisms by putting a new gloss on these principles. It will be claimed that epistemologists have lost sight of their real significance by construing them standardly as conditions on knowledge which has, in turn, given rise to the appearance of yet another series of Gettier-type examples for and against them. These principles, it will be argued, should be seen as giving expression to distinct cognitive goals for beliefs rather than stating requirements for knowledge. The consequences of seeing them as such are subsequently investigated in the light of the results of the first chapter.

The sensitivity of belief to experiential evidence, its consequences and the problems it poses are taken up in the next four chapters. In Chapters 4 and 5, an attempt is made to see how sensory experiences can confer justification on the beliefs they give rise to. Some theorists have claimed that nothing can count as a reason for a belief except another belief. Experiences do stand in causal relations to beliefs but this relation is not justificatory and reason-giving. This raises the question of non-doxastic justification, namely, the question of how causes of such nature can furnish grounds for the beliefs they give rise to. In Chapter 4, after highlighting the urgency of the issue, I try to provide a rather comprehensive survey of the current attempts to resolve the problem by reconstructing them as attempts to find a normative paradigm that would simulate the experience–belief transition. While finding them all wanting, I end by providing a diagnosis of why they fail.

In Chapter 5, I seek out a radically different solution to the problem of non-doxastic justification. To emphasize why a successful resolution of the problem requires a radical departure from the well-trodden paths, I look at another popular attempt at resolving the problem which appeals to the thesis of epistemic supervenience, namely, the view that epistemic properties supervene on non-epistemic, non-normative properties. I begin by critically examining the viability of the thesis of epistemic supervenience before setting out to explore and ultimately reject the claim that the thesis in question has the resources to resolve the problem of non-doxastic justification. I shall then suggest an account that places the experience–belief transition in a semantic context, thus giving rise to a notion of normativity that is manifestly content-sensitive. To this end, I appeal to a version of the functional-role-semantics (FRS) account of the content (meaning) of belief states. The explanation has the virtue of epistemizing semantic normativity, thus allowing us to see how beliefs resulting from sensory states can be justified.

Chapter 6 deals with another feature of the evidential sensitivity of perceptual beliefs to evidence, namely, the problem of the basing relation. While a justified perceptual belief is one where an agent's belief is said to be based on adequate perceptual grounds, no satisfactory analysis of the basing relation has been forthcoming. To set the stage for discussion, I begin by evaluating two major trends in the basing relation debate, namely the causal and doxastic theories. I shall focus, however, on causal theories as it is widely believed that some version of the causal theory must be true. The main obstacle on the way of providing such a theory is to accommodate the problem of deviant causal chains. After examining one recent prominent solution to this problem, I propose a version of the causal theory of the basing relation within a Davidsonian framework.

In Chapter 7, I shall try to deal with some of the consequences of the theses developed in Chapters 4 and 5, especially the thought that basic beliefs are justified by experiences that cause them. On some very plausible assumptions, this leads to the doctrine of basic knowledge, namely knowledge that an agent acquires from a certain source, even if he fails to know that the source is reliable. It has been claimed that, on such theories, bootstrapping and closure allow us far too easily to acquire knowledge (justification) that seems unlikely under the envisaged circumstances. Some philosophers have responded by claiming that closure arguments exploiting basic knowledge are not warrant-transmitting. In this chapter, I begin by examining different approaches to this issue before spelling out my own take on it. It will be claimed that, contrary to the received view, basic knowledge inferences are by no means epistemically uniform. A different account of transmission failure is proposed to explain why some of these arguments fail to transmit warrant and why others, despite being legitimate, strike us as unsatisfactory.

Chapter 8 focuses on the purported fallibility of basic beliefs. Although most contemporary theories of knowledge and justified belief claim to be fallibilist, they have had a hard time accommodating knowledge of necessary truths. This has proved to be a daunting task, not least because there is as yet no consensus on how the fallible/infallible divide is to be understood. In this chapter, after criticizing a number of recent accounts of fallible knowledge, I argue that the problems stem from the very coherence of that notion. It will then be claimed that the fallible/infallible divide in the domain of knowledge is best understood in terms of the externalist/internalist conceptions of knowledge (justification). I end by highlighting some of the consequences of the thesis which include, among other things, its surprising bearing on the recent controversy over the question whether internalism in the theory of justification is compatible with externalism in the theory of content.

In Chapter 9, I examine another epistemic feature of beliefs, that is, the epistemic significance of our knowledge of their contents. Recent discussions of externalism about mental content have been dominated by the question whether it undermines the intuitively plausible idea that we have direct knowledge of the contents of our thoughts. There have been two lines of argument in support of this claim. The first, mainly epistemological, argument exploits the so-called "slow switching" cases to argue that, if externalism is true, one could discover the contents of one's thoughts only after investigating the physical and/or social environment in which one exists. The second line of argument, due to McKinsey, draws attention to the absurd consequence of there being a non-empirical route to knowledge of empirical facts that seems to follow from the combined theses of externalism and privileged access. In this chapter, I specifically deal with the first line of argument. After examining various responses that have been made to the switching argument and finding them wanting, I set out to explain why it fails. It will be suggested that the argument trades on an ambiguity when claiming that our knowledge of our thoughts is susceptible to empirical contingencies. I shall try to show that it is only by relying on certain controversial assumptions about the concepts of justification and a priority that this claim, however construed, can stand a chance of establishing the incompatibility of privileged self-knowledge and externalism. Finally, drawing on an analogy with Benacerraf's argument against Platonism, I will offer some reasons as to why the switching argument fails to show that content externalism undermines our privileged knowledge of the contents of our belief states.

Having provided analyses of some of the main epistemological characteristics of belief in the preceding chapters, our conclusions combine to paint a coherent picture of the epistemology of belief, one that is particularly in harmony with some of the widely held theses in contemporary philosophical thought.

1
Truth and the Aim of Belief

Belief is the paradigm propositional attitude one of whose salient features is the way it is used to regulate our actions and guide us around the world. It functions, in Ramsey's word, like a map by which we steer. It has a content representing the world as being a certain way, and it is deemed correct or true in case its representational content matches what it is intended to represent. To believe something is to represent it as true. The representationality of belief is, thus, connected with its intentionality. Because a belief is about something, it represents it. Accordingly, what seems to be distinctive of the belief mode (as an attitude) is its constitutive link with the truth of its content. Adopting an attitude of believing toward a proposition seems to carry with it some sort of commitment toward the truth of that proposition. It is this distinctive feature of belief that is generally thought to be responsible for the puzzling situation that ensues following the assertion of a Moorean sentence like "I believe that p, but not-p."

Bernard Williams famously described this feature of belief in the form of the thesis that beliefs aim at truth (Williams 1973). He thought that the thesis explains a number of distinct characteristics of belief, for example, the so-called "normativity" of content, the idea that correct beliefs are true beliefs while false ones are those that are defective in some sense and ought to be avoided (call this the "norm of correctness"); the fact that beliefs seem to be governed by evidential norms in the sense that a rational belief is one that is supported by evidence; and, finally, the idea that we seem unable to form beliefs at will (the thesis of doxastic involuntarism). Furthermore, the aim-of-belief thesis is invoked in order to distinguish beliefs from other cognitive states such as assuming, supposing or (propositional) imagining. Despite the intuitive plausibility of the thesis, it has proved to be notoriously difficult to explain what is actually intended by it. In this chapter, I begin by critically evaluating a number of recent attempts at unpacking the metaphor. In Section 1.2, I try to highlight an important distinction between, what I call, the doxastic and epistemic goals and then proceed to illustrate how some of the recent accounts of the aim-of-belief thesis have failed to respect this distinction. Finally, I shall propose my own story of what the thesis involves while emphasizing its deflationary nature. I end by contrasting it with two prominent (inflationary) theories of the nature of belief.

1.1   Unpacking the metaphor: a survey and critique

There have been a number of attempts to interpret the metaphor that beliefs aim at truth. In this section, I shall focus on some recent treatments of the issue and seek to show that they all fail to provide a satisfactory analysis of the thesis in question. I start with Wedgwood, who interprets the aim-of-belief thesis as being equivalent to, what we called, the norm of correctness, namely, the claim that a belief is correct iff the proposition believed is true (Wedgwood 2002). He goes on to call this norm the "fundamental epistemic norm", claiming that it would explain the universal norm of rational belief (which specifies non-epistemic properties in virtue of which beliefs acquire rationality status). Before examining these further claims, let us look at Wedgwood's reasons for unpacking the metaphor of aim-of-belief in terms of the norm of correctness.

Wedgwood begins by providing two arguments to show that the norm of correctness is not trivial. But I think both arguments are unsuccessful. First, he notes that "belief" does not mean "the proposition believed." Belief is a particular mental state. Moreover, "correct," he says, is not the same as "true," and so concludes that the norm of correctness is not trivial. These observations, however, need to be substantiated in order to establish the non-triviality claim. For while one can go along with the distinction between a belief state and its content, the claim that "correct" is not identical with "true" (or "incorrect is distinct from false") is not borne out by Wedgwood's reasoning. His first reason for the claim in question is that "there is nothing wrong or defective about false propositions as such; what is defective is *believing* such false propositions" (Wedgwood 2002, p. 267).

This seems initially plausible. If one were to construe "correct" along epistemic lines intending it to apply only to mental states formed appropriately (from an epistemic point of view) – as Wedgwood seems to do when claiming that "[t]o say that a mental state is 'correct' is to say that in having that mental state, one has got things 'right'; one's mental state is 'appropriate'" (Wedgwood 2002, pp. 267–8) – then he is right. One could no longer speak of propositions being defective (when "defective" is understood epistemically). However, this comes at a price. In this (epistemic) sense a correct belief corresponds to justified or rational belief, that is, a belief formed appropriately from the epistemic point of view. But while this epistemic slant on "correctness" might make sense of Wedgwood's claim, it also undermines the norm of correctness. For now even false beliefs may be deemed epistemically appropriate as justified beliefs can be false. True beliefs, on the other hand, may be unjustified. The logical independence of justification and truth is a staple of contemporary epistemology.

Wedgwood's second reason for the non-triviality of the norm of correctness is equally problematic. He argues that "other mental states besides beliefs, such as choices or decisions can also be wrong or mistaken or incorrect. So 'is correct' also does not just mean 'is a belief in a true proposition'" (Wedgwood 2002, pp. 267–8). Fair enough! But now Wedgwood seems to be changing the subject for he is no longer arguing against identifying the property of "being correct" with the semantic property of "being true." Rather, he seems to be claiming that "correct" is not identical with the *doxastic* property of "believing a true proposition." But this was not the contention behind the triviality objection.[1] I conclude therefore that Wedgwood fails to make good his claim that the norm of correctness is non-trivial in the sense he intends.[2]

Another contentious issue concerns the alleged normative character of "correctness." After cashing out the aim-of-belief thesis in terms of the norm of correctness, Wedgwood immediately states that the term "correct" – in the sense he intends it – expresses a normative concept, and proposes the following (sufficient) condition for normativity: A concept F is normative for a certain practice just in case it is a constitutive feature of this concept that it plays a regulative role in that practice. What this means is that once one makes judgments as to which moves within a particular practice are F and which are not, one is thereby committed to regulate one's moves in accordance with those judgments. Thus, if one judges that "move x is F and move y is not F," one is thereby *committed* to making move x and avoiding move y. Clearly, this analysis of normativity falls short of providing a criterion to identify whether a concept F is normative. For all it says is that *if* F is normative, then certain consequences would ensue. To add some epistemic bite to his proposal, Wedgwood first construes "commitment" in terms of being "irrational" to make conflicting moves and then explains this as involving an incoherent set of mental states.

To give an example, consider the concept of a "legal chess move." Suppose now one is engaged in the practice of playing chess and judges a certain move y to be illegal, and yet persists in making that move. That incurs, according to Wedgwood, an incoherent set of mental states involving the aim of avoiding illegal moves, the judgment that y is an illegal move and the decision to make y anyway. Thus, the concept of a "legal chess move" turns out to be a normative concept by this criterion. But why, one may wonder, should judging that y is an illegal move conflict with the decision to make that move? To say that "one ought not to make move y" follows from "y is an illegal move" sounds very much like deriving an "ought" from an "is." This raises the suspicion that there must be another premise, with normative import, which in conjunction with "y is an illegal move" entails that "one ought not to make move y." And indeed that seems to be the case for Wedgwood takes one's engaging in a practice as "commit[ting] one to accepting that one (in some sense) ought not to make moves [with certain features] within [that] practice" (Wedgwood 2002, p. 268). Going back to the example of chess playing, this means that "engaging in the 'ordinary practice of playing chess' presumably involves aiming to win a game of chess by making *only* legal moves" (Wedgwood 2002, p. 268). So the reason why a certain commitment follows from judging that move y is illegal is because engaging in the practice of playing chess already involves the general commitment that one ought not to make illegal moves. So, far from showing that it is because of the normativity of a certain concept that a certain commitment follows, what carries the burden of normativity in Wedgwood's reasoning is a general commitment that he associates with one's engaging in a practice.

This immediately casts a shadow on Wedgwood's further claim that the concepts "correct" and "rational" are normative for the practice of theoretical reasoning: "For example, suppose that you judge that it is rational for you to suspend judgment about p and not rational for you to believe p. Then it is a constitutive feature of the concept 'rational' that you are thereby committed to not believing p" (Wedgwood 2002, p. 269). But, surely, consonant with the above analysis, the conclusion "one ought not to believe p" follows from "it is not rational to believe p" only if the latter is conjoined with the general commitment that "one ought not to hold irrational beliefs" that, on Wedgwood's account, is associated with one's engaging in the practice of theoretical reasoning. I conclude therefore that Wedgwood fails to show that, given his account of normativity, the concepts "rational" or "correct" are normative. This failure when coupled with his earlier unsuccessful attempt to show the non-triviality of the norm of correctness radically undermines his claim to have demonstrated that the norm of correctness captures the import of the thesis that beliefs aim at truth. I shall now turn to a different interpretation of the aim-of-belief hypothesis due to Owens.

Although Owens denies that believing, unlike guessing, is purposive in any interesting sense, it would be instructive to see how he unpacks the aim-of-belief metaphor, and why he thinks that guesses aim at truth (Owens 2003). He begins with the following interpretation of the metaphor.

(M)   Φ-ing that p aims at the truth iff someone who Φ's that p does so with the aim of Φ-ing that p only if p is true

Owens claims that guessing aims at the truth (in the above sense) because

> Truth is the standard of correctness for a guess and, I maintain, what explains this is the fact that a guesser intends to guess truly. The aim of a guess is to get it right: *a successful guess is a true guess and a false guess is a failure as a guess.*
>
> (Owens 2003, p. 290; emphasis added)

But there seems to be some confusion here as the quoted remarks do not seem to be quite in accord with the import of (M). For although, consonant with (M), Owens says that the aim of a guess is to get it right, yet, by way of explanation, he immediately adds that "a successful guess is a true guess." But, surely, all that (M) requires for a cognitive state to aim at the truth is for the agent to form the state in question with the *intention* of getting it right. It is no part of (M) that for successfully aiming at the truth one should hit the target (truth). So it is quite compatible with successfully forming a cognitive state that aims at truth that the cognitive state in question turns out to be false. The claim that "a successful guess is a true guess" is actually ambiguous depending on how "successful" is to be understood, either as an *adjective* (attached to a cognitive *state* like guessing) or an *adverb* (modifying the *process* of forming the state in question). So we arrive at the following statements.

(a) A successfully formed cognitive state Φ, qua a state aiming at the truth, is a true Φ.
(b) A successful cognitive state Φ, qua a state hitting its target (truth), is a true Φ.

Of (a) and (b), it is (a) that is relevant to the question of how a cognitive state aims at the truth (which is also what (M) is concerned with). However, as far as *this* question is concerned, and if (M) is to be our guide, (a) must be false. But it is (a) that Owens has in mind when saying that a successful guess is a true one as evidenced by his subsequent argument that imagination, unlike guessing, does not aim at the truth: "In this respect guessing is unlike, for instance, imagining…The act of imagining may be a complete success in that it is extremely gratifying or deeply revealing or merely distracting: Truth is not required for imaginative success" (Owens 2003, p. 290). But, as pointed out above, truth is not really required for a cognitive state to count as a state successfully aiming at the truth. So, *pace* Owens, the fact that truth is not required for imaginative success does not show that imagining does not aim at truth. Ditto for supposing.

These confusions, I think, are responsible for Owens' inadequate picture of why guessing differs from believing. To begin with, and contrary to what he says, guessing does not seem to be the kind of cognitive state that can be said to be really aiming at the truth. When we hazard a guess, we are, epistemically speaking, less ambitious than when we form a corresponding belief. We seem to be prepared to settle for something less than truth which explains why we get enough epistemic satisfaction when our guess turns out to have hit somewhere in the vicinity of truth (as in a quiz, for example). This also explains why a reasonable guess requires less, by way of evidential grounds, than a reasonable belief (with the same propositional content). Owens seems to have sensed the difference between guessing and believing though he expresses it in a rather paradoxical manner: "Both believing and guessing satisfy the definition of 'aiming at the truth'. A believer satisfies a further condition; in believing that p he actually believes that the aim of belief has been achieved, for he believes that p is true" (Owens 2003, p. 290). But this is an unsatisfying statement of the difference between the cognitive states in question as it seems to engender a regress that prevents the process of belief formation from being ever completed. For if in believing p the agent is required to believe that the aim of belief has been achieved, then this second belief would, in turn, require a further belief to the effect that the agent believes that the aim of believing that the aim of belief has been achieved, has been achieved and so on ad infinitum. The proceeding remarks, I think, are sufficient to show why Owens' account of the aim-of-belief thesis is inadequate.

Finally, I shall consider Velleman's pioneering study of the nature of belief and its purported aim (Velleman 2000). He begins by noting that believing a proposition to be true entails regarding it as true. He thinks this already distinguishes belief states from conative states such as desire. However, this feature of beliefs, which he calls "acceptance", is not sufficiently discriminative as it fails to separate belief states from other cognitive states like supposing, assuming, imagining and so on for they, too, involve regarding their propositional objects as true (i.e., accepting them). What distinguishes cognitive states, he says, is the aim with which their respective propositional object is accepted. When, for example, we assume p we accept it for the sake of argument, whereas imagining p involves accepting p for recreational or motivational purposes. To believe p, however, is to accept p with the "aim of getting the truth-value of that particular proposition right, by regarding the proposition as true only if it really is" (Velleman 2000, p. 252). This, says Velleman, is what the thesis that beliefs aim at truth involves.

There are a number of initial questions that need to be raised in regard to Velleman's proposal. To begin with, it does not seem to me that analyzing a belief in terms of "accepting a proposition with the aim of getting its truth-value right" and "accepting it only if it is really true" are equivalent. For the former analysis depicts the aim as being tied up to an ability to getting the truth-value of a propositional object right whereas the reference to such an ability is missing in the latter. Both are however problematic for reasons of their own. Consider the former analysis of belief. How is the "aim of getting the truth-value of a proposition right" supposed to illuminate the nature of belief? Suppose, I entertain the propositions that it rained at this stop and at this time of the day a million years ago, or that the universe was created ex nihilio. Suppose further that I have good reasons to think that there is no way one can get their truth-value right. I would obviously not aim at getting the truth-value of these propositions right if I have such entrenched beliefs. Does this mean that I would never be able to believe them? Then, what about those countless individuals in the history of philosophy who believed various metaphysical propositions while being hopeless of ever determining their truth-value for sure? Could one not come to believe a proposition while despairing of getting its truth-value right?

Velleman seems to be imposing too stringent a condition on forming a belief.

As for his second analysis of a belief state as involving accepting a proposition only if "it is really true," one may wonder what function "really" is supposed to serve here. It cannot merely serve to empha-size that the proposition be in fact true for that is what one takes for granted when regarding a proposition as true. It cannot, on the other hand, be expected to play an epistemic role involving knowledge of the proposition in question for such knowledge would already entail believ-ing that proposition. Perhaps it is meant to carry the implicature that one should not intend to systematically misrepresent facts when com-ing to form a belief. This sounds like a plausible requirement if the agent is deemed rational. But if rationality is all that the qualifier "really is true" is intended to highlight, then that seems to be redundant for this whole debate is being conducted against the background assumption that we are dealing with rational agents.

Let us now move to the "acceptance" ingredient in Velleman's account of the aim-of-belief thesis. He does not say much about the epistemic properties of this attitude beyond characterizing it as an atti-tude that plays a particular motivational role involving a disposition to behave as would be desirable if the relevant propositional object were true. He does, however, refer approvingly to the works of Stalnaker and Bratman, who also take "regarding as true" (acceptance) as being involved in cognitive states besides believing (Velleman 2000, p. 250, fn. 10). Bratman has, however, a lot to say about the epistemic charac-teristics of acceptance. So, in the remainder of this section, I shall try to find out if Bratman's arguments for the proposals he puts forward are valid (see Bratman 1999).

Bratman's main claim is that cognitive attitudes that guide our practi-cal reasoning go beyond our beliefs. He cites, what he takes to be, several features of belief (including their truth-directedness) in order to defend his claim. Of all these, the following, which we may call the "context-independent constraint," turns out to be most effective in his reasoning strategy:

> Reasonable belief is, in an important way, context-independent: at any one time a reasonable agent normally either believes something (to the degree n) or does not believe it (to that degree). She does not at the same time believe that p relative to one context but not relative to another.
>
> (Bratman 1999, p. 18)

Bratman's claim that reasonable belief is context-independent is quite controversial, but I shall not question it here. He then goes through a number of examples to illustrate why we need a different category of attitude other than belief, which he calls "acceptance", to account for the epistemic peculiarities of these examples. In what follows, I shall examine some of these cases trying to show that they fail to support Bratman's thesis.

He begins with the following example to prove that what we take for granted in our deliberations cannot be identified with belief. Suppose I plan to read a certain book to prepare myself for my seminar tomorrow. Knowing that I do not have a copy of the book, there are only two options before me; either to stop by the bookshop on my way home or to go to the library after dinner. In my deliberations over available options, there are propositions (like the book being at the bookshop or at the library) that I have to be content only with their likelihood, and there are those (like having a seminar tomorrow or not possessing a copy of the book) that I "take for granted." It is Bratman's contention that what one takes for granted in this way cannot be identified with belief. These are, rather, propositions that we "accept" in the cognitive background of our deliberations. The reason he gives involves seeing beliefs as degrees of confidence construed, in turn, as subjective probabilities. This would seem to imply that one should assign what one takes for granted (e.g., having a seminar tomorrow) a probability of 1. But this, says Bratman, is implausible for we are far from certain about this class of propositions.

I do not find this reasoning convincing. For one can equally describe these attitudes as "beliefs" but explain their privileged status in terms of the degree of justification they enjoy (as compared with the degree of justification of such propositions as, "The bookshop holds a copy of the book," etc.). We are unwilling to revise these beliefs or give them up precisely because, comparatively speaking, they possess a much higher degree of justification. Nevertheless, they stop short of being certain as is characteristic of all justified beliefs. Bratman's example gives us no reason to stop classifying these attitudes as beliefs.

To defend his thesis, he cites further examples relying mainly on the context-independent constraint. Here is the gist of his argument.

There are various kinds of practical pressures for accepting a given proposition in the background of one's deliberation. These pressures are context-relative in the sense that they apply in only some of

the practical contexts...Such pressures can sometimes make it reasonable for an agent to accept a proposition in a given context,
even though she reasonably would not...accept that proposition in
a different context...We need to distinguish such context-relative
acceptance from belief.

(Bratman 1999, pp. 20–21)

Let us now examine some of Bratman's illustrations. Suppose in planning my day, I take it for granted that it will not rain because it simplifies
my planning and the associated practical reasoning. Were I instead to
accept a monetary bet on it, I would not just take it for granted that
it will not rain. Here, says Bratman, what I accept/take for granted
reasonably varies across contexts: "Perhaps I find myself in these different contexts at different times in the day, and what I accept shifts as
I change contexts" (Bratman 1999, p. 29). To begin with, as we saw earlier, Bratman characterized the context-independent constraint in terms
of a fixed time saying that "*at any one time* a reasonable agent normally
either believes something or does not believe it." This leaves room for
the belief in question to have different epistemic status in different contexts at different times. So the fact that one may have different attitudes
"at different times in the day" in different contexts is quite compatible
with the attitude in question being belief.

More importantly, the story does not support Bratman's claim that,
unlike belief, "what is reasonable to accept in one context may not be
reasonable in another context." The impression that this is the moral of
the story rests on equivocating the senses of "reasonable." In the planning context, the term is used in a practical sense. So one may say that it
is *pragmatically* reasonable to accept that it will not rain today (because
of the practical consequences that ensues following the acceptance of
such an attitude). In the betting context, however, the pertinent sense
of "rationality" or "reasonability" is epistemic since the winning side is
determined on the basis of the truth of its prediction. In such contexts it
may not be *epistemically* reasonable to accept that it will not rain today.
This undermines Bratman's claim that the reasonability of what one
accepts changes as one moves from one context to another. It is, rather,
the type of reasonability that varies with context. And, once the equivocation is noted, one is longer bound to introduce a different type of
attitude (acceptance). For even a *belief* can be practically reasonable in
one context but epistemically unreasonable in another involving different concerns. I think this failing equally debilitates Bratman's other

examples. I shall consider just one more of the cases he conjures up in support of his thesis.

Suppose I am planning for a major construction project and I need to decide whether to do the whole project at once or, rather, proceed in a piecemeal manner. Suppose further that I am unsure whether I have currently enough money to do the whole project at once. Given this ambivalence, I decide to proceed cautiously taking for granted that the total costs will exceed the estimated range, and then try to see which option I should go for. However, says Bratman, if I am offered a bet on the actual total cost, with the winner being the one whose guess is closer to the truth, I would reason differently. But here, as in the previous example, the argument misses its target for it trades on the ambiguity of "reasonability" as it is being used in different contexts. It may well be true that while it is reasonable in the planning context to accept/take for granted that the total cost exceed the estimated range, it is not reasonable to adopt the same attitude in the betting context (which is characterized here in terms of truth-involving concerns). But that has nothing to do with the purported peculiarities of "acceptance." For it is not the epistemic status (reasonability) of the attitude in question (however described) that undergoes change as one moves from one context to another; rather, it is the *type* of "reasonability" that changes in so moving. So, as before, one can tell the same story in terms of the attitude of "belief" being practically reasonable in one context but epistemically unreasonable in another context involving different concerns.[3]

Given the proceeding remarks, one can reconstruct Bratman's argument for his claim that the attitude of taking for granted/acceptance (Φ) is distinct from belief as having the following from.

(1) Φ is reasonable in context C_1
(2) Φ is not reasonable in context C_2
(3) Reasonable belief is context-independent (the constraint of context independence)
(4) Therefore, $\Phi \neq$ Belief

However, as already pointed out, the argument is invalid because it equivocates on the sense of "reasonable" as it appears in (1) and (2). It is not the reasonability of Φ itself that changes from (1) to (2) but its type. Thus the following is quite consistent: While it is, say, practically reasonable to Φ in C_1, it is not epistemically reasonable to

Φ in C_2. Since "reasonable" has been used in two different senses in (1) and (2), it is mistake to regard the epistemic status of Φ as having changed when moving from one context to another.

Someone might, however, wish to defend Bratman on the ground that we have overlooked the fact that one of his criteria for distinguishing belief from acceptance is that the latter is typically voluntary whereas the former is not. A few remarks are, however, in order. First, although Bratman cites "being involuntary" as a mark of belief, nowhere in his article does he try to clarify the notion or even appeal to it in his arguments. Rather, he solely relies on his thesis about the context-independent character of reasonable (rational) belief (a highly controversial claim in its own) to establish the desired conclusion: "Examples (1)–(8) argue that there is an important phenomenon of acceptance that is context-relative in a way in which belief is not. I will not reasonably and at one and the same time believe that p relative to one context but not relative to another" (Bratman 1999, p. 27).

Secondly, the issue of doxastic voluntarism, as we all know, is quite tricky. According to the thesis of doxastic voluntarism, beliefs, like free actions, are under our voluntary control. This claim has, however, struck many philosophers as being, at least, psychologically implausible as no one seems to have the relevant sort of "direct" control over his beliefs that the thesis requires. But this does not mean that we can exercise *no* control over our beliefs. Many theorists recognize a rather weak degree of "long range" control over some of our beliefs, and certainly think that we can *indirectly* influence or exert control over beliefs provided there is something we could have done such that if we had done it we would not have had them (which incidentally explains why we might still be held responsible for them) (see, e.g., Alston 1988). It is not clear to me why this degree of voluntary control is not good enough to allow us to make sense of Bratman's examples without being forced to introduce the attitude of acceptance into the picture.

Finally, raising the issue of voluntarism would create a further (serious) problem for Velleman's analysis of belief. For, one may now wonder, how a belief could *fail* to be a voluntary mental act while its main ingredient, namely, acceptance, *is*.[4] I conclude, thus, that Bratman has failed to show that we need an attitudinal state (acceptance) different from belief. This also undermines Velleman's construal of the aim-of-belief thesis in terms of the attitude of accepting a proposition. Having criticized some of the current attempts to unpack the aim-of-belief metaphor, I shall now proceed to highlight a crippling error that most of them are susceptible to.

1.2 Truth as doxastic and epistemic goals: the anatomy of a confusion

So far we have been concerned with understanding the thesis that beliefs aim at truth. Understood thus, truth functions as a doxastic goal, an internal goal toward which a purposive state like belief strives. One might however understand the truth goal in an external sense, that is, as the goal of believing truths and not believing falsehoods. Interpreted this way, truth is seen as an *epistemic* goal. The distinction I am trying to highlight is one between (a) beliefs aiming at truth and (b) aiming at true beliefs. These are quite different for while (a) is intended to delineate the structure of belief, thus, providing a better insight into the nature of our doxastic behavior, (b) tells us what one should do if one's doxastic behavior is to count as rational. We have already become familiar with the import of (a), so let us say a few words about that of (b).

Beliefs can be evaluated from a number of perspectives. Depending on our choice of the standards and goals (moral, practical, etc.) the evaluation will yield different results. Epistemic evaluation, however, involves epistemic standards and appropriate epistemic goals. A theory of epistemic justification must, thus, address the question of the aim and objective of epistemic justification, that is, what is the point of epistemic justification and why we value it. It is generally thought that there is an intimate connection between justification and truth. This connection has, however, been formulated in substantially different ways. Sometimes it is conceived in a direct manner, "as a *means* to truth" (BonJour 1985, p. 7), thus, giving rise to the so-called truth-conducive accounts of justification (as advocated by the likes of Alston, BonJour, Goldman and others) where there is straightforward conceptual link between justification and truth. Sometimes, however, the link is thought to be more indirect. For example, on the so-called "deontological" conception of epistemic justification (where justification is matter of fulfilling one's intellectual obligations) truth comes in by virtue of the thesis that our chief intellectual obligation is often thought to consist in believing truth and avoiding falsehood (see, e.g., Chisholm 1987).

In any event, setting these differences aside, justification is widely understood as an evaluative concept whose attachment to a belief makes the belief worth having from the epistemic point of view which, as just noted, is, in turn, characterized in terms of a distinct goal, the truth-directed goal, namely, the goal of believing truths and not believing falsehoods, or, alternatively, the aim of maximizing truth and minimizing falsity in a large body of beliefs: "One's cognitive endeavors are epistemically justified only and to the extent that they are aimed at this goal" (BonJour 1985, p. 7).[5] Thus, whether it is epistemically rational for one to hold a certain belief depends solely on whether the forming of the belief in question tends to serve or promote the goal of having true rather than false beliefs. I think we can now have a better appreciation of the difference between (a) beliefs aiming at truth and (b) aiming at true beliefs. (a) concerns the structure of belief and designates what beliefs aim at (the doxastic goal), while (b) is concerned with the epistemic status of our doxastic behavior designating what justified beliefs aim at (the epistemic goal). The difference between (a) and (b) is rather analogous to the difference between (α_1) people desiring wealth and (β_1) desiring wealthy people, or between (α_2) birds desiring tropical forests and (β_2) desiring tropical birds. One may explain the difference by pointing out that while in (α_1) and (α_2) what does the desiring falls *outside* the scope of "desiring", in (β_1) and (β_2) that very same entity falls within its scope. Likewise, in (a) what does the aiming (viz., belief) falls outside the scope of the "aiming" whereas in (b) it falls within the scope of "aiming".

To get a better grip on this distinction, it would be instructive to address a number of potential questions. First, one might object to the viability of the distinction on the ground that talking of a belief aiming at truth (as in (a)) is, at best, metaphorical for it is the agent that does the aiming. This observation is correct and in fact my own account (in the next section) is formulated along these lines.[6] But this observation does not necessarily undermine the distinction between (a) and (b) for, even when reformulated accordingly, they still seem to be distinct: (a′) the agent aiming a belief at truth when forming it in the act of judgment, and (b′) the agent forming a belief in a way that it serves the aim of maximizing true belief and minimizing false belief. Suppose, however, that the agent fails to aim accordingly. The ensuing result in the case of (a′) is the absence of belief while in (b′) the agent still forms a belief, albeit an unjustified one (as when he forms the belief without taking all the relevant evidence into account).

Moreover, we hold beliefs for both epistemic and non-epistemic reasons. People can and do have non-epistemic aims and think that acquiring certain kinds of beliefs would help realize these aims. This results in the emergence of different notions of rationality (see, e.g., Foley 1987). It is widely known that these senses of rational belief can conflict (although the resulting state is nonetheless a belief state). Cases of such conflict actually give rise to the important problem of the "ethics of belief", that is, the question of what one ought to believe when our epistemic and non-epistemic reasons come to conflict with each other.

Finally, someone might wish to challenge the distinction by taking (b) as the most natural way of unpacking (a) and, in turn, construe (b) in terms of the following norm (N): One is entitled to hold belief B iff B is true. But this cannot be correct. For, consonant with the preceding remarks, realizing the epistemic goal (b) provides us with epistemic entitlement (justification) to hold a belief. This cannot, however, be the same kind of entitlement expressed in N for a justified belief can be false and a true belief may be unjustified. To get out of the impasse, the objector might invoke a distinction between aiming at truth and hitting it. Succeeding in aiming at a target, he might say, is not the same thing as hitting what is being aimed at, and so there will be no need to invoke the epistemic goal (b). But the aiming/hitting distinction can be equally made within both (a) and (b). To see this, consider what happens if the distinction is denied. In (a) this leads to the conclusion that belief, like knowledge, is factive (i.e., believing p entails p) while in (b) it results in the collapse of justification into truth. These outcomes are clearly distinct showing (a) and (b) to be genuinely different.

To conclude, our topic is the doxastic goal and it should be firmly distinguished from the epistemic goal although, as we have seen, it is easy to confuse them. In the rest of this section, I shall review two recent accounts of the aim-of-belief thesis where the above distinction is not sufficiently noted. This would, in turn, allow us to have a better grip on the import of the thesis in question.

Recall Wedgwood's claim that thesis should be understood in terms of the norm of correctness, namely, the claim that a belief is correct iff the proposition believed is true. As we saw, he particularly singles out a primitive norm that, he claims, can explain all the epistemic norms. This is the "fundamental epistemic norm" of correct beliefs which is none other than our old norm of correctness. Wedgwood then proceeds to show how the fundamental norm, when conjoined with other non-epistemic norms (truths), can explain the norm of rational belief.[7] One immediate problem on the way of providing a fully-fledged explanation is that, according to the fundamental norm, any belief in a true proposition is correct although it may be counted as irrational when judged by the norm of rational belief. Not all true beliefs are rational. To get the problem out of the way, Wedgwood reverts to the aim-of-belief metaphor: "Even though irrational beliefs can be correct, the only way in which it makes sense to *aim* at having a correct belief is by *means* of having a rational belief" (Wedgwood 2002, p. 276). My concern here is not with whether Wedgwood succeeds to make good his claim that the fundamental norm can explain the norm of rational belief but with the manner in which he tries to establish this as it seems to involve conflating the doxastic goal with the epistemic goal. Let me explain.

As the proceeding remarks quite clearly indicate, to solve his problem, he appeals to the thesis that *beliefs aim at truth* (i.e., the norm of correctness) but ends up saying that "the only way in which it makes sense to *aim at having a correct belief* is by *means* of having a rational belief." The shift from "beliefs aiming at truth" to "aiming at having correct beliefs" is precisely what we cautioned against when distinguishing between the doxastic goal (a) and the epistemic goal (b). This is not just an accidental lapse or a Freudian slip as what Wedgwood is trying to do here is to explain the norm of *rationality*. However, as emphasized earlier, beliefs are rational (justified) to the extent that they serve the epistemic goal of believing truth and not believing falsehood. Justification, as BonJour says, is a "means to truth" and this is precisely what Wedgwood addresses in his quoted remarks. He repeats the same mistake when, for example, claiming that "the fundamental epistemic norm implies that, for every proposition p one consciously considers, the best outcome is to believe p when p is true" (Wedgwood 2002, p. 273). This sounds very much like Chisholm's description of our chief intellectual obligation which, as we saw, is construed in terms of the epistemic goal and whose fulfillment constitutes the nature of epistemic justification according to the deontological approach. Let us now turn to another illustration of the same confusion.

Velleman, we may recall, interpreted the aim-of-belief metaphor in terms of the agent's accepting the relevant propositional object with the aim of getting its truth-value right. Seeking to elaborate his proposal further, he discusses the ways in which the aim in question may be realized and which he takes to form a broad spectrum. At one end of the spectrum, we have the agent intentionally aiming a belief at truth when forming it in act of judgment: "He entertains a question of the form 'p or not p?', ... [and] accepts one or the other proposition, as indicated by evidence or argument; and he continues to accept it only so long as he receives no evidence or argument impugning its truth" (Velleman 2000, p. 252). A belief, however, can be aimed at the truth, adds Velleman, without the agent himself directly doing the aiming. This will be the case when the subject's cognitive mechanism "regulates some of his cognitions in ways designed to ensure that they are true, by forming, revising, and extinguishing them in response to evidence and argument" (Velleman 2000, p. 253). Now, in this case the agent may either identify with the cognitive system and endorse it or simply be oblivious to it and even disapprove of it. Either way, says Velleman, since these "cognitions [have] aimed at the truth, they will still qualify as beliefs, according to my conception" (Velleman 2000, p. 253).

Thinking through these clarifications makes one wonder whether it is the doxastic or the epistemic goal that Velleman's remarks are targeted at, or, what is the same thing, whether he is talking about belief or *justified* belief. It seems to me that it is the epistemic goal that he is addressing when identifying different ways in which the truth-aim may be realized. Let us begin with the case where the agent is intentionally aiming at truth by forming a belief (in act of judgment) in response to evidence or argument. He does this, however, by regulating his acceptance of the relevant proposition "in ways he regards as truth-conducive." Being regulated for truth by evidence, the resulting cognitive state is surely not just a belief but an epistemically *justified* belief. So the target of Velleman's remarks is the epistemic goal whose obtaining confers justification on the relevant beliefs. Moreover, the regulation-by-evidence requirement fails to constitute a necessary condition for a cognitive state to count a belief. For beliefs can be formed on the basis of non-epistemic reasons and still be counted as aiming at truth. Of course, they may no longer be epistemically justified but this is just to say that the resulting attitude does not serve the *epistemic* goal of believing truth and avoiding falsehood.

The point comes into a sharper focus when we turn to Velleman's other cases where it is the cognizer's cognitive system (or the relevant module) that does the aiming by regulating his cognitions "in a way designed to ensure that they are true." Now, this sounds pretty much like describing and endorsing a reliabilist account of justification according to which beliefs formed by reliable cognitive processes are justified. And it is, surely, the epistemic goal that, when achieved, results in beliefs having a justified status. Not only does Velleman seem to be addressing justified beliefs, he also seems to be advocating an externalist account of justification. For, given the preceding remarks, it seems that Velleman is giving the agent's cognitive system rather than his intentions the right to veto when deciding whether a belief has satisfied the truth goal. If the agent's cognitive system is regulating his cognitions in a way designed to ensure its truth, then the resulting cognitive state has satisfied the truth goal regardless of whether he is "oblivious [of its workings], or ... disapproves of it." All these, I think confirm our suspicion that it is the epistemic, rather than the doxastic, goal whose realization Velleman is discussing in his remarks.

We may see this more clearly by considering the consequences of Velleman's views in dramatized epistemic circumstances. What I have in mind are the so-called demon world (or brain-in-a-vat) scenarios where, although the agent's cognitive system malfunctions, he is still disposed to produce the same cognitive attitudes in response to the sensory input that is, by hypothesis, ensured to be phenomenologically indistinguishable from what he would receive were his circumstances normal. The question is whether the agent has beliefs (aimed at truth) under such circumstances. On Velleman's disjunctive account, the agent's cognitive attitudes are beliefs presumably because he intentionally aims at truth when forming them. But, one wonders, if Velleman is willing to give priority to properly functioning cognitive systems (i.e., those designed to get at the truth), over the intentions of the agents, when deciding whether the resulting states have aimed at the truth, what makes him deny the cognitive modules the same privilege when they malfunction? There may be plausible rationales (initially, at least) either way when the question is whether beliefs produced in the demon scenarios are *justified* (depending on whether or not one's intuitions have externalist or internalist leanings). But when it comes to the question whether the agents have *beliefs*, these intuitive grounds disappear. In fact if Velleman's account is to be consistent and not ad hoc, he ought to allow cognitive systems to enjoy the same overriding power even when they malfunction. After all, it is the cognitive modules that determine what their outputs are going to be like (irrespective of the agent's intentions or stance). But this would mean that the agents in the demon scenario have no beliefs which is highly implausible. It is much more plausible to say they lack *justified* beliefs, but then, as stated earlier, this shows that it is the epistemic goal that Velleman is addressing when claiming to be clarifying what it means for beliefs to aim at truth – as we shall see later, Velleman does indeed deny that envatted brains have beliefs.

1.3   The aim of belief: aiming at a target and hitting the target

In this section, I am going to propose a deflationary account of the thesis that beliefs aim at truth and suggest an argument by way of its justification. I shall take my departure from Velleman's account while highlighting our substantial differences. Recall that, according to Velleman, what distinguishes cognitive states from one another is the aim with which we accept or regard as true their relevant propositional object (p). This gives us the following definitional schema,

(S)   P is a cognitive state iff one regards P as true for the sake
of............

where the gap for each distinct cognitive state is filled by a distinct
goal. For example, while assuming involves accepting a proposition for
the sake of argument that is, in order to see what it entails, imagining
involves regarding a proposition as true for motivational purposes.
Believing, on the other hand, pertains to accepting a proposition with
the purpose of getting its truth-value right. I have already made some
criticisms of Velleman's account in Section 1.1. What I wish to do now
is to argue that while S nicely covers many cognitive states, it fails to
incorporate beliefs. That is to say, while assuming or imagining that
p involve regarding p as true in order to reach certain specific goals,
believing p involves no such distinct goals. To believe p is to regard p as
true for its own sake, not to regard p as true "for the sake of something
else." In other words, regarding-p-as-true is not a *means* to some exterior
end but an end in itself. Before proceeding to offer an argument for this
claim, it would be instructive to see why "for the sake of" qualifier in
S is not needed in the case of beliefs.

To see this, consider Velleman's discussion of one of the ways in which
the aim of belief may be realized through the agent intentionally aiming
at the truth by regulating its formation and maintenance. In doing the
regulating, the agent *is* guided, says Velleman, by a methodology as to
how discriminate truth from falsehood. It is not necessary though that
the methodology be in fact truth-conducive. What is necessary, however, is whether he finds it so. So an agent's acceptance of a proposition,
according to Velleman, still counts as belief as long as it is "regulated in
ways that he *regards* as truth-conducive" (Velleman 2000, p. 252, fn. 17).
We therefore arrive at the following instance of S.

(B)   Believing p = (i) Regarding p as true and (ii) regarding the methodology for regulating (i) as truth-conducive.

As was pointed out in the previous section, however, (B) is actually an
account of what it is to be justified in believing p rather than the nature
of belief itself, for what gets addressed in clause (ii) is the epistemic goal
of forming true, rather than false, beliefs. The reference to the truth
conducivity of the ground of the belief is to emphasize that the belief
will be more likely to be true given what it is based on. So (B) is not an
account of what it is to aim at truth. Rather it is an account of what
ensures having true beliefs that is, when a belief is justified.

In fact, (B) suggests a very distinct species of epistemic justification, namely, subjective justification. For what the clause (ii) requires is not that the ground of one's belief be *in fact* truth-conducive but that it is *regarded* to be so by the agent. As it stands, (B) is an even more subjective an account than, say, Foley's well-known egocentric theory of epistemic justification (rationality). For, although being egocentric emphasizing the bearing of the individual's perspective on his cognitive performance, Foley constrains his account by requiring the resulting beliefs to arise in a process of deep reflection on the part of the agent conforming to his deepest epistemic standards. Nonetheless, Foley thinks that "truth is [not] a prerequisite of epistemic rationality" (Foley 1987, p. 155). Now, however one may think of Foley's account, it is clear that (B) offers an even more unbridled approach to justification as the sort of quasi-objective constraints that Foley imposes on his theory are absent in (B). There would thus be even less guarantee that beliefs complying with (B) would be true at all. Now, if that is the case, then one would naturally become suspicious of the role of the clause (ii) in (B). For if all that counts in forming a belief is whether the agent *regards* the methodology for regulating its formation as truth-conducive, then why not be content with the clause (i) and define believing p as simply regarding p as true (for its own sake)? This way we would also avoid conflating the doxastic and epistemic goals. Furthermore, the claim that the clause (ii) is not essential in capturing the import of the thesis that beliefs aim at truth can gain further support by the fact, highlighted earlier, that a belief formed on the basis of non-epistemic reasons is still a purposive state aiming at truth although, being held for non-epistemic reasons, it is obviously not a function of the truth conductivity of those reasons.

Finally, the thesis that "regarding p as true for its own sake" fully unpacks the aim-of-belief metaphor seems to be more in line with some of the isolated but intuitively plausible remarks of Velleman concerning the distinguishing features of belief states: "What distinguishes a proposition's being believed from its being assumed or imagined is the spirit in which it is regarded as true, whether tentatively or hypothetically, as in the case of assumption; fancifully, as in the case of imagination; or seriously, as in the case of belief" (Velleman 2000, p. 183). These plausible intuitions, I think, are better accounted for by my account of the nature of belief than by that of Velleman's. On my account, when cognitive states, other than belief, are analyzed in terms of "regarding a proposition (p) as true for the sake of...," the attitude of "regarding as true" is not the agent's primary objective. It is rather conceived as a *means* to bring about another aim, for example, knowing the likely consequences of accepting a proposition and so on. That is why when assuming or imagining p we do not seriously (really) regard p as true for our primary aim is what consequences (broadly understood) follow from accepting p. Thus, the obtaining of this attitude is just a means to the obtaining of another (primary) aim.

By contrast, our primary aim in believing p is its very acceptance as a true proposition. In this case, our regarding p as true is not intended to serve a different aim. Rather, our primary aim in believing p is to regard it as true for its own sake (period). It is, in other words, to regard it as true seriously. To give an analogy, compare a basketball player who plays to win games in order to earn as much money as he can with another player who plays only for the sake of winning regardless of its financial gains. We might say of the first player that he does not take winning seriously for his primary aim is to earn money. That is why if his club goes bankrupt he would very likely lose his motivation to win the games. He may even agree to sabotage the game to make his team lose in return for a lot of cash in a match-fixing deal. But such behavior is very unlikely of the second player. His primary aim is to win, period. He takes this aim seriously.

I think we can muster something in defense of the above thesis along the following lines. The line of argument I am going to exploit draw on Davidson's theory of radical interpretation (Davidson 1984). According to Davidson, an adequate semantic theory for a language should be such that if one comes to know the theory, one would partially understand the language. He thinks that a Tarski-style truth theory is the appropriate form for such a theory of meaning so that for each sentence (s) of object language (L), the theory should deliver a meaning-giving theorem of the form (T): s is true (in L) iff p, where p is the translation of the object-language sentence into the meta-language. However, because of the extensional nature of Tarski's truth theory as well as the fact that, on pain of begging the question, Davidson cannot help himself with the notion of translation, he is forced to impose, in addition to certain formal requirements, a further, "interpretive," constraint on the semantic theory. According to this constraint, known as the principle of charity, an adequate semantic theory should allow us to correctly interpret the speakers of L. This is how the principle is intended to function. Very roughly, he takes the evidence for the theory of meaning for L-speakers to consist in the conditions under which the speakers hold sentences true. Thus, he takes a sentence of the form

(1) John holds true "It is raining" iff it is raining in his vicinity.

to count as evidence for the meaning-giving sentence

(2) "It is raining", as uttered by John, is true iff it is raining in his vicinity.

But, as Davidson is quick to point out, the transition from (1) to (2) is not that simple, for the holding of a sentence to be true is not only a function of what the speaker means by that sentence but also depends on what she believes. If, for example, John, for some reason, failed to believe that it is raining, while raining in his vicinity, we could no longer use (1) as evidence for (2). The problem is due to, what Davidson calls, the "interdependence of belief and meaning," and it is here that the principle of charity enters the scene. We can solve the problem "by holding belief constant as far as possible while solving for meaning. This is accomplished by assigning truth conditions to alien sentences that make native speakers right when plausibly possible, according, of course, to our own view of what is right" (Davidson 1984, p. 137). Without assuming charity, we will not be able to break into the closed circle of belief and meaning which is why it is inevitable for the process of interpretation. It is important to note that, on Davidson's account, charity does not merely function as a useful regulative maxim facilitating the process of interpretation. Rather, he takes the principle to be constitutive of intentional ascription and the nature of belief itself: "If we cannot find a way to interpret the utterances and other behavior of a creature as revealing a set of beliefs largely consistent and true by our own standards, we have no reason to count that creature as rational, as having beliefs, or as saying anything" (Davidson 1984, p. 137).

   The principle of charity, thus, demands that we assume, for example, that the speakers believe that it is raining when raining in their vicinity. It requires us, in other words, to assume that people believe the obvious (*by our lights*), that is, *believe* what we, the interpreters, regard as obvious or *regard as true*. For our purposes here, we may simplify the situation by ignoring the interpreter/interpretee divide since, as both Quine and Davidson have emphasized, charity begins at home. The interpreter's beliefs are as much subject to the constraint of charity as are the beliefs of the interpretee. Given this simplification, the principle of charity yields the result that to believe p is to regard p as true which is precisely how we construed the thesis that beliefs aim at truth. Thus, seeing belief ascription as being constrained by the principle of charity would lend some support to our way of unpacking the aim-of-belief metaphor.

It should be noted, of course, that the invoking of Davidson's theory of radical interpretation was not intended to reveal everything about the nature of belief. For one thing, and this one respect in which our account is deflationary, "regarding p as true" is too close (semantically speaking) to "believing p" to be able to bring to surface the full nature of the latter. But, I think, it does have the virtue of showing that belief is a purposive state that is constitutively linked to truth. There is also a second, and more important, respect in which our account is deflationary. It is also deflationary in the sense that it respects the distinction between aiming at a target and hitting a target. One can aim at a target and yet fail to hit the target just as one can say of an item that it has a certain function despite failing to perform that function for some reason. A heart in fibrillation and the eyes of a congenially blind person still have their functions. Likewise, a belief can aim at truth and yet turn out to be false. This is clearly reflected in our account for we may regard a proposition as true and yet be mistaken in our assessment of its truth-value. I am actually inclined to take this particular deflationary aspect as an adequacy condition on theories of the nature of belief. Theories that fail to respect the distinction between "aiming at the truth" and "hitting the truth" are inadequate. This is by no means a trivial requirement. I end the chapter by considering two prominent theories that seem to violate it.

My first example of an inflationary account of the nature of belief comes from Davidson himself and his later views about the nature of intentional ascription. Davidson's early position, as explained above, is clearly deflationary in the respect just mentioned. As noted, he takes the psychological realm as being governed by a requirement of overall coherence and consistency. If the concepts of belief, desire and so on are not applied in accordance with the principle of charity, there is no reason, he says, to take them as applying at all. But the principle only requires that we take the interpretee to believe what we (the interpreter) regard as true. Clearly, this is not an epistemically loaded thesis having significant epistemic repercussions for the process of belief ascription. All that the principle of charity requires is the maximization of truth by the interpreter's own lights, and, for all we know, the interpreter's beliefs might very well be mistaken. Mere consistency between the beliefs of the speaker and those of the interpreter fails to ensure the (objective) truth of the either.

Davidson, however, felt increasingly dissatisfied with the deflationary nature of his theory. In order to add some epistemic bite to his theory, while being at the same time unhappy with foundationalist responses, which he took to conflate causes with reasons, Davidson adopted a radical externalist stance seeking to show that "coherence yields correspondence" (Davidson 1986, p. 307). What he sought was a full-blooded theory of belief ascription that was rich enough to rule out the possibility of massive error. A natural way of achieving this result would be to deny that the distinction between (beliefs) aiming at a target (truth) and (beliefs) hitting that target. Davidson's way of belittling the distinction appeared in two (apparently) different guises. Initially, he introduced the idea of an omniscient interpreter, playing the role of the field linguist, who believes all and only truths. Now if this omniscient being were to interpret a speaker, by maximizing agreement between himself and the latter, the ascribed beliefs (to the speaker) would, by hypothesis, be all true. Accordingly, the interpretee cannot be radically mistaken about her environment.

Subsequently, however, Davidson shifted the focus of his reasoning from the believer to the nature of belief itself. This he did by fortifying the principle of charity by having it to include the injunction that, as interpreters, we should identify the objects of beliefs with their causes. Beliefs are to be identified, he said, by matching them with facts in the world that prompt them:

> What stands in the way of global skepticism of the senses is, in my view, the fact that we must, in the plainest and methodologically most basic cases, take the objects of a belief to be the causes of that belief. And what we, as interpreters, must take them to be is what they in fact are.
>
> (Davidson 1986, pp. 317–18)

It is interesting to note that although these strategies are seemingly different, they are in fact functionally equivalent as far as the satisfaction of our deflationary constraint on a theory of belief, namely, respecting the distinction between aiming at a target and hitting it, is concerned. Either way, however, the resulting account of the nature of belief would be an inflationary theory where "[b]eliefs are [regarded] by nature [as] generally true" (Davidson 1986, p. 319). Thus, when, for example, a brain in a vat says "The sky is blue," in response to its sensory input, this belief, interpreted in accordance with the new principle of charity, has a content that involves its computer environment. The brain actually has no belief with the content "the sky is blue."

For my second illustration of an inflationary account of the nature of belief, I turn, once more, to Velleman. Although he does not explicitly address this issue, there are certain remarks of his that suggest close affinity with Davidson's later position. I have already raised doubts as to whether, on Velleman's account, the denizens of a demon or vat world can be said to have beliefs at all. There are, however, certain claims made by Velleman that seem to make the case for a negative answer stronger.

> In what sense are [false beliefs] faulty? The most plausible answer, I think, begins with the observation that we conceive of beliefs as constitutively regulated by input... The fact that beliefs are conceived to be faulty when false indicates that the regulation conceived to be constitutive of them is regulation for truth. Truth directedness thus appears to be enshrined in our concept of belief.
>
> (Velleman 2000, p. 278)

But this statement is ambiguous depending on how "input" is to be understood. If it is taken to refer to the proximate causes of a belief (viz., sensory experience), then we run into the following difficulty. Both our beliefs and those of our counterparts in a demon or a vat world are regulated in the same way by the same sensory input. Yet our beliefs are true while theirs are systematically false. So the regulation-by-input argument fails to show that "truth-directedness [is] enshrined in our concept of belief." On the other hand, if "input" is taken to refer to the distal causes of belief (objects in the world), then we have to deny that we and our vat-world counterparts hold the same belief when asserting, for example, that "The sky is blue." For, our beliefs, not theirs, are properly hooked up with the right objects. In fact, they have no beliefs with the content "the sky is blue." There are indeed some explicit statements by Velleman that supports this interpretation.

> I am especially worried about cases of delusion. Aren't there people who believe that they are Napoleon?... Don't such people have a belief that is not regulated for truth? I think the answer is that it isn't literally a belief. I suspect that we tend to apply the term 'belief' in a figurative sense to [such cases].
>
> (Velleman 2000, p. 281)

There is, thus, no belief with the content "I am Napoleon" in such cases because it is not hooked up in the right way to its cause[s]. One can then see Velleman moving away from the initial internalist account of belief where its regulation is done through the agent's intentions by adopting methodologies "he regards as truth-conducive but which may not in fact be" to an externalist position where it is the belief's connection with its actual cause that regulates its formation. This is a move that closely parallels Davidson's shift from the initial, deflationary account of intentional ascription to the later, epistemically loaded, externalist position. Whatever the epistemic merits of such externalist approaches to the nature of belief, they fail, I believe, to reflect the deflationary spirit of the aim-of-belief thesis.

Earlier it was pointed out that it is the truth-directed nature of belief that gives rise to the puzzling situation that follows the assertion of the so-called Moorean sentences like "I believe that p, but not-p." This phenomenon seems to be unique to belief-like states. For example, there is nothing wrong with saying "I wish it to be the case that p, but not-p." Although we have been trying to articulate what is meant by saying that beliefs are truth-directed, nothing we have said so far tell us how to resolve these so-called Moore paradoxes. Attempts at solving such paradoxes have often sought to identify the sense in which Moorean sentences are defective by appealing to various aspects of the nature of belief, epistemic and otherwise. Analyzing such attempts would thus help throw further light on the nature of belief. This is what I am going to do in the next chapter by highlighting what I take to be a salient feature of belief whose violation gives rise to such paradoxes.

2
Belief, Interpretation and Moore's Paradox

Moore famously observed that there is something odd or defective about sentences of the form "P but I do not believe that P", or <P & ~IBP> for short, in that asserting them would be absurd. Although such sentences can be true they cannot be sensibly asserted. For example, while one may countenance situations where it is raining but one happens not to believe it, one cannot properly assert the corresponding sentence. It is absurd to assert that it is raining but then go on to deny that one believes that it is. Moore noted that such an oddity is equally present when one utters sentences of the form <P & IB~P> (Moore 1942). We shall call such sentences "Moorean sentences". There thus appears to be something odd or defective about them, and the question that has caught the attention of philosophers ever since is to explain what underlies their defective nature.

There have been numerous responses to this question. Despite differing over details, all the attempted resolutions of Moore's paradox tend to see the absurdity of Moorean sentences as eventually stemming, one way or another, from the violation of the law of non-contradiction although such sentences seem to differ clearly from outright contradictions of the form <P & ~P>. While some philosophers construe the problem with such sentences as involving some sort of pragmatic contradiction arising from their assertion, others seek to locate the source of paradox in the alleged fact that such sentences cannot consistently be believed. Still others seem to think that what gives rise to the paradox is the violation of certain necessary conditions of epistemic justification (Wittgenstein 1953; Shoemaker 1996; Williams 2004). Now, one would be forgiven for wondering how such a seemingly simple problem could have its source in phenomena as diverse as the pragmatics of speech acts, and the nature of belief or justification. But perhaps, despite important differences between these approaches, they all share a substantive common ground. In what follows, I shall try to uncover a common pattern among all this diversity, and show how these disparate approaches to the paradox appeal to analogous strategies to resolve it. They are subsequently criticized by calling into question the principles they help themselves with to tackle the problem. Finally, I shall propose my own solution of the paradox according to which Moorean sentences are defective not because of some associated logical impropriety but because their assertion violates a certain interpretive constraint, namely, the principle of charity, on an adequate theory of meaning. I shall close by highlighting the merits of the proposal by comparing it with other suggestions.

2.1   Resolving the paradox: varieties of approaches

As just noted, Moorean sentences are widely known to have either of the following logical forms: (1) <P & ~IBP> and (2) <P & IB~P>. Unlike sentences of the form <P & ~P>, these sentences are consistent even though they cannot be sensibly asserted.

How is one supposed to explain this oddity? I think we can usefully classify the existing approaches to Moore's paradox into three main categories, by construing Moorean sentences as being either

(1) assertorically defective; or
(2) doxastically defective; or
(3) epistemically defective.

As claimed earlier, despite their different perspectives on the problem, all these proposals appeal to a common strategy, an "ascent" maneuver. The general idea (to be elaborated later) is that if, as most philosophers seem to agree, a solution to the paradox "must identify a contradiction, or something contradiction-like, in the Moorean claims" (Heal 1994, p. 6), one must first bring the conjuncts of Moorean sentences to the same (appropriate) level to show that they contradict one another.

These conjuncts, namely, "P" and "I believe that P", are, semantically speaking, of different orders (have different truth-conditions). Accordingly, to bring, say, "P" to the same semantic footing as "I believe that P", one must invoke what may be called an *ascent* principle of some sort. Before proceeding to explain what this idea involves and to evaluate its various implementations, I gather many would find it plausible that, as an adequacy condition on a solution to Moore's paradox, such a solution should be *complete* in the sense of offering a uniform treatment of both forms of paradox. Certainly a solution that possesses this feature is preferable to one that invokes different principles to deal with different Moorean sentences. Let us then start with the first group of solutions to the paradox.

2.2 Moore's paradox: the pragmatic approach

According to this approach, Moorean sentences are defective because their assertion leads to logical contradiction of some sort. There have been two ways of developing this theme. The first line of thought construes the incoherence in question as having a pragmatic nature. The general idea is that (sincere) assertion involves belief. Exactly how the link between assertion and belief is to be understood is, however, a controversial matter. Moore himself seemed to think that the link is more or less an inductive generalization in the sense that "in the immense majority of cases a man who makes such an assertion does believe or know what he asserts: lying... is vastly exceptional" (Moore 1942, pp. 542–3). More elaborate accounts have sought to explain the link using the apparatus of speech act theory (Baldwin 1990). The idea is that meaningful assertion constitutively involves having higher-order intentions of providing one's audience with information (belief) through their recognition of these intentions. We can call the belief whose communication is the purpose of standard utterances of a declarative sentence, the belief that the assertion of that sentence expresses. Accordingly, asserting P is thought of as an action that is done with the intention of producing the belief that one has the belief P. In so doing one *pragmatically* implies the (corresponding) belief. Thus the impropriety of Moorean sentences of, say, <P & ~IBP> variety may be explained in terms of the pragmatic contradiction that their assertion purportedly involves. In other words, what an utterer implies in asserting the first conjunct contradicts what she actually says in asserting the second conjunct (Shoemaker 1996, p. 74).

Another gloss on the idea that Moorean sentences are assertorically defective construes the defect in question as involving an explicit contradiction much like asserting <P & ~P>. The idea is originally due to Wittgenstein who propounded what might be called an "assertoric ascent" thesis according to which asserting a sentence with first-order content P is to assert a sentence with the second-order content "I believe P" ("IBP") and vice versa (Wittgenstein 1953).[1] This provides a neat solution to the paradox, for the assertion of <P & ~IBP> would now amount to contradicting oneself, that is, <IBp & ~IBp>, assuming the assertoric ascent thesis and distributivity of assertion across conjunction. To see this, suppose I assert that <p & ~IBp>, then since assertion distributes over conjunction, I assert that p and so by Wittgenstein's thesis, W, I assert that IBp. But since assertion distributes over conjunction I also assert that ~IBp. So I have made contradictory assertions.[2] Wittgenstein's ascent thesis is compatible with his view that "I believe" has no descriptive role to play when uttered by someone much in the same way that "I promise" functions when one says it. Accordingly, when one asserts that P, one is making the same conversational move as when one says "I believe that P". Wittgenstein's claim resembles his well-known thesis that when talking of one's sensations, say, "I am in pain", one is not describing anything. Rather, such utterances are verbal substitutes for the relevant natural nonverbal behavior.

But it is very unintuitive to claim that in (sincerely) asserting "I believe that it is raining", I am not reporting my own belief. Even if I am asserting that it is raining, there is no reason why I cannot be reporting my own belief as well. In fact by endorsing the principle that to assert P is to assert "I believe that P", Wittgenstein would have to agree with the point just made. Moreover, by reducing Moorean absurdities to flat-out contradictions like <P & ~P>, Wittgenstein is not just saying that my Moorean assertions *involve* me in making (*other*) contradictory assertions, but that my Moorean assertions just *are* contradictory assertions. But, as we saw, what underlay the oddity of Moorean sentences was the fact that, while not sensibly assertable, they could nevertheless be true (see also Williams 1998).

Wittgenstein's proposal is, thus, too radical and unintuitive to be acceptable. Despite this negative conclusion, our discussion, I hope, has served to accentuate the strategy adopted in the current approach (in its Wittgensteinian variety) in explaining the absurdity of Moorean sentences, namely, the assertoric ascent maneuver, for, as we shall see, a similar strategy is at work in other approaches to the paradox. Let us then proceed to evaluate another proposal.

2.3   Moore's paradox: the doxastic approach

According to this approach the fault with Moorean sentences lies in the fact that such sentences cannot be truly believed.[3] In other words, the reason why these sentences cannot be sensibly asserted is that they are doxastically defective or incoherent. The doxastic approach has been advocated by a number of philosophers, though I shall focus on Shoemaker's version of the story as it is the most fully developed of such accounts (see also Hintikka 1962; Baldwin 1990; Kriegel 2004). According to Shoemaker, what is crucial in explaining the absurdity of Moorean sentences is that they cannot be believed (despite the fact that they can be true). However, since sincere assertions of such sentences involve believing their content, once an explanation for the impossibility of believing them is at hand, "an explanation of why one cannot assert a Moore-paradoxical sentence will come along for free" (Shoemaker 1996, p. 76).

To defend this line of thought, Shoemaker starts with the Higher Order Thought (HOT) theory of consciousness (see, e.g., Rosental 1986). According to this theory, a mental state M is conscious when, and only when, one is aware of it (i.e., one truly believes that one is in that state). Thus, to consciously believe p, one must not only believe p but also have a second-order belief that one has that (first-order) belief, that is, $xBp \rightarrow xBx^*Bp$.[4] Now, with HOT in force, and assuming that conscious belief distributes over conjunction, consciously believing the Moorean sentence <P & ~IBP> will involve contradictory beliefs such as IB~IBp and IBIBp.[5] This seems to provide an explanation as to why a Moorean sentence is absurd because, for the reason just mentioned, it is doxastically defective.

Again, what is important to note in this solution is that it invokes an ascent principle to the effect that if one consciously believes P then one believes that one believes it. Without this assumption it would be impossible to show that Moorean beliefs suffer from logical impropriety (in the way envisaged by the doxastic approach). The move is similar to the one we saw in the previous approach where a similar (assertoric) ascent principle was involved. The difference, in this case, is that the relevant ascent principle is doxastic, commensurate with the doxastic nature of the approach.

Shoemaker is nevertheless critical of certain aspects of the HOT approach. For one thing, it only shows that Moorean sentences cannot be *consciously* believed. Moreover, the HOT approach, he claims, cannot explain why mental assent conditions for P entail those for "I believe P" (where a mental assent is an episodic instantiation of belief) (but see Larkin 1999). So he suggests another view according to which the content of the Moorean sentence cannot be believed at all, consciously or non-consciously. To elaborate, he introduces what he calls the "self-intimation" thesis:

(SI) If x believes that p, then if x considers whether she believes that p, then x believes that she believes that p.

What is important to note, according to Shoemaker, is that the link between first-order beliefs and those second-order beliefs that constitute one's awareness of first-order beliefs is a necessary constitutive relation not a contingent one. By applying (SI), Shoemaker is able to solve the paradox in the manner of the HOT approach, namely, by unpacking the Moorean belief into a complex set of beliefs some of which are contradictory. That is, by assuming (SI) and the distributivity of belief across conjunction, IB(P & ~IBP) would entail the following: IBP & IB~IBP & IBIBP & IBIB~IBP, where the second and third conjuncts report the fact that I have contradictory beliefs.[6]

Shoemaker's resolution of the paradox invites a number of questions. To begin with, what reason is there for accepting (SI) beyond the fact that, as Shoemaker admits, "without something like this, the explanation [of the Moorean absurdity] does not go through" (Shoemaker 1996)? The question assumes more significance once it is noted that Shoemaker's solution violates the completeness constraint. It is unable to deal with Moorean sentences of the form <P & IB~P>. For one thing, unlike <(P & ~IBP) & IB(P & ~IBP)>, the conjunction <(P & IB~P) & IB(P & IB~P)> is not self-contradictory which is why Shoemaker is eventually forced to introduce a (more controversial) principle to deal with them (Shoemaker 1996, p. 87). If the resolution of the paradox is the prime virtue of (SI), then it is clearly ad hoc.

Indeed, there are some significant reasons that tell against (SI). To begin with, it seems to engender an infinite regress. For if in believing something one believes that one believes it, then the latter belief would, in turn, require a higher-order belief and so on ad infinitum. Shoemaker is aware of this problem but thinks that the presence of the clause emphasizing the availability of belief in (SI), namely, "if the agent considers whether he holds the target belief", blocks the regress because "there is no threat of an infinity of considerings" (Shoemaker 1996, p. 81). But now this raises a new problem which is analogous to the one that Shoemaker himself raises for the HOT approach, namely, that it fails to explain the absurdity of Moorean beliefs that are not available to the agent (including those that the agent is not considering). To explain, as Shoemaker admits, it is perfectly legitimate to assume that one has beliefs that are not available to her, that is, one does not consider whether one has them: "[L]ots of the beliefs that one can be said to have at a time are not available to one at that time" (Shoemaker 1996, p. 80). This should be equally true of Moorean beliefs. Now, if, as Shoemaker claims, Moorean beliefs are absurd, they remain absurd even when they are unavailable to agents, including cases where one does not consider whether one possesses them. If so, Shoemaker's approach is ineffective to deal with such Moorean beliefs (just as the HOT approach, he claimed, was unable to account for non-conscious Moorean beliefs). This gives rise to the following dilemma: Either the self-intimation thesis can be expressed without requiring that the target belief should be available to an agent in which case it engenders an infinite regress of beliefs or it incorporates that requirement in which case Shoemaker is unable to explain the absurdity of Moorean beliefs that are not available to an agent (Kriegel 2004).

Another problem with Shoemaker's doxastic ascent maneuver is more direct; it blocks the formulation of certain legitimate instances of a Moorean sentence. Some Moorean sentences, we may recall, have the following schematic form: (1) <P & ~IBP>. Now, although we lack clear-cut intuitions as to the precise structure of Moorean sentences, we have initially identified them as those satisfying the minimum requirement of being possibly true but not sensibly assertable. Our examples have thus far consisted of sentences with first-order content, like "it is raining", as substitution instances of "P" in both types of Moore-paradoxical sentences, but that does not seem to constitute a necessary feature of Moorean sentences. Indeed, Sorensen has offered a catalogue of Moore-paradoxical sentences some of which lack this feature. Although Sorensen's claim that all those sentences are Moorean is controversial, some of his examples are genuinely Moore-paradoxical because they are structurally similar to the original Moorean sentences and they satisfy our noted minimum requirement. In particular, in some of these cases, what is substituted for "P" has a *second-order* content expressing a propositional attitude (Sorensen 1988, p. 47).

Bearing this point in mind, let us, then, take "I believe P" as a substitution instance for "P" in (1) to get the following Moorean sentence (consonant with our minimum requirement).

(M*)   <IBP & ~IBIBP>

Being Moorean, (M*) can be true though not assertable. According to (SI), however, since believing P commits one to believing that one believes that P, (M*) would be impossible. But that can hardly be regarded as a resolution of the mystery of how sentences with *consistent* truth conditions fail to be assertable. Self-deception seems to show that a case such as (M*) is possible. For example, it might be the case that "I believe that women are inferior but I do not think I believe they are." Now suppose I hold a true belief in the latter sentence. I now have a Moorean belief, the absurdity of which cannot be explained by (SI). Accordingly, with (SI) in operation, M*-type sentences are no longer paradoxical for they are simply (necessarily) false, in the same way that <P & ∼P> is. Consequently, there will be no absurdity to be accounted for as there is nothing puzzling about necessary falsehoods. This undermines the legitimacy of (SI) in explaining the absurdity of Moorean sentences.

Finally, there is something intuitively unsatisfying about Shoemaker's proposal. As we saw, Shoemaker claims that the absurdity of Moorean sentences lies in the fact that believing them results in having contradictory beliefs: "[I]t is a feature of the contents of Moore-paradoxical sentences that if they can be believed at all, the subject of such a belief could not, logically, believe that she had it" (Shoemaker 1996, p. 76), or, alternatively, "such [contents] cannot be believed without the subject believing a self-contradiction" (Shoemaker 1996, p. 77). But this is not quite right. Even when (SI) is applied to IB(P & ∼IBP) we only get IBIBP and IB∼IBP, not a self-contradictory belief. I shall now turn to one last approach in dealing with Moorean sentences that construes their absurdity as being of an epistemic nature.

2.4   Moore's paradox: the epistemic approach

According to this approach, Moore's paradox arises out of violating certain necessary conditions of epistemic justification. Put differently, Moorean sentences are absurd because they cannot be justifiably believed. Two attempts in this direction, though exploiting different principles (by Lee and Williams), have both sought to exploit the following observation of Gareth Evans as the basis of their resolution of Moore's paradox (Lee 2001; Williams 2004; see also de Almeida 2001).

> [I]n making a self-ascription of belief, one's eyes are, so to speak, or occasionally literally, directed outward – upon the world. If someone asks me "Do you think there is going to be a third world war?", I must attend, in answering him, to precisely outward phenomena as I would attend to if I were answering the question "Will there be a

third world war?"...We can encapsulate this procedure for answering questions about what one believes in the following simple rule: whenever you are in a position to assert that p, you are *ipso facto* in a position to assert "I believe that p".

(Evans 1982, pp. 225–6)

Lee takes these remarks as supporting the principle that if one should judge that p, then one should judge that one believes that p:

[Suppose] I consider whether I believe that the person in front of me is Smith...If my procedures for answering the question lead me to judge that the person in front of me is Smith, then I will also judge that I believe that the person in front of me is Smith.

(Lee 2001, p. 365)

This principle, he claims, can be used to show why one cannot rationally believe a Moorean sentence like M = <P & ~IBP>. Suppose one has adequate evidence for "P". Then one should believe P. Since one knows that one sincerely assents to "P", one should judge that one believes that P too and so should reject the second conjunct of M. Thus, one cannot rationally believe a Moorean sentence.

A different account, exploiting Evans's remarks, has been adopted by Williams who also provides a clear argument for it. I shall focus on Williams's account in the remainder of this section and try to see if it provides an acceptable solution to Moore's paradox. According to Williams, Evans's observation yields the following principle.

(EA)   Whatever justifies me in believing that p also justifies me in believing that I believe that p.

Alternatively, one may describe (EA) as a thesis sanctioning epistemic ascent for what it says is that to justify my belief that p is to justify the higher-order belief that I believe that p. Seeing (EA) in this light, one is automatically reminded of other (structurally) similar ascent theses, namely, the assertoric and doxastic theses which state, respectively, that to assert P is to assert "I believe P" and to believe P is to believe that one believes that P. In any case, it is not difficult to see how the application of (EA) can establish that one cannot justifiably believe, say, <P & ~IBP>. For suppose one has justification for believing the sentence in question. Assuming that whatever justifies one in believing a conjunction justifies one in believing the relevant conjuncts, it follows that I am justified in believing that P and justified in believing that I do not believe that P. But, given (EA), being justified in believing that P implies that I am also justified in believing that I believe that P: "This is logically impossible, because anything that justifies me in believing that something is the case renders me unjustified in believing that it is not the case and vice versa" (Williams 2004, p. 352).[7]

But why should we accept (EA)? Williams proposes the following argument in its defense.

(1)   Circumstances that justify me in believing that p are circumstances that tend to make me believe that p.

(2)   Circumstances that tend to make me believe that p are circumstances in which I am justified in believing that I believe that p.

(EA)   Circumstances that justify me in believing that p are circumstances that justify me in believing that I believe that p.

There are, however, some problems with Williams's resolution of Moore's paradox. To get a better grip on (EA) it is worth taking note of the following objection (Vahid 2005; see also Williams 2006). Williams's argument, if successful, not only establishes (EA) but can also be used to generate highly implausible conclusions of the form (EA*), namely, that "circumstances that justify me in believing that p are circumstances that justify me in believing that I believe that I believe that . . . I believe that p." One can easily show this by constructing a different instance of the argument in the following manner. Having derived (EA), we start with the premise (1′) that "circumstances that justify me in believing that I believe that p are circumstances that tend to make me believe that I believe that p." This would be true for precisely the same reason that Williams offers in support of the first premise of the original argument.

Now, this premise together with an appropriate analogue of the second premise (of the original argument) would result in the conclusion that "circumstances that justify me in believing that I believe that p are circumstances that justify me in believing that I believe that I believe that I believe that p." Iterating the above reasoning procedure, we will eventually arrive at the highly implausible conclusion of the form (EA*) (which is even impossible to entertain). It is worth noting that if this objection is valid the fault must lie with the premises of Williams's argument. Since, as noted earlier, the first premise is plausible, it is the second premise that has to be rejected. Williams has, however, replied that this argument depends on whether (1′) refers to conscious occurrent belief. On his account, he says, what justifies me in believing that I believe that, say, it is raining is my apparent perceptions of rain. However, these perceptions are not reliably connected with a conscious belief that it is raining. Rather, they are reliably connected to my disposition to believe that I hold the belief that it is raining. Construed thus, (EA*) seems plausible. But there are still problems with Williams's argument. Let us look at its premises again.

The first premise is plausible but the second premise is not at all obvious. Suppose I see rain falling down from the sky leading me to form the belief that it is raining. This belief is justified given the plausible assumption that my apparent perceptions of rain are reliable indicators of the truth of my belief, but, as Williams notes, "[these] perceptions...also tend to make me believe that it is raining" (Williams 2004, p. 350), thus, the first premise. He further claims that the second premise is also plausible:

> For my apparent perceptions of rain are also reliably connected with my coming to believe that it is raining. So my apparent perceptions of rain justify both my belief that it is raining and my belief that I believe that it is raining in virtue of different sets of reliable connections.
>
> (Williams 2004, p. 350)

But the second sentence in the quote is not entirely supported by the sentence that precedes it. For, while one can admit that the reliable connection of my perceptions of rain with the belief that it is raining renders this belief justified, no reason has been given for thinking that these perceptions are also reliably connected with, thus justify, my believing that I believe that it is raining.

Williams's reason for this claim seems to be that "my apparent perceptions of rain are also reliably connected with my coming to believe that it is raining." This can be granted if "coming to believe" that it is raining is intended to mean "forming the belief" that it is raining. Williams's conclusion follows, however, only if we take "coming to believe that p" to mean "forming the belief that I believe that p." But I see no grounds for taking this route. Williams's remarks seem to speak to the causal origin of my second-order belief rather than its epistemic status. This problem, I believe, highlights the question of how Evans's observation is supposed to yield an epistemic principle like (EA). I take Anthony

Brueckner to be making this point, in his recent criticism of William, when he claims that:

> [T]he Evans claim from which Williams proceeds... is not about evidence or justification. It is instead primarily a point about the genesis of belief. Once I form a belief on the basis of considering [an external state of affairs], I can simply tell you what belief is. The vast majority of my beliefs about what I believe are just not justified on some evidential basis.

> (Brueckner 2006, p. 266)

Brueckner further points out that in cases typified by Evans's example, the sorts of propositions that are said to lend evidential support to propositions about my beliefs are not typically propositions about my behavior or my mental states. They rather purport to describe certain mind-independent states of affairs and cannot therefore be expected to confer justification on one's beliefs. He goes on to argue that while one's evidence, e, may justify me in believing that p, it does not justify me in believing that I believe that p. Rather, justification for the latter (second order) belief derives from premise (1) together with the assumption that e justifies me in believing that p. So, contrary to what (EA) states, it is not true that what justifies me in believing p also justifies me in believing that I believe that p. Having shown that none of the ascent maneuvers, that I have considered, has successfully pinned down the source of the absurdity of Moorean sentences, I shall close by offering a different explanation.

2.5   Moore's paradox: the interpretive approach

All the attempted resolutions of the paradox examined thus far have sought to show, via some appropriate ascent thesis, that the absurdity of Moorean sentences lies in the fact that their being asserted, believed or justified eventually leads, one way or another, to logical impropriety of some kind (self-contradiction, etc.). As noted before, however, such an explanation is a bit far-fetched, for, intuitively speaking, we are disinclined to assimilate the absurdity of Moorean sentences to that of explicit contradictions. What I am claiming in this section is that it is not some logical impropriety that underlies the oddity of Moorean sentences. Rather, it is the contravention of a constitutive principle of interpretation that renders them absurd. These sentences are, to put it differently, interpretively defective. To elaborate on this suggestion, it is worth reminding ourselves of the main features of Davidson's theory of radical interpretation.

As we saw in Chapter 1, Davidson imposes the following adequacy condition on any semantic theory for a language: should one come to know the theory, one would partially understand the language (see Davidson 1984). He thinks that a Tarski-style truth theory is the appropriate form for such a theory of meaning which is expected to yield, for each sentence (s) of object language (L), a meaning-giving theorem (T-sentences) of the form (T): s is true (in L) iff p; where p is the translation of the object-language sentence into the meta-language. The bulk of Davidson's writings on this topic have been taken up with enunciating the conditions of adequacy for such theories. However, because of the extensional nature of Tarski's truth theory as well as the fact that, on pain of begging the question, Davidson cannot help himself to the notion of translation, he is forced to require, in addition to certain formal requirements, a further, "interpretive", constraint on his semantic theory, the principle of charity, to the effect that an adequate semantic theory should allow us to correctly interpret the speakers of L.

This is how Davidson applies the idea. When an interpreter finds a sentence of the speaker which the speaker assents to regularly under conditions he recognizes, he is entitled to take those conditions as the truth conditions of the speaker's sentence. The idea is, thus, to recover the meaning of the speaker's utterances, at least in the methodologically most basic cases, from the environmental circumstances that prompt them. More formally, as noted in Chapter 1, Davidson takes the evidence for the theory of meaning for L-speakers to consist in the conditions under which the speakers hold sentences true. The holding of a sentence to be true by a speaker turns out, however, to be a function of both what she means by that sentence as well as what she believes. This means that belief cannot be inferred without prior knowledge of the meaning, and meaning cannot be deduced without the belief. Thus the fact that a sentence is assented to under certain environmental circumstances does not warrant taking the latter as constituting the truth conditions (meaning) of that sentence, for the sentence might have either truth-value in those circumstances. It is here that the principle of charity enters the scene.

Without assuming charity, we will not be able to break into the closed circle of belief and meaning to get a non-question-begging empirical foothold on what a speaker means and believes. But truth (agreement) is just one strand in the principle of charity. Indeed, in Davidson's later refinements of the principle it comprises a multitude of principles and constraints that epistemically regulate our own beliefs including canons of inductive and deductive reasoning and norms of rationality in general. Accordingly, to be a speaker is to exhibit a large degree of rationality. We cannot take someone to be a speaker and also be largely irrational. It is important to note that, on Davidson's account, charity does not merely function as a useful regulative maxim facilitating the process of interpretation. Rather, he takes the principle to be constitutive of intentional ascription and the nature of belief itself: "If we cannot find a way to interpret the utterances and other behavior of a creature as revealing a set of beliefs largely consistent and true by our own standards, we have no reason to count that creature as rational, as having beliefs, or as saying anything" (Davidson 1984, p. 137).

> [C]harity is not an option, but a condition of having a workable theory of [interpretation] . . . . Charity is forced on us; whether we like it or not, if we want to understand others, we must count them right in most matters. If we can produce a theory that reconciles charity and the formal conditions for a theory, we have done all that could be done to ensure communication.
>
> (Davidson 1984, p. 197)

The preceding remarks may give the impression that charity is only a constraint on the interpretation of an alien language, but it is equally applicable to cases where the object-language and meta-language are identical (i.e., when translation is homophonic). As both Davidson and Quine have emphasized, charity begins at home. When trying to translate (homophonically) my neighbor's sincere English assertions, we have to resort to the principle of charity as much as we invoke it in the case of radical translation (interpretation), for, epistemologically speaking, the circumstances are on the same footing. To give an example, take someone regularly assenting to the sentence, "It is raining," in the middle of a downpour. One's default position, no doubt, will be to take this as evidence for the T-sentence, " 'It is raining' is true iff it is raining." But there may well be "deviant" truth theories that are, extensionally speaking, equally adequate. Such theories would yield different T-sentences pairing different meta-language sentences with the original sentence in the object language like " 'It is raining' is true iff it is raining and there is no largest prime number" or " 'It is raining' is true iff it is raining and $2+2=4$." It is obvious that necessary truths, such as "$2+2=4$", would hold in all circumstances including when it is raining in the speaker's vicinity. So the speaker's assent to "It is raining" would be compatible with the truth of all those deviant T-sentences.

The problem then is which of these T-sentences should be identified as giving the meaning of the object-language sentence in question. On the other hand, given the obvious fact that the meanings of the speaker's words are such that by her utterance she expresses beliefs, then, commensurate with each T-sentence (as above), we can infer a corresponding belief (attributed to the speaker) ranging from the belief that "it is raining" to the belief that "it is raining and $2 + 2 = 4$" and so on. We can solve our problem if we know what belief the speaker holds under the circumstances in question. It is here that the principle of charity is expected to discharge its function (see Davidson 1976). Charity requires us to interpret the speaker's utterance in such a way that she comes out as maximally rational by our own norms of rationality. Thus, by holding belief constant, we can identify " 'It is raining' is true iff it is raining" as the proper meaning-giving T-sentence for we normally believe that it is raining when it is raining in our vicinity.

The bearing of the preceding observations on the topic of this chapter should by now be clear. The idea might be cast as two-stepped. The first step is the claim that by asserting Moorean sentences one violates the principle of charity, the second that such violation results in absurdity. Given the preceding remarks the reason behind the first claim is obvious enough. For once the principle of charity is recognized as being constitutive of intentional ascription, of what it is to be a speaker at all, we can see how the assertion of such sentences undermines charity. Consider an instance of <P & ~IBP>, say, "It is raining but I do not believe that it is raining." By asserting P, or assenting to "P", one is performing a speech act to communicate certain information that P. Thus, when an agent assents to "It is raining" the default position is to interpret the utterance in such a way that it is true just in case it is raining, that is, take it to mean "it is raining." And, assuming Davidson's strictures on interpretation, to infer, in accordance with the principle of charity, that she believes that it is raining. For – recalling our discussion of deviant T-sentences – without imputing this belief, the speaker's utterance cannot be taken to mean "it is raining." So when, having assented to "it is raining," the speaker goes on to assert that she does not believe that it is raining, this would be a clear case in which the principle of charity is undermined.

As for the second step in our proposal, we may recall that charity is not a contingent assumption but, rather, constitutive of what it is to be speaker at all. Accordingly, having assented to "it is raining," the agent cannot go on to assert that she does not believe that it is raining. To do so would be tantamount to jettisoning and undermining her status as a speaker or as an agent at all. Once the agent asserts P, she cannot, on pain of contravening the principle of charity, go on to deny that she believes that P. On this approach Moorean sentences are absurd not because their assertion, believing, and so on involve some logical impropriety, but because their assertion is *interpretively* defective. It is the very status of the utterer as a speaker or agent, rather than the logical propriety of her utterance, that is put at risk when she violates the principle of charity by choosing to assert a Moorean sentence.

That charity is needed to make sense of how an interpreter can see, on the basis of his evidence, another as a speaker may be further explained as follows. Attribution of attitude content is constrained by the fact that attitudes be assigned in a way that would make sense both of the speaker as a rational agent and of her possessing concepts that make up the contents of her attitudes. Such attributions would be warranted in virtue of bringing about a best fit between the speaker's attitudes and language and all the pertinent evidence. On this picture, the speaker would emerge as a rational agent producing appropriate responses to her fellow speakers and to her environment. Since there is so much at stake in violating the principle of charity, Moorean sentences can be said to be (interpretively) defective because their assertion undermines that very principle.

In the remaining part of this section, I shall argue that the interpretive approach is superior to those that have already been discussed. To begin with, it differs from the assertoric approach in that it is not just based on the presumption that a speaker is sincere, but holds that this presumption is necessary if we are to take the assertor as a speaker at all (this presumption can be overridden by knowledge or conjecture of the desire to deceive). The necessity of charity stems from the constitutive interdependence of belief and meaning requiring that in fixing meaning we fix, at the same time, what people believe and desire. Accordingly, on the interpretive approach, the absurdity of Moorean sentences is traced to certain important facts about meaning, content and agency. This goes well beyond the peculiarities of the assertoric approach and such familiar claims that sincere assertions express beliefs.

As for the doxastic approach, there are important differences that set it well apart from our proposal. To start with, it is worth noting that what all explanations of Moorean absurdities have in common is the violation of some norm of rationality. Where they differ is over the type of norm they pick out to account for the absurdity in question.

In this respect, the doxastic and epistemic approaches are closer to each other than to the interpretive account. For their proposals both involve exploring the consequences of believing the Moorean sentences. The doxastic approach claims that such sentences cannot be *truly* believed (by postulating some as hoc principles, as I have argued) while the epistemic approach states that these sentences cannot be *rationally* believed. The interpretive account, by contrast, does not concern the peculiarities of believing these sentences. Rather, it seeks to reveal the *mechanism* that underlies the absurdity of their assertion. This may involve attributing contradictory beliefs to speakers but any associated similarity with other approaches is only superficial. For it is the violation of the principle of charity, as a *normative* constraint on interpretation, that explains the absurdity of asserting Moorean sentences. Charity is presupposed by interpretation such that to be a speaker is to exhibit a large degree of rationality which, in turn, requires the speaker's beliefs to be found to be largely consistent. This is quite different from showing, as in the doxastic approach, why believing Moorean sentences is problematic.

Secondly, unlike the doxastic (and, indeed, the epistemic) approach, our proposal does not depend for its success on the syntactic structure of Moorean sentences. Charity is not a syntactic or formal constraint on an adequate interpretation. Rather, it is a constitutive requirement that Davidson adds to certain other formal constraints to render his Tarski-style truth theory of meaning interpretive.[8]

Thirdly, whereas Shoemaker tries to establish why Moorean sentences are not assertable indirectly, by showing that they cannot be coherently believed, our proposal seeks to achieve this goal in an entirely different way. Although this point may look trivial, it actually says something important about the relation between language and thought. Both doxastic and epistemic approaches take Moore's paradox to be essentially a paradox about belief. Thus they give priority to thought over language and meaning. This is evidenced by Shoemaker's remark that "what can be (coherently) believed constrains what can be (coherently) asserted" (Shoemaker 1996, p. 76). The interpretive approach, by contrast, upholds no priority thesis. Linguistic meaning and mental content must be explained together, or not at all.

Finally, unlike the doxastic approach, our proposal is not ad hoc. We saw that Shoemaker's proposal violated the completeness constraint on an adequate solution to Moore's paradox since it was unable to deal with sentences of the type <P & IB~P>. This led Shoemaker to postulate yet another (and more controversial) principle to tackle such sentences. The interpretive account, however, does not infringe the completeness requirement. For once the necessity of attributing "I believe that P" to a speaker, who asserts P, is recognized, then this fact would not only render sentences of the form <P & ~IBP> unassertable but it would equally afflict the assertion of sentences of the form <P & IB~P>. Such sentences are equally absurd since their assertion is interpretively defective. For when one asserts P, we are required, by the principle of charity, to infer that she believes that P. So, when having assented to P, the speaker goes on to assert that she believes ~P, charity is thereby undermined. The interpretive account thus provides a uniform treatment of both types of Moorean absurdities. To conclude, I take the preceding remarks to give the interpretive approach a clear edge over its rivals.

In Chapter 1, we tried to provide an account of the truth-directed nature of belief and what is meant by saying that beliefs aim at truth. In this chapter, we considered some of the consequences of truth-directed nature of belief by seeing how best one can resolve the associated problem of Moore's paradox. It was concluded that the paradoxes arise as a result of contravening a principle of interpretation, charity, that turns out to be constitutive of intentional ascription and the nature of belief itself. This squares nicely with the account of the aim-of-belief thesis in the previous chapter as that account itself was founded on such a constraint on belief ascription as a participle of rationality to ensure that the total set of such states ascribed to a subject will be as rational and coherent as possible. What these findings indicate about the nature of belief is that when we ascribe beliefs and desires to a certain creature, we are, in effect, trying to make rational sense of its doings. In the next chapter, I shall further stress the importance of the truth-sensitive character of belief by showing how two well-known requirements on knowledge are best seen as giving expression to this feature of belief.

3
Belief, Sensitivity and Safety

Much recent work on knowledge and skepticism has been concerned with delineating requirements whose satisfaction is supposed to lead to the obtaining of knowledge and thwarting the threat of skepticism. One of these conditions, sensitivity, has been the subject of much discussion, not least because it seems to call into question the principle of closure. In response, some theorists have proposed an alternative requirement, known as the principle of safety, as what a belief requires in order to count as knowledge. Needless to say, both principles have been criticized for a variety of reasons. In this chapter, while focusing mostly on safety, I shall try to evaluate these criticisms by putting a new gloss on these principles. To reinforce the conclusions reached in previous chapters, it will be argued that these principles should be seen, not as stating requirements for knowledge, but rather as giving expression to distinct cognitive goals involving the truth-directed character of belief. Accordingly, while we may then be able to preserve what is plausible about such principles, it will also follow, *pace* the standard account, that they can coexist because they involve different cognitive tasks.

3.1 Sensitivity and safety

In his influential analysis of knowledge, Nozick observes that, in addition to the truth and belief conditions, certain other requirements have to be added to ensure that what a cognizer believes is somehow dependent on the truth of what she believes (Nozick 1981). Nozick's important insight was to express this dependence relation in terms of subjunctive conditionals. This crucial condition in his account, known as sensitivity, is stated thus.

(SEN)   If p were false, S would not believe that p.

Utilizing SEN, Nozick seems to able to neutralize one important skeptical argument that exploits the so-called principle of closure according to which if one knows that p and that p entails q, then one knows that q (where q is the negation of some skeptical hypothesis like "I am a brain in a vat (BIV)"). It can be shown that while our common-sense beliefs are sensitive, beliefs in the denials of typical skeptical hypotheses are not. Even those theorists who propound a different account of knowledge seem to think that SEN contains a great deal of truth. Thus, to give an example, some contextualists are keen to incorporate the insight behind SEN in a "rule of sensitivity" in order to substantiate their claim that knowledge attribution is a function of the attributer's conversational context (see, e.g., DeRose 1995).

Nonetheless, many theorists believe that, on the whole, Nozick's account of knowledge is deficient in many ways and have accordingly proposed counter-examples to it, perhaps the most well-known of which are Kripke's cases. Suppose a film set needs a barn in a certain location when there is already a (real) red barn. If no barn had existed in that location, a green fake barn would have been erected there (all the available fake barns are green). Now, while an agent's belief that there is a real red barn there is sensitive, thus, a candidate for knowledge, she does not know that there is a real barn there since the latter belief fails to be sensitive. Or, consider the propositions p and "I am not wrong in thinking that p." Now, even if one can track and thereby know that p, one could never know that one is not wrong in thinking that p because the latter belief is not sensitive which is odd (Vogel 1987). In response to these problems, some epistemologists have proposed to replace sensitivity with another principle known as safety as a necessary condition on knowledge. In the following section, I shall consider various formulations of the safety requirement and the arguments that have been adduced in its support.

3.1.1   Safety: different formulations

There are currently a number of formulations of safety on offer. Although they are consistent with one another and indeed complementary, it will nevertheless be appropriate to treat them separately since the arguments and considerations offered in their support are different. It will be useful to distinguish three ways of delineating safety; intuitive, epistemic and doxastic though they are driven by the same motive, namely, that to count as knowledge, one's belief should be safe ensuring that it is non-accidentally true and could not easily be false where this is taken to mean that "one's belief as to whether P is true match the fact of the matter as to whether P is true, not only in the actual world, but also at the worlds sufficiently close to the actual world" (DeRose 1995, p. 204). Let us start with the intuitive formulation.

3.2 Safety: the intuitive version

The intuitive formulation of safety, safety$_i$, can be simply seen as highlighting the rationale just mentioned. Safety$_i$ brings together three notions of knowledge, reliability and easy possibility. Knowledge is thought to resemble reliability. Just as a machine is said to be reliable in case it could not easily go wrong, a reliably produced belief is one which could not easily have been false. Such a belief is said to be safe$_i$ which, to quote Sainsbury, may be expressed as follows (Sainsbury 1997, p. 112; see also Williamson 2000).

(safety$_i$)   If you know you could not easily have been wrong.

Accordingly, the absence of easy possibility is regarded as a necessary condition for the obtaining of knowledge. Although safety$_i$ appears to be an initially plausible thesis, its plausibility is undermined once one digs deeper into what is said to underwrite it. To count as plausible, safety$_i$ needs to be qualified as we shall see. To elaborate on this claim, it will be instructive to begin by considering the reasons that Sainsbury offers in support of the thesis.

Sainsbury does not present any direct argument for safety$_i$. He proceeds, rather, by offering examples which, he claims, lend support to the thesis. Comparing safety$_i$ with sensitivity, he says, while one's belief that one is not a BIV is not sensitive, thus, not a candidate for knowledge, the belief in question is safe$_i$ because one could not easily been wrong in holding it: "[T]o have been wrong, you would have had to be a brain in a vat, and it seems that this is not easily possible. So [safety$_i$] seems not to preclude your current belief that you are not a BIV from counting as knowledge" (Sainsbury 1997, p. 113). But this example hardly lends any credibility to safety$_i$ for knowledge is a cognitive achievement. A knower is not just a passive register of facts but an epistemically responsible agent whose belief is sensitive to his evidence. Knowledge is not about being always right but about how reliably one has acquired his true belief.[1] This is precisely the feature that is missing in Sainsbury's example. It is true that the agent's belief that he is not a BIV, assuming that he lives in a normal world, could not have easily being wrong, but this is entirely due to the circumstances external to the agent and outside his ken. It would still be safe$_i$, by Sainsbury's lights, had he formed it in a most haphazard and irresponsible way. What determines knowledge is how reliably (i.e., non-accidentally) one has *arrived* at his beliefs. To put it differently, the pertinent kind of reliability for a belief to count as knowledge is the reliability of the method or process generating that belief, that is, the reliability (safety) of the knower rather than the known.

Sainsbury's other reasons (couched in terms of examples) fare no better. Suppose I come to believe that Mary is married because I see her wedding ring. However, Mary hardly ever wears her ring and it is only by accident that she was wearing it on this occasion. Moreover, I have no particular interest in her marital status. Sainsbury claims that while my belief is not sensitive, it is safe$_i$ for "I could not easily have been wrong (given the uniformly prevailing convention in my culture that only married persons wear such a ring)... [Thus, I know] that Mary is married" (Sainsbury 1997, p. 114). But this example is hardly convincing. To begin with, it is not clear why Sainsbury thinks that the belief that Mary is married is insensitive. For if the belief were false, then, given the convention that only married persons wear such rings, one would not believe that Mary is married. Perhaps Sainsbury is confusing sensitivity with the condition that if the proposition that Mary is married were true, one would believe that she is married. It is true that this condition (Nozick's fourth requirement) fails in this example because in most of the nearby worlds where Mary is married but does not wear her ring, one would not believe that she is married. But this has no bearing on the sensitivity of the belief in question.

Moreover, it is not also entirely clear that the belief is safe since the example's structure easily renders it exposed to the generality problem. For if one takes the belief-forming process to be a token of the type "seeing Mary wearing a ring on that particular occasion," namely, the process token itself, then, given the mentioned convention, the ensuing belief would inevitably be an instance of knowledge. But this would make the example quite ineffective for the purposes it was designed for. On the other hand, if the process is seen as a token of the type "seeing people who rarely wear their rings," or alternatively, "seeing people who sometimes wear their rings but often do not," then the latter is hardly a reliable enough process to produce knowledge about people's marital status. How can such a process lead to false belief? Given Mary's habit of not wearing her ring, it follows that in most of the nearby worlds she fails to wear it on her finger. Then, assuming (quite plausibly) that married people generally wear their rings, seeing Mary under these circumstances would prompt us to falsely believe that she is unmarried.

Sainsbury's final example is, however, more plausible, but, as it happens, it supports only a modified version of safety$_i$ that should be acceptable to most theorists. Suppose you come to believe a mathematical truth in some haphazard way (e.g., by simply guessing and so on). Sainsbury claims that this belief is not safe$_i$, and, thus, not a candidate for knowledge "as you could have easily been wrong" (Sainsbury 1997, p. 114). However, it is clear that this particular belief (being necessarily true) could not have been false. Every world where one forms this belief is a world where it is true. What *is* right about this example is that, given the method used, one could easily have *gone* wrong. This is just another way of saying that to have knowledge, one's belief should be responsive to one's (adequate) evidence. This suggest a modification of safety$_i$ from "If you know, you could not easily have *been* wrong" to "If you know, you could not easily have *gone* wrong," suggesting that it is the reliability (safety) of the way one arrives at a belief that is relevant to the obtaining of knowledge rather than the safety of the proposition believed. Thus understood, safety$_i$ comes very close to expressing a justification condition for knowledge and something that many epistemologists would be happy to take on board (I shall take up this issue again later). I shall now proceed to examine a different style of expressing the safety requirement.

3.3 Safety: the epistemic version

This version of the safety requirement, safety$_e$, often associated with Williamson is one that has uniformly informed some of his epistemological projects. What is distinctive about safety$_e$ is that it goes well beyond the intuitive version by unfolding the mechanism through which a belief's safety bears on its being a piece of knowledge. We may call it the epistemic version of safety because of its alleged potential for clarifying certain philosophical controversies. A well-known case where the thesis is put to good effect is in Williamson's anti-luminosity argument where it is claimed that no non-trivial mental state is such that being in that state is sufficient for one to be in a position to know that one is in it. This is how Williamson articulates the thesis (Williamson 2000, p. 128).

(safety$_e$)   For all cases α and β, if β is close [i.e., sufficiently similar] to α and in α one knows that C obtains, then in β one does not falsely believe that C obtains.

It is important that to understand "closeness" here in an epistemic sense requiring, rather vaguely, sufficient similarity in the agent's evidential circumstances in the pertinent cases.

Safety$_e$ has been the subject of many discussions offering counter-examples to the thesis. I think some of these examples miss the point of safety$_e$. In this section, I begin by showing why they fail while high-lighting what I take to be the main problem with safety$_e$. The first set of counter-examples to be considered is due to Neta and Bohrbaugh (2004). Consider the following scenario. Suppose I am drinking a glass of water and judging truly and knowingly that "I am drinking pure, unadulterated water". Standing next to me is a person who has just won a lottery although he could have easily lost. Had he lost, he would have poisoned my water with a tasteless, colorless, odorless toxin such that I would still have believed (falsely) that I was drinking pure water. Now in the actual case, claim Neta and Bohrbaugh, my belief is an instance of knowledge despite being unsafe$_e$. But this counter-example is inad-equate for the real content of the belief in questions is "I am drinking water free from any external substance," bearing in mind that the pres-ence of some of these substances, like toxin, is phenomenologically undetectable. Understood thus, I do not, *pace* Neta and Bohrbraugh, think that I know I am drinking pure water in the actual case, for my per-tinent evidence in this situation is unable to establish that I am actually drinking water with no admixture of phenomenologically undetectable substances. Anyone who is inclined to dispute this claim should be pre-pared to accept that he knows he is not a brain in a vat by merely examining his phenomenological circumstances.

The authors' other counter-example falters on different grounds. We are asked to imagine a psychological experiment in which two groups of people are to report the number of flashes they see during the trial. Before starting the experiment, those people are asked, randomly, to drink a glass of liquid filled with either orange juice or some chemi-cals negatively affecting the working of the memory. Consider now an agent, S, who happens to drink orange juice and subsequently judges truly and knowingly that he sees seven flashes. However, had he drank the chemical, and been shown six flashes, he would still have believed that he had seen seven. Neta and Bohrbraugh claim that, in the actual case, S knows that the number of flashes is seven despite having an unsafe$_e$ belief. Again the example does not support its conclusion. For, we may recall, a necessary condition for safety$_e$ is that the agent's evidential circumstances must be sufficiently similar in the pertinent cases. This requirement is violated in the above scenario for, unlike the actual case, the agent's belief in the counterfactual case is based on unreliable grounds (faulty memory) and this undermines the case as being a genuine counter-example to safety$_e$.

There are, however, other counter-examples that seem to be damaging. Suppose a generally well-informed citizen, S, who, at t, one millisecond before Lincoln dies, believes that Lincoln is President. By all accounts this belief is an instance of knowledge. Now consider a possible world (w) where Lincoln dies at t instead of a millisecond later. W is very close to the actual world with the agent's evidential situation in w being quite similar to his epistemic circumstances in the actual world. But while S knows that Lincoln is President at t in the actual world, this belief is false in w. It is, thus, unsafe$_e$ (Brueckner and Oreste Fioco 2002). The moral of the example is actually symptomatic of a more general problem that concerns the ambiguity of the notion of closeness that is being employed in safety$_e$. To see this more clearly, let us consider various ways in which this notion might lend itself to interpretation.

These interpretations, coming in different strengths, would cast the notion of closeness in terms of the similarity of the agent's knowledge, justified beliefs, or his phenomenological and doxastic states in the pertinent states. Let us begin with the strong interpretation involving the similarity of knowledge states. Accordingly, the two circumstances of α and β are close just in case an agent knows as much in both cases. But this construal of "closeness" leads to the trivialization of safety$_e$ as it immediately entails that in β the agent knows, thus, truly believes, that C obtains. On a weaker interpretation "closeness" may be construed in terms of the similarity of the agent's justified beliefs in the relevant situations. But now safety$_e$ would be false as the following example illustrates. Suppose that, in α, S knows that there is a vase before him when he sees it in good light. In β, however, what he is seeing is an exact holographic image of the same vase in α. S is thus justified in believing that there is a vase before him on the very same grounds that provided justification in α. But this belief is false in β.

A still weaker interpretation might construe "closeness" merely in terms of the similarity of the relevant phenomenological states of the cognizer. Once again, safety$_e$ would be false on this interpretation. Suppose an agent, S, is seeing a red book in α under normal conditions. S thus knows there is a red book before him. In β, S, seeing a white book lit by red light, comes to falsely believe that there is a red book in front of him. However, when told (by some reliable source) of the abnormal lighting condition, he still persists on holding to the belief. Under these circumstances, S's relevant states in α and β are phenomenologically, but not epistemically, similar as he is no longer justified in believing that there is a red book before him. Finally, one might construe "closeness" in terms of mere doxastic similarity such that the agent's belief systems in α and β are similar. Once again, safety$_e$ is trivialized. So, on all such construals, safety$_e$ is either rendered false or trivial. This is not to claim that our survey covers all possible interpretations. But, in the absence of a clear account of what "closeness" consists in, safety$_e$ remains an ineffective thesis. I shall now turn to one final formulation of the safety requirement.

3.4   Safety: the doxastic version

The doxastic version of safety, safety$_d$, has been defended most explicitly by Sosa (Sosa 2000; see also Williamson 2000). It is effectively a counterfactual analysis of the safety thesis intended to highlight the tenacity of a belief if it is to count as knowledge. Thus, a belief is said to be safe$_d$ if, to quote Sosa, S would not have held it without it being true.[2]

(safety$_d$) $Bp \;\square\!\!\rightarrow p$

In support of safety$_d$, Sosa suggests the following illustration. Suppose a person has dropped his garbage down a chute in an apartment building, and that person believes that (p) the garbage will soon be in the basement. Given the long track record of correlation between the two events, the belief is certainly an instance of (inductive) knowledge. Consonant with the safety requirement, it is also safe$_d$: If one believes, in this situation, that the garbage would soon be in the basement, it would be true. However, despite constituting knowledge the belief is not sensitive for if it were false, one would still believe that the garbage would soon be in the basement. This, says Sosa, lends support to the claim that it is safety, not sensitivity, that is necessary for knowledge.

In a recent discussion of these issues, Kvanvig has claimed that, on their own, neither safety nor sensitivity are adequate to explain the nature of knowledge or how it obtains. Rather, both are needed to explain different species of knowledge. The reason why Sosa's example strikes us as convincing, he says, is that it involves a case of inductive knowledge. However, with cases involving perceptual knowledge, it is sensitivity that is needed to explain their obtaining for such species of knowledge require discriminatory capacity to enable one to differentiate truth from error. So "sensitivity is more at home in the realm of perceptual knowledge and safety in the realm of inductive or statistical knowledge" (Kvanvig 2004, p. 215).

I am not, however, sure that Sosa's example lends any support to safety$_d$. Neither is it clear, as he claims, that the pertinent belief is insensitive. Let us start with the latter claim. It is true that if p were false, one would still believe that the garbage will soon be in the basement (relying on the relevant good track record). But a sensitivity theorist might respond by proposing a recursive account of sensitivity in the following manner. Suppose belief q is sensitive and p's truth value (or its likelihood) varies with (tracks) the truth value of q such that if q is true/false, then so is p. Then one can say that belief p is sensitive because its sensitivity is dependent on the sensitivity of belief q. This seems to be true of Sosa's chute example as the truth value of p, "The next garbage bag will land in the basement," is, other things being equal (inductively), dependent on the truth value of q, "Garbage bags have been landing in the basement." Belief q is obviously sensitive (assuming that we have observed the bags in the basement). Thus, on our account, belief p will also be sensitive.[3]

Now to the claim that Sosa's example supports safety$_d$. As we saw, safety$_d$ is represented by the following counterfactual: Bp $\square \rightarrow$ p. On the Nozickian semantics for counterfactuals, this counterfactual requires that in the closest possible worlds to the actual world in which Bp, p is the case. Assuming, as in this example, that p is true in the actual world (i.e., that the garbage will soon be in the basement), there will surely be very close worlds where one believes that p, but p fails to be true because, say, due a slight technical glitch, the chute is blocked at that time. We are, of course, assuming that the agent's evidential situation, involving a good track record of correlation between the relevant events, remains the same across such worlds. Obviously a good track record need not be absolutely perfect. Thus, in the absence of a principled account of what makes worlds count as close, it would be fair to conclude that Sosa's example hardly supports his claim that the belief that the garbage will soon be in the basement is safe$_d$ and, thus, a candidate for knowledge. This is a defect that Sosa's account shares with Williamson's.

Sosa, however, goes on to say that safety$_d$ is just a first approximation and thus proposes a more refined version which, he claims, is immune to the problems afflicting safety$_d$. Before examining the revised safety, it would be instructive to get a better grip on the content of safety$_d$.

Following Vogel's useful analysis of, what he calls, "neighborhood relia-bilism," we can understand "$Bp \; \square \!\rightarrow p$" as saying that a belief is safe just in case it turns out to be true whenever it is held in the neighborhood N of worlds not too far away from the actual world.

(safety$_d$)   In N, $Bp \rightarrow p$

This captures the intent behind safety$_d$ for it plausibly construes a belief's tenacity in terms of its not being false in a neighborhood of possible worlds around the actual world.

Sosa gives his reasons for revising safety through the following exam-ple. Seeing a sailfish arching over water, I come to know that there is a fish nearby. Suppose, however, that the circumstances are in such a way that (a) the sailfish might easily have been swimming away while (b) the whale nearby might have surfaced and (c) I would on that basis have believed that there was a fish nearby. Accordingly, given a, b and c, I might have easily formed the false belief that there was a fish nearby. So while I know there is a fish nearby when I see a sailfish, the cor-responding belief is not safe$_d$. Couched in our neighborhood N-worlds terminology, what Sosa seems to be saying is that, given the easy possi-bility expressed by a and b, some of the N-worlds are worlds where the sailfish is outside my visual field and I falsely judge that there is a fish nearby on the basis of seeing a whale. The belief in question is thus not safe$_d$.

Accordingly, Sosa qualifies his thesis by shifting the emphasis from the safety of a belief to its safe basis (e): "[The belief should] be based on an indication or deliverance that *would* be true only if veridical. In the example of the fish, the basis would be an ostensibly sound argument from the arching sailfish to the presence of a fish nearby" (Sosa 2000, p. 41). The revised version of safety may then be stated as follows.

(safety$^{*}_{d}$) Bp based on $e \; \square \!\rightarrow p$

Or alternatively,

(safety$^{*}_{d}$)   In N, Bp based on $e \rightarrow p$

Safety$^{*}_{d}$ appears to avoid the problem with the fish example. For if we wish to take the relevant basis to be "seeing a sailfish," then that would safely give rise to the belief that there is a fish nearby. But now the gen-erality problem shows its ugly head again. For if we take one's evidence or the process responsible for producing the belief in question to be a token of the type "seeing a fish-like creature," then our basis would be unsafe*$_d$ as it would give rise to some false beliefs in some N-worlds. If, on the other hand, we take the belief-forming process to be a token of the type "seeing an arching sailfish," then that would be a safe*$_d$ basis. Sosa clearly takes the latter basis as being relevant and, thus, regards the belief that there is a fish nearby as a piece of knowledge. But that is a rather curious conclusion if the belief can, by hypothesis, be easily false since it is false in many of the N-worlds.

Another advantage of safety*$_d$, according to Sosa, is that, unlike safety$_d$, it saves closure for knowledge. How does safety$_d$ fail the closure? Consider the following example (due to Cohen). Suppose the residents of a region decide to erect some real and fake barns there by flipping a coin. All the replicas happen to be green. An agent, S, who is unaware of the fake barns comes to believe that there is red barn before him upon seeing a real red barn. Thus, S knows that there is a red barn before him because the corresponding belief is safe*$_d$. But S does not know that there is a barn before him since in some of the N-worlds in which S holds the belief, it is false. However, safety*$_d$ appears to save closure for knowledge. Here is how Cohen argues for this claim (Cohen 2004). S's belief that there is a barn before him is based on the deliverance of a red barn which is safe*$_d$ because the deliverance would occur if there were a red barn before him. Closure is thus saved. But safety*$_d$ avoids closure failure, says Cohen, only at the cost of producing the result that S knows he is seeing a barn in a region infested with fake barns. This conclusion is highly counterintuitive as Goldman famously illustrated it when he introduced the barn example to undermine the causal theory of knowledge.

In response, Sosa denies that we either know it is a red barn we face or that it is a barn (Sosa 2004). So neither closure nor our intuitions are undermined by such cases. But how does safety*$_d$ entail that we do not know there is a red barn before us when looking at one? According to Sosa, the problem arises because we take the content of our evidence for the belief that we are seeing a red barn to consist of an experience with a unified red-visual character, whereas our experience has both a barnish as well as a reddish character grounding the beliefs that here we see a barn and here we see something red respectively. From these two beliefs, we then infer that we see a red barn. Now since the belief that we see a barn is not, in that example, a safe*$_d$ belief, neither is the belief that we see a red barn.

Sosa's response raises a number of questions. To begin with, do people usually form their beliefs in the inferential manner suggested by Sosa?

Do they usually exercise such a fine-grained capacity to discriminate between various characters of their experiences and then recombine them via an inferential procedure? Is this how children and unsophisticated people go about forming their ordinary beliefs? Secondly, Sosa escapes the charge that his theory commits him to the unintuitive conclusion that one knows one is seeing a barn only at the cost of denying the intuitive claim that one knows one is seeing a red barn when looking at one. If I see a real *red* barn alongside a number of *green* fake barns, it seems that, at least, at an intuitive level, one knows one is seeing a red barn. There is no reason to think that the belief in question is accidental in that it could easily be false in the envisaged circumstances where the fake barns are green. Moreover, Sosa's claim does not conform to his verdict in the fish example where he claimed that by seeing a sailfish one knows that there is fish nearby despite the sailfish's ability to swim away while whales are swimming around. For the knowledge in question is certainly based on the safe*$_d$ basis that one knows one is seeing a sailfish.

Sosa might insist that the belief that one is seeing a red barn is based on the unsafe*$_d$ belief that one is seeing a barn. But this strategy runs into problem with the original Kripke example. There is a real red barn in a certain location. But if no barn had existed there, a green fake barn would have been erected instead (all the available fake barns are green). The belief that one is seeing a barn is not safe*$_d$. On Sosa's proposal, the belief that one is seeing a red barn is equally unsafe*$_d$ for it is based on the unsafe*$_d$ belief that one is seeing a barn. But it would be quite implausible to deny that one does not know one is seeing a red barn when, as in Cohen's version, one is looking at one in a location where the real red barn is the only standing construction.

Another problem concerns the procedure by means of which we decide which bases are supposed to support the pertinent beliefs, and, thus, whether the beliefs are to be regarded as safe. We saw, for example, that Cohen took the deliverance of a red barn as the basis of the belief that one is seeing a barn and so regarded the latter belief as safe while Sosa chose to move in the opposite direction. Rejecting arbitrariness, it seems that what underlies the differences of opinions is our old generality problem. While Cohen is inclined to take "seeing a real red barn" as the type of process whose token provides the basis for the belief that one is seeing a barn, Sosa chooses "seeing a barn in a fake barn country" as the process responsible for producing the belief in question which is why they differ over its safety status.

Finally, Sosa's revised version of safety has a sense of déjà vu about it. Recall that, according to safety*$_d$, a belief is safe iff it is held on a basis that the belief would not have been without being true. If we take "holding on a basis" as referring to the property of justification, then Sosa's proposal would sound very much like one of the early attempts to meet the Gettier problem, namely, the claim that a belief counts as knowledge only if it is conclusively justified in the sense that the belief's justification entails its truth.

To conclude this part of the chapter, neither versions of safety has proven capable of defusing the objections raised against them. Moreover, as we have seen, the situation is no rosier in regard to sensitivity. We thus seem to find ourselves in a bind. In the remainder of this chapter, I shall try to put a new gloss on the sensitivity and safety theses that is, hopefully, capable of explaining their attractions as well as their vulnerabilities. Before embarking on this task, it should be noted that from now on I shall take safety$_d$ to represent the safety thesis (thus, dropping the subscript) as it is some version of this thesis that actually constitutes the core of other formulations.

3.5 Safety and sensitivity as distinct cognitive goals

Despite their differences, the theories we have discussed and criticized thus far share one single characteristic in that they all view safety and sensitivity as necessary conditions for knowledge. But there is an alternative way of looking at these theses which construes them as cognitive principles expressing distinct cognitive goals, namely (a) aiming at truth and (b) aiming at true beliefs. To explain, let us remind ourselves of some the points that were raised in Chapter 1.

It seems that adopting the attitude of believing toward a proposition carries with it some sort of commitment toward the truth of that proposition. Bernard Williams famously described this feature of belief in the guise of the metaphor that beliefs aim at truth. As noted in Chapter 1, truth functions, in some manner, as an *internal* goal toward which a purposive state like belief strives. It is this feature of belief that is said to mark it from other cognitive states such as supposing, assuming, imagining and so on. For we may assume or suppose something, even if it is false, just, say, for the sake of argument or to see where it leads. But it seems that one can only believe a proposition with the aim of regarding it as true for its own sake, that is, seriously (see Chapter 1).

In any case, the aim-of-belief thesis constitutes a substantial fact about the nature of belief. Accordingly, it seems that, as a first shot, one may want to say at least this much of believing a proposition, p, that it sustains the following conditional.

(C)   Necessarily, if a proposition p is false, then one does not believe it.

But C seems too strong and indeed false for it threatens the reductio that no belief can be false, and that no one believes a false proposition. We thus need to weaken C by considering, *a la* Vogel, only the nearby possible worlds (N) to the actual world rather than all the possible worlds. Accordingly, to say that a belief p aims at truth is to say that in N-worlds in which the truth value of p is different from it actual value, one's belief varies with that truth value. That is to say, we need to move to some subjunctive version of C.

(C*)   If p were false, one would not believe it.

Now it seems that C* avoids the reductio. Not every true proposition is such that if it were false one would not believe it. Presumably because, on the standard semantics, the truth of C* requires that in the closest worlds to the actual world in which $\sim$p, $\sim$Bp is the case. However, this does not rule out the existence of remote worlds where $\sim$p but one believes that p.

C* is not, however, true of other cognitive states such as assuming or supposing. Supposing, for example, involves regarding a proposition as true regardless of whether it is true. When someone asks us to suppose that p, he is not inviting us to believe p but only to highlight where it leads. Thus, C* allows us to differentiate belief from other cognitive states by giving expression to the aim-of-belief-thesis. One might put this by saying that a belief is a cognitive state that sustains the counterfactual C*. (Compare: Laws are said to support or sustain certain counterfactuals in a way that accidental generalization do not.) But C* is precisely what the sensitivity thesis asserts, namely, our old SEN. However, instead of seeing C* as a requirement for *knowledge*, on our account, it turns out to underline a distinctive feature of *belief* – while allowing the possibility of false beliefs. For, to say that beliefs aim at truth is not to say that they are true. As we saw in Chapter 1, aiming at a target is not the same thing as hitting the target. So instead of saying that knowledge is sensitive belief, we may say that belief is a cognitive state that is sensitive to truth. Accordingly, if sensitivity is really just a way of expressing the aim-of-belief thesis, it may be no wonder that incorporating it in an account of knowledge, as Dretske and Nozick have done, would create insurmountable difficulties for those theories which they subsequently faced.

Another feature of the interpretation offered here is that it seems to be able to account for one of the most controversial features of sensitivity (as a condition on knowledge), namely, the fact that it undermines the principle that knowledge is closed under entailment (on Nozick's account it does not matter whether the relevant entailment is known or not). The idea is that while your belief that, say, you have hands is sensitive, thus, an instance of knowledge, your belief that you are not a BIV is not sensitive. While Nozick and others have taken this to be a virtue of their subjunctive account of knowledge (as it seems to neutralize one effective argument for skepticism involving closure), other theorists tend to see it as actually the reductio of the account offered for, among other things, it seems to commit one to, what they call, an abominable conjunction, namely, that while you know that you have hands, still you do not know you are not a bodiless BIV. Steering away from the controversy over the validity of closure, I think our gloss on sensitivity can explain why sensitivity fails closure. For, on our account, sensitivity pertains to the nature of belief rather than knowledge, and it is widely thought that belief is not closed under entailment (but see Stalnaker 1984). Looked at this way, much of the controversy surrounding sensitivity, vis-à-vis the question of the validity of closure, ought to be seen as pointless

Now to the other goal (b), namely, "aiming at true beliefs." To repeat what was said in Chapter 1, to say that beliefs aim at truth is different from saying that one aims at true beliefs. A belief can aim at truth and yet turn out to be false. Aiming at a target (truth) does not necessarily involve hitting it, otherwise belief would be factive. While (a) is intended to delineate the structure of belief, thus, providing an insight into the character of our doxastic behavior, (b) tells us what one should do if one's doxastic behavior is to count as rational. Let us then remind ourselves of what (b) actually involves.

As noted in Chapter 1, (b) is crucial to epistemic evaluation in the following sense. It is too familiar a fact that beliefs can be assessed from a number of perspectives. Depending on which standards and goals one adopts, such assessments will yield different results. Beliefs can be evaluated from, say, moral, practical and epistemic standpoints. What distinguishes epistemic evaluations from other species is the involvement of epistemic standards and appropriate epistemic goals. Now an important type of epistemic evaluation is to check beliefs for whether they are justified. Being a goal-directed notion, justification's attachment to a belief is thought to render the belief worth having from the epistemic point of view characterized, in turn, in terms of an appropriate epistemic goal.

In any event, whether one's belief is epistemically rational or justified depends on whether the forming of the belief in question tends to serve or promote the truth goal, namely, the goal of having true rather than false beliefs: "One's cognitive endeavors are epistemically justified only and to the extent that they are aimed at this goal" (BonJour 1985, p. 7). But for a belief to serve the truth goal it does not have to be true. That is, a successful promotion of the truth goal does not require the following strong principle.

(T)   Necessarily, Bp → p

It is a staple of modern epistemological thought that justified (rational) belief can be false and true beliefs unjustified. To avoid this implication, theorists often choose to express the truth goal subjunctively for then not every true belief would be such that one would believe only if true (David 2001; Sosa 2003). So one may express the truth goal in the following fashion (Sosa 2003).

(G)   Being such that (x) (one would believe x only if x were true)

Construed thus, what the promotion of the truth goal really requires is the weaker principle (T*) according to which a belief serving G is not false in the neighborhood (N) of worlds not too far away from the actual world.

(T*)   In N, Bp → p

Accordingly, a belief that satisfies T* can be justified without being necessarily true as T* leaves open the possibility of false belief promoting the truth goal. But now T* seems to express precisely the content of the safety thesis, namely, Bp □→ p. So safety can be thought of not as *condition* on *knowledge* but as an *aim* whose promotion renders a belief *justified* – while allowing the possibility of justified false beliefs. Accordingly, if the safety of a belief is to bear on its epistemic status, it is its status as being justified rather than knowledge that is really relevant in the context. These results have important ramifications for our discussions here. First, one should no longer conceive of sensitivity and safety as competing theses for they belong to different conceptual planes. While sensitivity concerns the structure of *belief* and designates what such states aim at, safety gives expression to an aim that *justified* beliefs are said to serve (viz., the truth goal).

Secondly, seeing safety in this light would no longer make it vulnerable to the objections raised against it. For those objections were precisely aimed at safety as a condition on knowledge whereas, on our account, safety is constitutive of justification, an aim whose realization renders a belief justified. In this connection, it is interesting to recall Sosa's revised version of safety (i.e., safety*$_d$) which comes very close to associate safety with the justificatory status of a belief by replacing "the requirement that the belief itself be safe with the requirement that it have a safe *basis*: that is, that it be based on an indication or deliverance that *would* be there only if veridical" (Sosa 2000, p. 41). To put this in more familiar terms, what this qualification seems to suggest is that a belief is safe only if it has a safe basis (where the latter is, in turn, couched in terms of reliability). But now all this sounds like a justification clause for knowledge, for one may alternatively describe a belief based on safe (reliable) grounds as justified. The same sentiment is echoed by Lehrer:

> S's belief that p is safe iff the following: S has evidence e for believing that p and if S were to believe that p on the evidence e S has, then p ... [So] the truth of p should be a result of the belief being based on the evidence one has rather than of the belief simpliciter.
>
> (Lehrer 2000, p. 35)

Finally, it seems that our account is also able to accommodate the intuition behind the safety thesis, namely, the link between knowledge and reliability. The idea was that "knowledge in some ways resembles reliability," or, to quote Sosa again, a safe belief, as a candidate for knowledge, is one that has a safe and reliable basis. If you rely on it, you could not, like reliable machine, easily go wrong. Accordingly, knowledge is not a one-off, lucky achievement, for reliability inevitably takes the past as well as the future performance of belief-forming processes into account. It is, in other words, a *historical* concept, a feature that the concept of safety inevitably inherits. Now, one may capture this historical aspect of safety, on the account presented here, by advocating a diachronic conception of the truth goal understood in terms of the overall maximization of truth and minimization of falsity in one's belief repertoire in the long run. The diachronic conception makes justification of a belief sensitive to how the belief has been formed or sustained in a non-accidental and reliable way.

Thus, contrary to what Neta and Bohrbaugh claim, justification (knowledge) is not just a dramatic achievement like a "horse which wins by a nose [or a] leap across a chasm" (Neta and Bohrbaugh 2004, p. 404). Such analogies are actually more fitting in the case of *true belief* rather than justification (knowledge). A true belief can be a one-off achievement obtained by sheer luck. If hard pressed for an analogy, knowledge seems to resemble a victory obtained by exercising a brilliant strategy rather than a victory brought about by luck and accident. Just as aiming at "winning battles in the long run" requires a well-conducted campaign, a reliability-based account of justification ought to maintain that the truth goal is the diachronic goal of "having true beliefs in the long run." To conclude, the preceding observations lend, I believe, considerable support to the interpretation of safety and sensitivity as distinct cognitive goals rather than conditions on knowledge.

As argued in Chapters 1 and 2, rationality, truth and coherence are of the essence of belief. But beliefs are also distinguished by the fact that they are sensitive to evidence. The idea is that beliefs seem to be governed by evidential norms in the sense that a rational belief is one that is supported by evidence. But evidence can be either of a doxastic nature (a belief state) or of a nondoxtasic one (sensory experience). The question that we will be concerned with is how, as in certain epistemological theories, one can appeal to sensory experiences to give an account of the justification of perceptual beliefs. This is to be investigated in the next two chapters.

4
Basic Beliefs and the Problem of Non-doxastic Justification

Beliefs, as noted earlier, are also distinguished by the fact that they are sensitive to evidence. Evidence, however, can be either doxastic or experiential. It is the bearing of the latter type of evidence on belief that we will be concerned with in this chapter. The question of the epistemic liaison between sensory experience (perception) and belief has long been a controversial one dividing the foundationalist and coherentist theories of the structure of our justified beliefs. The debate has been further fueled by the recent controversy over the character of experience; whether its content is of a conceptual or non-conceptual nature. In this chapter, after highlighting the urgency of the issue, I try to provide a rather comprehensive survey of the current attempts to resolve the problem of non-doxastic justification by reconstructing them as attempts to find a normative paradigm that would simulate the experience–belief transition. While finding them all wanting, I conclude by providing a diagnosis of why they fail and examine the prospects of finding a satisfactory solution to the problem.

4.1 Experience and reason: the problem explained

Most of our knowledge (justified beliefs) about the world comes to us through our senses. This raises the question of the type of structure our body of knowledge (justified beliefs) enjoys. On a foundationalist account, our system of justified beliefs consists of a "foundation" and a "superstructure" which, in turn, requires distinguishing between basic, that is, foundational and non-basic beliefs. Basic beliefs are those that acquire their justified status without standing in any relevant relation to other beliefs, whereas non-basic beliefs are arrived at by reasoning (broadly construed) from basic beliefs. Reasoning can only confer justification if the beliefs from which we have reasoned are themselves justified. So there has got to be a set of (basic) beliefs whose justification obtains independently of other beliefs or else the regress of justification will not come to an end. Thus, foundational beliefs provide prima facie justification for beliefs belonging to the superstructure. Foundationalism has therefore two major questions to address: (1) The precise nature of the transmission of justification from the foundation to the superstructure; and (2) the way basic beliefs acquire their justification. It is the second question that will be the focus of this chapter.

The reason why I am justified in believing, say, that the book on my desk is red is simply the fact that it looks red to me. We typically cease to offer justification in terms of the other beliefs we hold when we reach a basic source. It is precisely this intuition that underlies the postulation of basic beliefs in foundationalist theories. This helps terminate the regress of reasons but brings into focus the question of how sensory experiences can confer justification on the beliefs they give rise to. This has prompted certain philosophers to reject foundationalist theories that rely on sensory experience to terminate the regress of reasons. According to these theorists "nothing can count as a reason for a belief except another belief" (Davidson 1986, p. 310; see also Rorty 1980; BonJour 1985). Once sensory experiences are construed as non-cognitive and non-judgmental, they neither need any justification nor are capable of giving it. Experiences do stand in causal relations to beliefs but this relation is not justificatory and reason-giving. Thus, the problem for foundationalists is that of showing how a cause can be transformed into a reason (let us call this the problem of "nondoxastic justification"). The problem has been succinctly stated by Davidson (who conceives of experiences as sensations, thus, lacking propositional content).

> The relation between a sensation and a belief cannot be logical, since sensations are not beliefs or other propositional attitudes. What then is the relation? The answer is, I think, obvious: the relation is causal. Sensations cause some beliefs and in *this* sense are the basis or ground of those beliefs. But a causal explanation of a belief does not show how or why the belief is justified.
>
> (Davidson 1986, p. 311)

To illustrate the severity of the issue, I shall now proceed to examine variety of attempts to resolve the problem to show why it cannot easily go away by the standard means.

4.2 Resolving the problem: normative paradigms

In the rest of this chapter, I set out to examine some recent solutions to the problem of the of non-doxastic justification. To obtain a more accurate picture of the territory and see what divides philosophers over the issues involved, it would be instructive to construe the problem as a challenge to map one important feature of epistemic justification, namely, its normativity, onto the experience–belief transitional process. Epistemic justification is a normative and evaluative concept which pertains to what an agent ought or ought not believe, so that to say of an agent that he is justified in holding a belief is to say that there is something alright and satisfactory with the way things are with that agent. If one can do the required mapping, one will have shown that the transition in question is not only causal but also normative, thus going some way toward explaining the rational bearing of experience on the beliefs it gives rise to.

A natural way of addressing this issue is to find a normative paradigm that would simulate the transition in question. This would also help us carve up the conceptual territory in terms of the specific features of the paradigm in question. What would these normative paradigms look like? A most obvious candidate is one that involves the norms of logic, thus allowing us to evaluate the normativity of experience–belief transitions in terms of their conformity with such norms. Other, less obvious, paradigms are those like the exercise of skills whose supposedly normative dimension manifests itself when those skills are evaluated for correctness according to publicly known standards. Let us examine these approaches in turn.

4.3 Inferential paradigms

By far the most likely candidate for being a normative paradigm is an inferential transition where one moves from premises to a conclusion in accordance with certain rules or norms. Such a transition usually comes in deductive, inductive and abductive varieties. Typically, inferential relations require contentful structures, that is, logical or inferential relations hold between items that have both content and structure. This is most obvious in the case of inferences involving beliefs. An agent who believes, say, that a is φ, and that b is φ, and that a and b are distinct will be disposed to believe that at least two things are φ. A most natural explanation for the validity of this inference is to assume that the states in question have structured contents. Let us begin with deductive inference as the most obvious example of a normative inferential transition.

4.3.1   Experience–belief transition as (broadly) deductive

There is no doubt that appropriate deductive transitions – where new beliefs are derived from other justified beliefs in accordance with the norms of logic – are justification-conferring, and, as was noted, they require their relevant premises to have structured content. One may however discern two major divisions within the deductivist approach depending on how the notion of content is to be understood as one's view of the nature of content would directly bear on how one thinks that content is structured. There are, on the one hand, the conceptualists who claim that the content of experience is conceptual (with concepts generally understood as the inferentially relevant constituents of intentional states like beliefs) and there are those, the non-conceptualists, who deny this. I have no intention to enter the conceptual/non-conceptual controversy here. Rather, I am only interested to see how the theorists on either side of the divide seek to show that experience justifies beliefs. I shall start with the conceptualist camp.

4.3.1.1   *Conceptualist approaches*

It is widely recognized that perceptions have (representational) content, that is, representing the world as being a certain way. What has, however, divided the theorists on this issue is the nature of the content in question. Thus, according to McDowell's conceptualist picture, "[a] judgement of experience does not introduce a new kind of content, but simply endorses the conceptual content, or some of it, that is already possessed by the experience on which it is grounded" (McDowell 1994, pp. 48–9). Now, with the content of experience conceived as conceptual, the kind of structure that would naturally go with it can only be propositional. That is to say, if perceptions and beliefs are to stand in evidential relationship to one another, then, at the risk of leaving it mysterious how such a relation obtains, thereby undermining our epistemic contact with the world, one must assume that both sides of the relation are conceptually structured: "We cannot really understand the relation in which a *judgement* is warranted except as relations within the space of concepts" (McDowell 1994, p. 7).

However, in the absence of further elaboration of what the notion of justification requires, McDowell's remarks do not undermine the non-conceptualist's claim that states with non-conceptual content can play the role of justifiers. And, indeed, McDowell goes on to clarify his conception of epistemic justification. He complains that the non-conceptualist severs "the tie between reasons for which a subject thinks as she does and reasons she can give for thinking that way" (McDowell 1994, p. 165). However, as it turns out, these elaborations actually tend to obscure the picture of how non-doxastic justification is possible. To begin with, it is quite unclear how, on McDowell's account, experiences can confer justification on beliefs while our imaginings and hopes fail to do so when they all lack the required epistemic status. To see the point, let us begin by noting that McDowell propounds a strongly internalist conception of justification.

> If [the semantic] relation [between perceptual states and beliefs] are to be generally recognizable as reason-constituting, we cannot confine spontaneity within a boundary across which the relations are supposed to hold. The relations themselves must be able to come under the self-scrutiny of active thinking.
>
> (McDowell 1994, p. 53)

The internalist character of justification is further emphasized by demanding that the "[r]easons that the subject can give, in so far as they are articulable, must be within the space of concepts" (McDowell 1994, p. 165).

Thus, by McDowell's lights, if a cognizer's belief is to be justified, he must have some sort of strong access (in the form of, say, justified belief) to the grounds (reasons) of that belief, for, in his words, the agent must be able to articulate and rationally evaluate the force of those reasons bringing them under "the self-scrutiny of active thinking." Such an undertaking, however, requires considering how the world appears to the agent, for the articulation of his reasons is tantamount to expressing certain beliefs. So although McDowell takes experiences themselves to justify perceptual beliefs, this task always requires the cognizer to form beliefs or judgments about how the world appear to him (henceforth, "appearance beliefs").

Now although the preceding remarks help reveal the real import of McDowell's conceptualism, this is done at the cost of weakening his argument for the claim that experience justifies beliefs. For now, with the intrusion of appearance beliefs, these beliefs seem, by McDowell's own lights, to be better placed to play the role of justifiers for perceptual beliefs. To begin with, it would be implausible to see them as being mere epistemic epiphenomena if, as McDowell himself holds, they are supposed to play an important part in his picture of how experiences justifies beliefs.[1] On the other hand, McDowell is inclined to conceive of experience–belief transition as having a deductive structure. Against this background, it would be plausible to suppose that appearance beliefs are more suited to play the role of premises in such structures than perceptual experiences. For one thing, being beliefs, their content is conceptual. Moreover, unlike experiences, they are the sort of thing that can be justified, and, thus, able to transmit justification to the beliefs that are derived from them. In general, we have a better grasp of how beliefs can justify other beliefs.

This also poses a dilemma for McDowell. Either these appearance beliefs are justified or they are not. If they are, then this raises the question of how they acquire such a status. The natural answer would be to say that the very same experiences justify such beliefs. But to say this is to raise the question of non-doxastic justification at a different level. Suppose, on the other hand, that appearance beliefs are not justified. But then it would be puzzling how the addition of these further elements, lacking positive epistemic status themselves, to experiences can take the sting out of the problem of non-doxastic justification. These complications in McDowell's argument seem to suggest that, instead of highlighting the conceptual character of content, he should have proceeded to establish why experience can justify beliefs in the first place. This is in fact what Bill Brewer has undertaken to do by presenting an account that closely tracks McDowell's overall strategy (Brewer 1999).

Following McDowell, Brewer claims that only if experience has conceptual content can it justify the beliefs it gives rise to. However, unlike McDowell, this is not his starting point. Rather, he first tries to show that (R) perceptual experience provides reason for perceptual beliefs and then goes on to argue that this is possible only if experience has conceptual content. His argument, which he labels the "switching argument," and attributes it to Peacocke, has the following form:

(P1)   There is a class of beliefs about the spatial world ("a is F") whose members have the content which they do only in virtue of their standing in certain relations with various actual or possible perceptual experiences.

(P2)   Only reason-giving relations between perceptual experiences and beliefs could possibly serve the content-determining role required by (P1).

(R)   Perceptual experiences provide reasons for empirical beliefs.

According to (P1), relations with certain perceptual experiences play an *essential* role in the determination of the contents of empirical beliefs (making their truth-conditions *about* the mind-independent reality). So suppose an agent S actually believes that p because her actual perceptual experiences determine this, as opposed to q, as the empirical content of her belief. Had her perceptual experiences been appropriately different, she would have believed q rather than p. This much follows from (P1), assuming that it is true. Brewer then proceeds to argue for (P2) by highlighting the absurd consequences that would follow if it were false. So let us suppose

> These content-determining relations between experiences and beliefs are not reason-giving relations. So S's actual perceptual experiences give her no reason to believe that p rather than q. Thus, she has, and could have no more reason whatsoever to believe that p rather than that q, or vice versa. For recall, nothing other than their relation with experiences decides between the two contents – this is how q was introduced. Which belief she actually has is due entirely to the course of her perceptual experience ... [T]here could be no reason for her to decide between them. She does not really *understand* them as *alternatives*. Believing that p and believing that q are identical to her. Hence the supposedly content determining role of S's perceptual experience is empty.
>
> (Brewer 1999, pp. 50–1)

It is, however, difficult to see how the preceding remarks lend any support to (P2). All they do is to emphasize the causal link between experience and the relevant belief by expressing it counterfactually: If S's experience had been different, S would have had a different belief (with a different content *a la* (P1)). This is something that no causal theory of content would want to quarrel with. Brewer, however, goes on to add that if these content-determining relations were also not reason-giving relations, they would cease to be content-determining. Why? He makes several loosely related remarks none of which is convincing. First, he claims that if (P2) were false, S would "have no reason whatsoever to believe that p rather than that q." But could S not decide between p and q by checking to see which one best coheres with the rest of her beliefs? Nothing that Brower has said so far rules out coherence as a justification-conferring factor.

Secondly, Brewer asserts that if (P2) were false, this would imply that any supposed "difference between believing that p and believing that q is...nothing to [S]; for there could be no reason for [S] to decide between them." But this claim is ambiguous depending on what he intends by "deciding." If it means being able to distinguish between the contents of p and q, then this has already been secured through the appropriate causal chains linking experiences to the relevant beliefs. If, on the other hand, it is intended in an epistemic sense, then, as noted earlier, S could decide between the beliefs by appealing to an appropriate coherence relation. If one were to insist that only experiences could discharge this function, then that would immediately render Brewer's reasoning question-begging.

Thirdly, says Brewer, if (P2) were not the case, S would "not really understand [p and q] as alternatives." But why should the absence of reasons for p and q prevent S from *understanding* them as alternatives? Understanding has to do with truth-conditions and, surely, in virtue of having different causal links, p and q would have different truth-conditions (intentional contents) which S should be able to discriminate. One may have no reason for, say, the hypothesis "There was a tree at this spot one million years ago" and its negation, but that is no reason for failing to see them as alternatives. Perhaps what Brewer has in mind is some form of an argument from arbitrariness, namely, the idea that if some experience (e) supported propositions p and q to an equal degree but had no reason-giving function, then it would be quite arbitrary to believe p rather than q or, in fact, anything else. But this does not accord with the intent of his switching argument. For, we may recall, the claim was that had the agent's "perceptual experience been appropriately different..., she would have believed that q, and not believed that p" (Brewer 1999, p. 50). If, under such circumstances, one wonders what to believe, all one has to do is to identify which belief is actually the upshot of the experience in question. The arbitrariness worry would only arise if the relevant competing beliefs were equally supported by the *same* experience.

I think it is this confusion that leads Brewer to offer a subsequent illustration which is clearly not in accord with the structure of his argument. He invites us to conceive of the following scenario where the experiences normally produced in us by red objects (having specific microphysical properties) are labeled "red'" experiences. By (P1) these experiences determine the intentional contents of the relevant beliefs. Now suppose these experiences were *not* reason-giving, thus, providing the agent S with no reason to take the world as having just that property rather than another: "Indeed, had it been a quite different property in the world...which happened to be the normal cause of red' experiences, then [S's] beliefs about redness would, on this account, have been beliefs about that indeed" (Brewer 1999, p. 56, my emphasis). Now, unlike the switching argument, what the above example involves is the *same type* of experience (red' experience) giving rise to *different* beliefs. It would then be quite arbitrary which belief one were to embrace.

Setting this confusion aside, does the reasoning suggested by Brewer's example establish (R)? The immediate reaction to this version of the switching argument would be to say that the kind of externalism it highlights is, as the Twin Earth-style considerations have taught us, innocuous. The contents of many of our concepts (beliefs) are actually determined by our socio-physical environment. In response, Brewer proposes to restrict (R) to beliefs whose concepts are observational (unitary) in that they "cannot correctly be understood on...the model of natural kind concepts" (Brewer 1999, p. 75), namely, "concepts for which Twin Earth thought experiments cannot be given ... [like] colors, shapes, textures...and so on" (Brewer 1999, pp. 76–7). But this maneuver is both ad hoc and damagingly restrictive. Moreover, far from resolving the problems, it generates further complications of its own. For if (R) is now said to obtain only in connection with "concepts for which subjects' conception of their semantic value uniquely determines their semantic value" (Brewer 1999, p. 78), then, given that Brewer ties the content-determining role of experience with its reason-giving potentials, one would expect to see an epistemic counterpart of the preceding semantic thesis which is precisely what we get. He seems to think that the reason-giving nature of experience should enable the agent to know what his beliefs are about: "[I]n most, if not all, of the cases in which a person forms a belief about the world around him on the basis of perception, a belief which actually succeeds in making reference to a particular mind-independent thing...he also knows that he is referring to that thing" (Brewer 1999, p. 33).

This observation is further underlined when, later on, seeking to delineate the mechanism whereby experience justifies beliefs, Brewer says of the perceiving subject that "[s]imply in virtue of grasping the content that [that] thing is thus, he has a reason to believe that that thing is indeed thus: for he necessarily recognizes that his entertaining that content is a response to that thing's actually being thus" (Brewer 1999, pp. 204–5). Accordingly, the epistemic potentials of (a veridical) experience follow entirely from its content and the fact that the agent necessarily recognizes that he can be entertaining that content only if it is true. Brewer in fact likens the way experiences tend to be justification-conferring to the way a piece of knowledge is deemed a priori (Brewer 1999, p. 206). This is in fact tantamount to saying that grasping the content of an experience is to see that it is true. But it is all too familiar a fact that for every true perceptual content which a person entertains, he could have been in a subjectively indistinguishable situation which is all but illusory. In response, Brewer denies the claim that every "true perceptual demonstrative content has a subjectively indistinguishable yet illusory possible correlate" (Brewer 1999, p. 330). The agent can actually find out which state he is in.

But this is quite implausible. For if, by hypothesis, a veridical perception or hallucination is phenomenologically indistinguishable for an agent, it is only too natural that the agent is unable to find out in which state he is by merely reflecting on his psychological states. Veridical perception and hallucination share the same experiential content. And this is what underlies the widely held intuition that the victims of demon world scenarios enjoy as much justification for their perceptual beliefs as their counterparts in normal circumstances. If our perceptual experiences, under normal conditions, can confer justification on the beliefs they give rise to, there is no reason why they should fail to do so in demon world scenarios. But not only does Brewer's theory of non-doxastic justification fail to accommodate this fact, he actually denies that "[w]hen having a vivid hallucinatory experience, a person . . . [has] the same reasons for empirical beliefs as she does when she is actually perceiving the way things are in the world around her" (Brewer 2001, p. 451). But this is an implausible claim for, as far as the problem of non-doxastic justification is concerned, both veridical and hallucinatory perceptions pose the same challenge. I conclude therefore that neither McDowell's argument nor Brewer's modified version really establish the rational bearing of experience on perceptual beliefs. I shall now turn to the non-conceptualist camp to see if they can do any better.

4.3.1.2   *Non-conceptualist approaches*

In this section, I shall focus on the non-conceptualist attempts that, along with the conceptualist strategies, fall within the inferential paradigm. The paradigm, we may recall, demanded that perceptual experiences have both representational content and structure. Where conceptualists and non-conceptualists differ is over the nature of this structured content. Proponents of non-conceptual content often invoke certain alleged facts about the content of perceptions, for example, their specificity and richness of detail, or the fact that some agents, despite lacking conceptual resources, have, nonetheless, the ability to perceive the world to support their position, even though there are disputes involving both the intension and the extension of the notion of conceptual content. Despite their differences, since both groups appeal to the same normative paradigm to explain why the experience – belief transition is justificatory, their arguments often proceed in parallel directions though from different starting points.

Nonetheless, since, by assuming experience to have conceptual content, conceptualists are in a better position to offer an explanation as to why the experience–belief transition can be inferential, it is not surprising to see non-conceptualists trying to emulate the conceptualist strategies as closely as possible. Accordingly, given that content and structure were singled out as the most prominent features of the inferential paradigm, one could in fact delineate the non-conceptualist accounts along the following dimensions: Either postulate a sort of inference-like relation between experience and belief or construe experience itself as being belief-like. The first strategy has been pursued by Millar who calls such inferences "quasi-inferences" (Millar 1991). Millar takes inferential justification as his paradigm of how a belief derives its justification, and then seeks to show that analogous conditions hold in the case of experience–belief transitions linking experience types (described in terms of the situations and objects that typically produce them like red-book type experience) to belief contents. Making quasi-inferences, he claims, is part of mastering the relevant concepts. So the reason why your belief that something having the look of a red book before you is justified is that the content of this belief is quasi-inferable from the type of your current experience and the absence of countervailing facts.

The obvious difficulty with Millar's proposal is that while beliefs can transfer justification by standing in inferential relations to one another – in accordance with the norms of logic – this cannot be said of experience–belief transitions. For Millar's quasi-inferences are not really proper inferences. Even assuming that experiences can somehow play the role of premises in an argument, that still leaves us with the problem of how experience confers justification on a belief because, to transfer justification to their conclusions, the premises of a valid inference must *themselves* be justified and experiences are not the sort of thing that can be said to be justified. Indeed, quasi-inferential links, where causes are said to come into contact with reasons, look very much like the epistemic analogue of the Cartesian pineal gland which Descartes thought is the place where the mind comes into contact with the body.

A non-conceptualist could, on the other hand, try to assimilate experiences to beliefs while retaining the claim that their content is non-conceptual. This is the line taken by Richard Heck whose target is McDowell's claim that only if we assume that experience has conceptual content can we explain its reason-giving potentials. He accepts the widely held view that perception is distinct from belief but thinks that it is, nonetheless, an attitude of some kind: "In fact, I suggest, perceptions are attitudes, attitudes that are like belief in so far as to be in perceptual state is to hold an assertive, or presentational, attitude towards a certain content" (Heck 2000, p. 509). So how do perceptions justify beliefs? "Pretty much the same way beliefs do – whatever that may be" (Heck 2000, p. 509).

> When I look around, the result is not just that I come to be in a state with a certain content, but that I come to have a *presentational attitude towards* a particular nonconceptual content; then there is an inference or transition – call it whatever you like – from perceptual state to some belief I recognize it to underwrite. My belief will then be justified by perception on which I base it, in much the same way it might have been justified by another *belief* upon which I based it. Moreover my perception is my *reason* for my belief: At least, we have not yet seen any reason it should not be.
>
> (Heck 2000, p. 511)

It is very difficult to see how these remarks are thought to cast light on the epistemic nature of experience–belief transition, for they seem to rely heavily on metaphors and analogies rather than providing an explanatory account of the purported normative nature of the transition. Experiences are said to be belief-like (or quasi-beliefs) and it is further postulated that there is an inference – or "call it whatever you like" – from perceptual states to beliefs (following Millar, we may call it "quasi-inference"). But can such semantic baptisms really illuminate the epistemic puzzle we are trying to resolve?

Heck's emulation of McDowell's reasoning strategy does not end here. He also embraces McDowell's internalist conception of epistemic justification which requires us to evaluate the force of our reasons for our beliefs (Heck 2000, p. 512). To be able to do this, however, we need to know what our reasons are which, in turn, involves making judgments about the content of our experience and how it presents the world as being, that is, forming appearance beliefs. But how could one form such beliefs if the content of experience is supposed to be non-conceptual? This problem does not arise for McDowell, says Heck, because, on the latter's account, appearance judgments *record* the contents of our perceptual states. One cannot, however, say the same thing about Heck's version of the story where experience is said to have non-conceptual content. Once again, the non-conceptualist can try to mimic the conceptualist's strategy and that is precisely what Heck does. Appearance judgments, he says, *reflect* or conceptualize rather than record those contents. Presumably we are expected to understand "reflecting" as being somehow analogous to recording. But, again, it is difficult to see how the mimicking strategy can take the non-conceptualist's case far enough.[2] I shall now bring this section to an end by considering one final position within the inferential paradigm, namely, one that sees the contents of experience as standing in an abductive relation to perceptual beliefs.

4.3.2   Experience–belief transition as abductive

Some theorists within the inferential paradigm have tried to resolve the problem by construing the experience–belief transition as having an abductive structure. One such account has been propounded by Moser in which the notion of explanation plays a central role (he calls his account "experiential explanationism") (Moser 1991). Moser offers a broadly foundationalist account of epistemic justification in which the justification of empirical propositions are ultimately provided by the non-propositional evidential bases. He defines an epistemic reason as that which indicates that a proposition is true. So on his account an epistemic justifier of a proposition (belief) is simply a certain sort of truth indicator, or, what he calls, an "evidential probability-maker" for that proposition. But how can basic (unconditional) probability-makers, being non-propositional, non-conceptual items, lend any support to a proposition? Moser's initial response is to say that one's subjective non-conceptual contents, C, can make a proposition, P, evidentially probable to some extent for one, that is, being an evidential probability-maker for P, in virtue of those contents *being explained for one* by P. To take account of the rivals of the proposition in question, the notion of *maximal* evidential probability-maker is introduced requiring the proposition P to be a better explanation of C for a person, S, than is every probabilistic competitor for S.

But, without further elaboration of the mechanism whereby experience can be said to have justification-conferring ability, this account is unsuccessful. All Moser offers by way of a solution is to say that the non-conceptual content (C) of, say, seeing a red book justifies (makes probable) the proposition (P) "There is a red book before S", because P is the best explanation for S of why C occurs as it does. Although the idea behind inference to the best explanation (IBE) is intuitively plausible, it has proved to be notoriously difficult to delineate its structure (see Vahid 2001). The question actually splits into two questions. (1) What makes one explanation a *better* explanation than another? This is a request to identify the canons of theory choice. (2) Why does a theory's possessing these explanatory virtues make it more likely to be true? Answers to question (1) have often been formulated in terms of such largely unanalyzed notions as simplicity, parsimony, non-ad hocness and so on. This has significantly affected the status of the second question prompting theorists to either forgo their truth-conduciveness by declaring IBE a purely methodological principle or to resort to such equally unclear metaphysical assumptions as the simplicity and uniformity of nature.

Until these questions receive satisfactory answers, appealing to IBE would turn out to be no more than a mere name-dropping practice. These concerns are especially pertinent to Moser's case because he resolutely defends a truth-conducive conception of epistemic justification. Unfortunately, Moser's cursory remarks about such worries are far from helpful. For example, when trying to articulate what makes an explanation better than its rivals, he finds it sufficient to say that "an explanation is better than another if, other things being equal, the first does not posit gratuitous items whereas the second does" (Moser 1991, p. 98). And he then goes on to dismiss (in one sentence) the rival, skeptical, hypothesis that a Cartesian demon might be stimulating our brain so that it appears to us that there is an external world on the ground that the demon hypothesis "posits a gratuitous item" (Moser 1991, p. 98).

Moreover, even if we set all these fundamental problems aside, Moser's account still fails to achieve its intended goal. For not only our sensory experiences feature in the causal link leading from, say, a red book to the belief that there is a book before one, but also there are various neurophysiological states of the agent that form various stages of that causal link. By parity of reasoning, one might claim that since the proposition "There is a red book before me" is the best explanation of why those states occur, they, too, provide justification-conferring grounds for the corresponding belief. But this claim is absurd. The explanationist strategy has to be supplemented with further constraints to identify genuine justifiers from among these candidates but Moser's account lacks such a fastidious tendency.

4.4   Non-inferential paradigms

A radically different attempt, though in accord with the general strategy outlined so far, has been made by Reynolds (1991). Instead of inferential transitions, he picks out, as his normative paradigm, the exercise of such skills as playing the piano or speaking a natural language. He thinks that the exercises of such skills have a normative dimension which manifests itself when they are evaluated for correctness according to publicly known standards. Of course rules for correct performance in these cases are rarely stated and, in any event, performers are usually unable to state them or have any beliefs about them. But Reynolds thinks that we may nevertheless see the performers' attempts to meet the public standards of correctness, by monitoring their performance (in a somewhat nondoxastic way), as a matter of trying to "follow" the relevant rules (loosely understood). He claims that the normative character of experience–belief transition can best be explained by analogy with the correctness of the exercises involving such skills. When we arrive at our perceptual beliefs, we are, in effect, exercising our recognitional skills, that is, we are responding to experiential situations by forming appropriate sorts of beliefs. By thus locating the normativity of the experience–belief transition, we can see, says Reynolds, why beliefs arising appropriately from experience are justified.

To get a better grip on the proposal, I shall evaluate Reynolds' responses to a number of disanalogies that he himself brings to the fore in the course of defending his view. These responses, I shall argue, are inadequate, eventually undermining his account. One disanalogy, with such skills as piano playing, concerns the difficulty of spelling out the relevant rules for the experience–belief transition. Reynolds offers some suggestions as to how our recognitional abilities are structured. Our skills for arriving at perceptually justified beliefs are actually composed, he says, of lesser skills which can be combined in an unlimited number of ways. For example, "[a]rriving at the justified perceptual belief that Sam is standing requires recognizing the referent of 'Sam' by, [say], a pattern of visual qualities produced by light reflected from his face; it requires recognizing an instantiation of the predicate 'is standing', by another pattern of visual qualities" (Reynolds 1991, p. 285) and so on. By decomposing perceptual skills to re-combinable sub-skills, Reynolds thinks that cognitive science will eventually be able to answer the question of "[h]ow could one hope to write rules for perceptual judgement?" (Reynolds 1991, p. 283).

But this response is inadequate as it stands. To begin with, Reynolds' decompositional strategy invoking sub-skills such as various visual recognitional capacities (as in Marr's theory of vision) seems to be an appeal to the so-called "unconscious" processes that lead up to experience and eventually to belief. Marr's theory, for example, describes the stages by which variations in illumination are parsed to yield an image of objects in space in terms of representations which are themselves the product of a limited series of specialized processes (Marr 1982). His idea is to specify computational processes that result in visual representations of the world. Now, there is no harm in describing these information-processing systems as being governed by "rules." But these rules are more like computational algorithms than the sort of *prescriptive* rules that constitute such skills as piano playing and which are supposedly responsible for their normative character. If this is how Reynolds conceives of the structure of our perceptual capacities and skills, then describing them as processes where we "follow rules" is to stretch this notion far beyond its customary context. (One might as well describe the process of digestion as a case of following certain rules.)[3]

Another problem sees the analogy with skills as cutting loose the link between justification and truth. One can hardly think of correctness in exercising the skill of, say, piano playing as having anything to do with truth. Reynolds counters by declining to characterize epistemic justification as an evaluation relative to the goal of acquiring truth and avoiding falsehood.

> It seems more plausible to regard 'epistemically justified', not as an evaluation relative to a goal of achieving true and avoiding false beliefs, but instead as an evaluations indicating an acceptable degree of conformity to epistemic norms. In the case of perceptual beliefs, it indicates an acceptable degree of conformity to the rules that would describe the appropriate recognitional skill.
>
> (Reynolds 1991, p. 288)

But this response does not really take the sting out of the problem. For, nowhere in his article does Reynolds tell us what he means by an "epistemic norm." At one point, however, he refers to Pollock's views that epistemic norms are relevant to beliefs' justification (Pollock 1986). If this is meant to be an expression of support for Pollock's view of such norms, then it does not help to clarify the situation. According to Pollock, epistemic norms are of the following kind: If something looks red to you and you have no reason for thinking otherwise, then you are permitted to believe it is red. But if this is what an epistemic norm looks like, then it fails to accord with Reynolds' final statement (in the above quote), namely, that, in the case of perceptual beliefs, conformity to epistemic norms is to be construed as "conformity to rules that would describe the appropriate recognitional skill." For, as noted earlier, rules that purportedly describe recognitional sub-skills are more like algorithms that are intended to compute functions.

Setting these problems aside, it is still unclear how Reynolds' response is supposed to allay fears that his skills approach is likely to sever the link between justification and truth. Early on in his paper, when professing to adhere to an internalist conception of justification, he says this position "may be argued for from a deontological conception of epistemic acceptability" (Reynolds 1991, p. 274). Indeed this is Chisholm's and BonJour's chosen route to internalism (in fn. 9 he cites them as the main proponents of the deontological theory). But for BonJour justification is constitutively linked to truth, and in fact Chisholm construes our chief intellectual obligation in terms of the goal of believing truth and avoiding falsehood. Reynolds, however, recoils from spelling out what makes a norm epistemic, or, alternatively, what distinguishes epistemic from, say, prudential or moral norms. So it is not clear how he could work with a notion of epistemic justification that is internalist, deontological *and* distinct from other species of justification but, at the same time, not tied to the goal of believing truth.

Moreover, there is a tension between Reynolds' conception of justification and the way he conceives of arriving at justified perceptual beliefs in terms of re-combinable sub-skills involving information-processing systems. For, as just noted, the internal states that carry this information are usually thought of as "subdoxastic" states because, although contentful, they are, unlike perceptual states, not tied to consciousness. This is unfortunate for Reynolds' position because early on in his paper he makes it clear that he defends an internalist conception of epistemic justification: "[J]ustification has a pronounced 'internalist' character. One must be able to tell whether one's beliefs are justified" (Reynolds 1991, p. 274). Construed thus, this internalist account of justification requires the cognizer to have some sort of cognitive access to the adequacy of the grounds of his beliefs. But this does not square well with Reynolds' explanation of the way we arrive at our justified beliefs in terms of sub-skills that involve rule-governed subdoxastic processes and states whose contents are, by definition, not phenomenologically salient. Given the preceding remarks, it is, I think, fair to conclude that Reynolds' version of the non-inferential strategy fails to resolve the problem of non-doxastic justification.

A somewhat similar account to Reynolds' has been recently proposed by Markie (2004; 2006) according to which a particular perceptual experience confers justification on a belief as a result of our having learned to identify objects and their characteristics by experiences of that phenomenological sort. On this account, as in Reynolds', knowing how to do something (e.g., reasoning or riding a bike) consists in introducing norms that describe certain goal-directed behaviors. Markie's proposal is subtle and seems to escape some of the objections that were leveled against Reynolds' account, in particular, the problem concerning the link between justification and truth. But there is still a worry here. Unlike others, Markie rightly recognizes that an adequate account of non-doxastic justification should explain why perceptual experience justifies beliefs in normal as well as demon world scenarios. But Markie goes on to distinguish three ways in which a perceptual belief might be epistemically appropriate (justified) and takes the beliefs of the demon-worlders to be justified in an "undefeated evidence" (EU), rather than a "reliably based" (R), sense. On both conceptions one has internalized appropriate epistemic norms but only in R's sense does one's evidence also make the truth of belief objectively likely. This seems to suggest that EU (which Markie takes to be "the most basic" form of epistemic appropriateness) expresses something like a deontological conception of justification while R is a truth-conducive sense. (This strategy resembles Goldman's distinction between weak and strong justification in order to account for the justification of the beliefs of the demon-worlders (Goldman 1988).) Given the widely held view that deontological justification is not truth-conducive, we have, once again, the problem of the nature of the link between justification and truth resurfacing at a different level. It thus seems that non-inferential strategies are unable to improve significantly on the inferential approaches. I shall now proceed to provide a diagnosis of the failure of the proceeding accounts and examine the prospects of finding a satisfactory solution to the problem of non-doxastic justification.

4.5   Way forward

As we have seen the preceding attempts to show how experience justifies beliefs have, in one way or another, ended in failure although their strategy to identify a normative process simulating the experience–belief transition seems to be on the right track. In what follows, I shall try to uncover what underlies their failure and identify the obstacles that lie on the way of initiating a promising approach to the problem of non-doxastic justification.

To set the stage for discussion, let us begin by reminding ourselves that epistemic justification is a normative concept (more on this in the next chapter). Accordingly, to show that experience justifies beliefs, one should look for an *appropriate* normative paradigm that would simulate the experience–belief transition. As we saw, a number of options presented themselves to do the job with the inferential paradigm being the most obvious candidate to fulfill this role. The problem, however, was that while in a (valid) deductive inference justification can be transferred from its premises (beliefs) to its conclusion, it seemed difficult to conceive of perceptions as playing the role of such premises. For perceptions seem to lack the required positive epistemic status to be able to stand in a suitable evidential relation to the contents they are supposed to justify. This suggests the existence of an evidential gap between experience and beliefs given the presumed inferential nature of the support relation between the two. To remove this obstacle, a natural move was to introduce certain mediating elements to bridge the gap. We saw that, at the hands of McDowell, these mediating elements turned out to be species of, what we called, "appearance beliefs." Instead of solving our puzzle, however, this move merely reintroduced the same questions regarding the epistemic status of these new beliefs.

Following McDowell's footsteps closely, Brewer suggested instead that we take the recognition of our "openness" – that is, recognizing that our grasp of the content of our experience is a response to its being true – as the mediating element to bring perceptual experience to bear on the epistemic status of our beliefs. This required tying the content-determining role of experiences to their reason-giving potentials. Regardless of the nature of the element of "recognition" in Brewer's account, we saw that his suggestion had, among other things, the unpalatable consequence of ruling out the possibility of perceptual error. To leave room for error (justified false beliefs), while respecting the content-sensitive character of normativity, the link between justification and truth had to be weakened. One could see Moser's offering of an explanationist theory of justification as a move along this line. But, as noted earlier, the notions of explanation and justification stand too far apart. It seems that an explanation for why an agent believes that p is just a different sort of thing from a justification for believing that p. Weakening the link had also the untoward consequence of letting in items that could hardly be regarded as justifiers (on any theory of justification).

Given these problems, one may choose to move from the "knowing-how" end of the spectrum of normative processes and, thus, identify perceptual beliefs with the exercises of our recognitional skills (as in Reynolds' skills account). Although Reynolds' move seemed to avoid the problem of error, it did so only at the cost of stripping the associated notion of normativity of its content-sensitive character by effectively severing the link between justification and truth. This meant that, in Reynolds' account, the resulting notion of normativity was no longer responsive to truth, thus ruling out the justification of the ensuing perceptual beliefs as being truth-conducive.

Moreover, there are also some general problems with the inferential approach which, together with failure of the skills approach, seems to require a radically different account of the problem of non-doxastic justification. These problems concern the kind of picture that emerges from the inferential approach about the nature of our doxastic and epistemic activities. The thought is that the inferential paradigm seems to suggest an over-intellectualized and deliberative picture of our belief-forming activities. We are led to think that, when forming a belief, we are in full control of the choices that we make vis-à-vis our epistemic resources, that, for example, we are free to decide which body of evidence to ignore and what grounds to take as justification-conferring.

But much of our beliefs are not formed in such a deliberative manner. Often we find ourselves with our beliefs that may or may not have positive epistemic status depending on whether or not they are appropriately grounded. In this respect, our belief-forming endeavors resemble the exercise of skills along the lines suggested above. But if the skills approach is to deliver the goods, it should identify an appropriate normative framework where a right balance is struck between the content-sensitivity of the normativity of epistemic justification and the possibility of perceptual error compatible with the fact that our experiences can justify our beliefs in cases we are hallucinating. Moreover, this should be done without compromising the truth-conducivity of epistemic justification. We have, however, seen that the skills approach seems unable to deliver such a package. Exactly how this can be achieved is what has made the problem of non-doxastic justification so intractable. In the next chapter, we shall suggest a radically different approach to this problem.

5
Experience as Reason for Beliefs

Let us begin by emphasizing some of the points raised at the end of the previous chapter. It was pointed out that although attempts that seek to identify a normative process simulating the experience–belief transition were on the right track, their main problem was to identify an appropriate normative framework that respects both the content-sensitivity of the normativity of epistemic justification and the possibility of perceptual error as well as the fact that experiences can justify beliefs in cases of hallucinations. In this chapter, we shall present an account that, it will be argued, can accommodate these concerns.

Before embarking on this task, however, I would like to discuss one further attempted resolution of the problem of non-doxastic justification which appeals to the thesis of epistemic supervenience, namely, the view that epistemic properties supervene on non-epistemic, non-normative properties. It is important to examine this proposal thoroughly as it is claimed that the thesis in question provides a neat and straightforward solution to the problem we are grappling with. The first part of this chapter is thus devoted to investigating the supervenience proposal. I begin by briefly surveying what the notion of supervenience involves before examining the viability of the thesis of epistemic supervenience itself. I shall conclude that, despite being an initially plausible thesis, these arguments are unsuccessful. This is not, however, to deny the possibility of epistemic supervenience. The point is, rather, to draw attention to the fact that if supervenience is really as rich a concept as it is claimed to be, which seems to be the case judging by the variety of functions it is said to perform, then a lot more needs to be said in its defense. Finally, waiving such worries, I set out to investigate whether the thesis of epistemic supervenience has the resources to resolve the problem of non-doxastic justification. The upshot of our discussion is that the prospect of solving our problem along these lines is extremely dim and that a successful resolution requires a more radical departure from the well-trodden paths.

5.1   The supervenience thesis explained and applied

A set of properties, A, is said to supervene on another set of properties, B, when and only when there could be no difference of sort A without some difference of sort B. Variation in the supervenient A-properties, in other words, requires variation in B-properties. This constitutes the core idea of supervenience. Thus, mental properties are said to supervene on physical properties if and only if there could be no difference of a mental sort without a difference of a physical sort. Once the physical properties are fixed, mental properties are fixed as well. So understood, supervenience is a modal relation that is both reflexive and transitive but neither symmetrical nor asymmetrical. Jaegwon Kim has identified a number of features as marking the concept of supervenience (Kim 1990). To say, according to the core idea of supervenience, that B-indiscernibility entails A-indiscernibilty is just another way of saying that variations in A-properties are correlated with variations in B-properties. Kim calls this the "covariance" component of supervenience. What it does is to put a constraint on the distribution of supervenient properties relative to the distribution of their subvenient properties. But if the holding of a supervenience relation between two sets of properties is supposed to express a substantive metaphysical fact about them, the relation in question must be more than a mere property covariation. For what initially stirred up interests in supervenience was that many theorists thought they had eventually hit on a new type of dependency relation that would enable them to navigate freely between reductionism and unbridled autonomy. So "dependency" and "non-reducibility" should be counted as the other two components of supervenience, and this is what is meant by "supervenience" throughout this chapter.

   The core idea of supervenience admits, however, of a number of interpretations depending on whether we take the relata of supervenience relations to involve individuals or whole worlds. For the purposes of this chapter, I shall focus on the relation of supervenience as holding between properties of individuals. But even within this restricted scope one can distinguish between varieties of supervenience relations depending on whether it is within the same world or across different possible worlds that individuals are being compared. Accordingly, the following distinct types of covariance can be discerned. Suppose A and B are, respectively, supervenient and subvenient sets of properties.

(WC) Weak Covariance Necessarily, if anything has some property a in A, there exists a property b in B such that the thing has b, and everything that has b has a.

$$\forall x \forall a (ax \rightarrow \exists b (bx \& \forall y (by \rightarrow ay)))$$

(SC) Strong Covariance Necessarily, if anything has some property a in A, there exists a property b in B such that the thing has b, and necessarily, everything that has b has a.

$$\forall x \forall a (ax \rightarrow \exists b (bx \& \forall y (by \rightarrow ay)))$$

As can be seen, (SC) implies (WC) but the converse relation does not hold. Moreover, if the modal operator in (SC), or (WC), is taken to involve only nomologically possible worlds, then we get, what might be called, strong and weak "natural" supervenience; whereas if the class of worlds that fall within its scope involves all possible worlds, we obtain logical supervenience. I shall, however, take (SC) (in its logical sense) as being the preferred version of the covariance relation, and, indeed, that seems to be how the proponents of epistemic supervenience choose to formulate their thesis. In what follows, I drop all the modifiers and use "supervenience" to refer to strong logical supervenience alone.

As noted earlier, a number of epistemologists have maintained that epistemic properties supervene on non-epistemic, non-normative properties (e.g., Alston 1976; Sosa 1980; Van Cleve 1985; Kim 1988). Thus, epistemic justification is thought to be supervenient on such properties as indubitability, coherence, being appropriately caused by experience, being produced by a reliable process and so on. To uphold the thesis of epistemic supervenience is to assert that one's reasons for a belief being justified must be grounded in certain non-epistemic properties of that belief. By subscribing to the supervenience thesis one can deny the autonomy of epistemic properties without being driven to identify them with non-epistemic properties. Indeed, according to some theorists, this feature of epistemic justification is actually "what underlies [the] belief in the possibility of normative epistemology" (Kim 1988, p. 236) despite the attempts made to undermine it by the proponents of "naturalized epistemology." The supervenience thesis has also been invoked in a number of attempts aimed at undermining certain anti-foundationalist strategies. Sosa, for example, has claimed that supervenience commits one to, what he calls, "formal foundationalism" (Sosa 1980). Formal foundationalism holds that the class of justified beliefs is recursively specifiable in terms of a non-epistemic basis and a non-epistemic generator. This is precisely what is entailed by the supervenience thesis. The thesis is, thus, of some help to foundationalists as it seems to rule out certain forms of infinite justificatory regress.

More importantly, for our purposes, epistemic supervenince has been invoked, most notably by Van Cleve, to resolve the problem of non-doxastic justification (Van Cleve 1985). The idea is quite simple. If the supervenience thesis is true, that is, if property of being justified supervenes on the property of, say, being caused by experience, then one can say that it is *in virtue of* those non-epistemic (experiential) properties that a belief is justified. It thus looks as if the supervenience thesis is capable of serving many functions. But what reasons are there for it truth?

5.1.1   General arguments for the supervenience thesis

General arguments for the supervenience thesis are usually of a reductio form, highlighting the absurd consequences that would follow if the thesis were denied. These consequences either involve the violation of certain formal requirements on making epistemic judgements or touch on more substantive problems. Let us start with the formal variety.

According to Van Cleve the case for supervenience in epistemology is analogous to the case for supervenience in ethics. To show that moral supervenience holds of necessity, he cites the often quoted passage by Richard Hare.

> Suppose that we say "St. Francis was a good man". It is logically impossible to say this and to maintain at the same time that there might have been another man placed exactly in the same circumstances as St. Francis, and who behaved in exactly the same way, but who differed from St. Francis in this respect only, that he was not a good man.
>
> (Hare 1952, p. 145)

The idea is that if moral supervenience is denied, then we ought to admit that two objects could differ in respect of the property of goodness, but be indiscernible as far as their natural properties are concerned. And this is absurd. Similar absurdity, says Van Cleve, follows if epistemic supervenience is denied. For it implies that two beliefs may share their non-epistemic properties, but while one is justified, the other is not: "I shall therefore take it as established that epistemic properties supervene on non-epistemic properties" (Van Cleve 1985, p. 99).

But no such consequence follows from the above considerations. All that follows from Hare's remarks is that, when making moral judgements, we ought to treat like cases alike (in the form of either (WC) or (SC)). This is actually the import of the so-called principle of universalizability according to which an agent who makes a moral judgment is committed, on pain of being inconsistent, to making the same judgment of any relevantly similar action. So all that can be extracted from Hare's remarks is a version of, what Klagge calls, "ascriptive" supervenience which only says that an agent's *judgments* of a certain (supervening) kind about things cannot differ unless judgments of other kind about the things differ (Klagge 1988). This is to be contrasted with "ontological" supervenience, which involves a connection between two classes of *properties*. We cannot infer ontological supervenience from ascriptive supervenience for, as Klagge points out, "from the fact that it is reasonable to place certain constraints on our judgements, it does not follow that the world is constituted in a particular way" (Klagge 1988, p. 464). If this inference were legitimate, then one would have to count Hare himself as being committed to ontological supervenience and, thus, moral realism which he flatly rejects. Likewise, from the fact that it is reasonable to subject our epistemic attributions to a consistency constraint, nothing follows about the constitution of epistemic properties, and, in particular, their purported supervenience on non-epistemic properties.

It might be objected that if one takes a *realist* attitude toward a given stretch of discourse, then constraints on judgments made within that stretch of discourse should be seen as reflecting facts about that discourse. This is a plausible suggestion., but it is not of much help to the supervenience thesis. To begin with while epistemic supervenience (construed ontologically) is arguably sufficient for realism about a discourse, it is certainly not necessary. A realist might advocate autonomy (as dualists do in regard to the mental realm) and reject any sort of dependence relation between the properties in question. Moreover, the transition from methodological considerations to ontological conclusions can only be made possible against the background of some added information (Klagge 1988). To explain, suppose we take belief attributions to supervene on behavioral facts in the sense that if we posit some belief states as best explaining the behavioral dispositions of an agent, we must posit the same psychological states in the case of other agents who are indiscernible in so far those dispositions are concerned. This is a clear case of ascriptive supervenience involving a consistency constraint on belief attributions. But, on its own, this thesis does not immediately yield an ontological interpretation. This would be so if the constraint in question is put forward within an explanatory framework, that is, if we are told what it is *in virtue of* which those postulated belief states provide the best explanation of the corresponding behavioral dispositions. In the absence of an explanatory framework methodological constraints (of Hare-type variety) only ensure the consistency of one's judgments rather than the obtaining of the desired supervenience relation.

To reinforce this point, let us consider the question in a setting that might be more agreeable to the objector. Let us concede to him the point that methodological constraints (like those we have been considering) express facts about the properties (as well as the judgments) involved. Does Van Cleve's appeal to Hare-type arguments give us now the desired supervenience thesis? Hardly. For all that the argument can be said to establish, under the present construal, is that properties of certain sort covary with properties of another sort, that is, no difference of one sort without differences of another sort. But, as we saw, supervenience is more than an expression of property covariation.[1] It also involves a dependence relation which is intended to rule out the possibility that the domains in question are completely autonomous. The relation of dependency is precisely what enables us to say that it is *in virtue of* its base properties that a thing has a supervenient property, or, alternatively, that the former *explains* why the latter obtains. This relation is essentially asymmetric, whereas what (strong) covariance expresses is a relation of entailment that is neither symmetric nor asymmetric. As Kim and Heil have both emphasized, there is no obvious way of supplementing (strong) covariance to accommodate the element of dependence (Kim 1990; Heil 1992). They cite examples of cases in which strong covariance fails to be asymmetric (as when the surface area of a sphere, for instance, strongly covaries with its volume, and conversely, without either determining the other in an asymmetric way), and cases of strong covariance which, though expressing an asymmetric relation, still fail to yield dependence (as when the relation in question can be explained by invoking a third common factor). This means that dependency is an independent feature of epistemic supervenience, and not something that follows from the mere holding of a covariance relation between epistemic and non-epistemic properties.

It might be thought that all we need to do in order to rectify the situation is simply to add to the above considerations the idea that there is also a dependence relation between the properties involved. This would then give us the desired supervenience thesis. But the problem with this suggestion is that the mere postulation of a (supervenience) dependence relation between epistemic and non-epistemic properties fails to have any significant impact on what is really at issue. Any account as to why the supervenience thesis holds must be able to say what it is in virtue of which non-epistemic properties determine epistemic ones. Merely affirming that there is a supervenience dependence relation between them deprives the supervenience thesis of any significant explanatory potential that it might otherwise enjoy. It is indeed this problem that has led Kim himself to revise his earlier views on the uniqueness of the supervenience relation: "It now seems to me a mistake, or at least misleading, to think of supervenience itself as a special and distinctive type of dependence relation" (Kim 1990, p. 137). In any event, and regardless of the explanatory constraint on the supervenience relation, merely asserting a dependence relation would not provide a good argument for supervenience. Are there other arguments for the thesis?

An argument of sort can be gleaned from Kim's attempt to explain why moral properties supposedly supervene on natural properties (Kim 1993, p. 166). The answer, according to Kim, involves the very nature of valuation. If the supervenience of valuational properties on non-valuational ones is denied, we would be faced with an endless descending series of valuations, each depending on the one below it as its criterion of application. To avoid infinite regress, valuations must terminate in non-valuational grounds. The argument, if valid, would equally account for the supervenience of epistemic valuations such as justification on non-valuational grounds. It does not seem to me, however, that it succeeds in establishing the supervenience thesis. To begin with, being of an infinite regress type of argument, it stands or falls with the validity of such arguments, and it is quite controversial just how much infinite regress arguments can establish (see, e.g., Sosa 1980). Secondly, the argument shows, if anything at all, that to avoid regress the descending chain of justified beliefs must terminate in non-epistemic grounds. But whether these grounds are also (cross-worldly) *sufficient* for epistemic justification (which is what the supervenience thesis requires) is not something that is addressed by the argument. The claim that a descending series of justified beliefs must eventually terminate in non-epistemic grounds is quite consistent with the *possibility* of beliefs having the same grounds but differing in their justificatory status, something which contravenes the thesis of epistemic supervenience.

Moreover, by defending the supervenience thesis on the ground of the implausibility of an endless descending series of justified beliefs, we deprive it of its ability to serve the functions that foundationalists expect it to serve. The supervenience thesis, we may recall, was invoked to rule out certain forms of infinite justificatory regress, namely, an endless series of beliefs each of which is justified only because some other belief in the series is justified. It underpinned Van Cleve's reasons for introducing generation principles. In all these cases the supervenience thesis is called upon to defuse certain forms of the regress of justification. But now if the thesis itself depends for its validity on the implausibility of an endless descending series of valuations (justified beliefs), it cannot certainly be relied upon to defuse the regress of justification. If epistemic supervenience is to be established on the sort of grounds that Kim suggests, it would fail to provide independent support for the relevant foundationalist tenets. I conclude, therefore, that the proposed general arguments for the supervenience thesis fail to lend it sufficient credibility. I will now turn to more specific arguments for the thesis.

5.1.2   Arguments from particular theories of justification

While general arguments for the supervenience thesis aim at establishing the supervenience of justification on *some* non-epistemic property, other arguments might pick up a *particular* non-epistemic property of beliefs (coherence, being reliably produced etc.), and, relying on the corresponding theories of justification, seek to prove that epistemic justification supervenes on that property. Construed thus, these arguments would be taking their cue from the relevant theories of justification (coherence theories, reliability theories, etc.), so that any defense of these theories would be automatically regarded as lending support to the corresponding supervenience theses. Given our construal of strong supervenience (incorporating SC), these supervenience theses can be understood as saying that, necessarily, if a belief is justified, then it possesses the non-epistemic property n, and, necessarily, if a belief possesses n, then it is justified. Thus each particular supervenience thesis (corresponding to a particular non-epistemic property) would provide us with cross-world necessary and sufficient conditions for having the property of justification. The problem with such arguments (riding piggyback on particular theories of justification) is twofold. To begin with they stand or fall with those theories themselves; and, secondly, even if the theories could secure necessary and sufficient conditions for the application of the concept of justification, they would still have to go a long way to establish the corresponding supervenience theses. In this section, I will try to illustrate this point by following the lead of coherence and reliability theories of justification and taking "n" to denote the properties of "coherence"[2] and "being reliably produced."

It is obvious that justification would fail to supervene on n if the corresponding necessary and sufficient conditions fail to obtain. That is to say, supervenience would fail if there are worlds where justification is exemplified in the absence of n, or a belief has n but lacks justification. So, for example, if n is taken to be the property of coherence, then justification would fail to supervene on this property if there could be a coherent set of beliefs whose members, nonetheless, lack justification (failure of the sufficiency condition). And if n is taken to be the property of being reliably produced, supervenience would fail if there could be a belief that is justified despite being unreliably produced (failure of the necessary condition).

Now, such possible failures are completely isomorphic to those that are standardly associated with the corresponding coherence and reliability theories of justification. Coherence theories are often thought to be inadequate on the ground that, among others, there could be many equally coherent systems of beliefs that are mutually incompatible. Mere coherence is not sufficient for justification (this is part of the so-called "isolation problem"). Reliability theories, on the other hand, usually get into trouble over the so-called problem of the Cartesian demon world. Consider a possible world (D) that is indistinguishable from the actual world as far as our experiences are concerned, but in which a Cartesian demon has seen to it that our perceptual beliefs are invariably false. Since D is indistinguishable from the actual world, beliefs in D should enjoy as much justification as they do in the actual world. But these beliefs are, by hypothesis, not reliably formed, and are thus, according to the reliability theory, unjustified. Hence reliability is not necessary for justification. Given this structural isomorphism, the fate of the arguments for the supervenience thesis exploiting particular theories of justification seems then to depend entirely on the fate of those theories themselves.[3]

But even if one could find ways of fixing the failures of necessary and sufficient conditions for the application of the concept of justification, thereby saving the corresponding theories of justification, that would not necessarily give us epistemic supervenience. For, as we saw earlier, if it is to be a substantial claim, the supervenience thesis must also yield a dependency relation between supervenient and subvenient properties. All that the obtaining of cross-world necessary and sufficient conditions for having the property of justification entails is a strong form of property covariance which only says that the distribution of supervenient properties are constrained (in the way indicated by (SC)) by the distribution of their base properties. But we noted that strong covariance fails to give us dependence, which is essentially a metaphysical relation (suggesting the ontic priority of the base properties relative to the supervenient ones). Until the relevant dependency relation has been shown to hold, arguments from particular theories of justification will not be in a position to claim that justification supervenes on a particular non-epistemic property. Having examined the arguments for the supervenience thesis, I shall now examine its bearing on some issues in epistemology.

5.1.3   Supervenience and the basing relation requirement

Supervenience is a transitive relation. If x supervenes on y and y supervenes on z, then x supervenes on z. The problem this would raise is that if justification is to be supervenient on a certain non-epistemic subvenient property, then every other non-epistemic natural property on which the subvenient property itself happens to supervene would automatically turn into a justifier, and this would run foul of the basing relation constraint on what is to count as a justifier. Let me elaborate. When holding a belief for a reason, the reason should enter into some specific relation with the belief. It is not enough to merely *have* a reason for the belief. If the belief is to be justified it must also be *based* on the reason in question. As Harman says, "Reasons for which one believes are relevant to whether one is justified in believing as one does. Reasons for believing something are not relevant unless they are also reasons for which one believes" (Harman 1973, p. 26). Despite the fact that a belief's being based on a reason is a necessary condition of its being justified, it has proved to be notoriously difficult to articulate just what this relation consists in. It seems, nonetheless, plausible to think that an adequate analysis of the basing relation must incorporate some sort of causal ingredient. We form our beliefs *because* of, or in the words of Harman, *in virtue* of the reason or evidence we come to possess. Merely having reasons for a belief only makes it justifi*able*, whereas for the belief to be justi*fied* we must come to hold it in virtue (or because) of our reasons for that belief. What I am going to argue is that the supervenience thesis leads to the violation of the basing relation requirement when it is considered in conjunction with certain peculiar characteristics of the supervenience relation.

Suppose we take justification as being supervenient on some non-epistemic property (N_1) into which the basing relation requirement has already been built – N_1 can be, for example, the property of being appropriately caused by experience, where the inclusion of "appropriately" in the description is meant to incorporate the basing relation requirement. It is important to note that by building the basing relation requirement into the relevant non-epistemic property, the resulting property remains non-epistemic (at least given the current accounts of the basing relation as involving either a causal or a doxastic ingredient or both). Now consider an agent who forms a justified belief (b), say, "This is a red book" by instantiating an appropriate form of N_1. Given the supervenience claim, this means that it is in virtue of possessing N_1 that b is justified. This seems unproblematic since the ground of b is, by hypothesis, justification-conferring, and the basing relation requirement has also been satisfied. But, surely, the agent does not come to possess N_1 without first satisfying some antecedent conditions. It is quite plausible to think that she comes to possess it in virtue of having *another* non-epistemic, natural property (N_2) and so on (just think of the various processes – neural or otherwise – that eventually result in the belief in question). This layered conception of the world is precisely what motivates the supervenience picture.

> We require a conception of supervenience insofar as we regard our world as *layered* or *sedimented*, as consisting of *hierarchies* of characteristics in which the upper tiers of the hierarchy are fixed by those in the lower tires.... This conception of the world as comprising layers of subvenient and supervenient characteristics, then, stands in contrast to non-layered, nonhierarchical, *flat* images of the world.
>
> (Heil 1992, pp. 59–60)

So, given the non-epistemic nature of N_1, N_2 and the other properties in the hierarchy, it would be plausible to take them as being strongly supervenient (with at least *nomological*, i.e., natural necessity) on one another. That is, N_1 supervenes naturally on N_2, N_2 on N_3, N_3 on ... and so on.[4] Let us take some property, N_n, in this hierarchy of supervenient properties. Given the transitivity of the supervenience relation, N_1 would supervene naturally on N_n. Since b's justification is supervenient on N_1, it follows, again by transitivity, that the justification in question is also supervenient on N_n. Now, as we have seen, to say of some property that it supervenes on another property is to say that it is because of the obtaining of the latter property that the former obtains. To say, for example, of goodness that it supervenes on natural properties would be to say that it is *in virtue* (or because) of those properties that something is good.

This feature actually stems from the dependency constraint on the relation of supervenience. As was noted earlier, if the supervenience relation is to express a substantive metaphysical fact between two sets of properties, the relation in question must be more than a mere property covariation. Dependency of supervenient properties on subvenient properties must be regarded as another feature of the supervenience relation. In fact, it is the dependency relation that explains or accounts for the property covariation. What this implies for the claim that b's justification supervenes on N_n is that it is *in virtue* of (or *because* of) possessing N_n that b is justified, which, in turn, given our account of the basing relation, implies that b must be *based on* N_n.

But this is quite implausible. N_n could be some complex neural property of the brain, and it is certainly not the case that b, "This is a red book," is justified because it is based on this complex neural property (at least not under the current conceptions of the basing relation requirement). The reason why the claim of b's justification supervening on N_1 seemed unproblematic is because we can say of N_1 that it is in virtue of its possession by b that b is justified. N_1 is, in other words, the sort of property that answers to such descriptions as "in virtue of..." or "because of..." that supervenience claims give of their base or subvenient properties. And this is so because N_1 incorporates the basing relation requirement. But this is not true of N_n. N_n is not the sort property of which one can say that it is in virtue of its possession by b that b is justified. But this is precisely what the (initially plausible) claim of the supervenience of b's justification on N_1 entails when one also takes into account certain peculiar features of the supervenience relation.

5.1.4   Supervenience and normative epistemology

Supervenience was earlier heralded, by many theorists including Kim, as a way of articulating a physicalistic metaphysical picture that no longer incorporates reductionist tendencies which are nowadays thought to be wrongheaded. It was, however, Kim himself who first raised doubts about the non-reductive character of the supervenience relation (see, e.g., Kim 1990). While weaker versions of supervenience can be consistent with autonomy, strong supervenience, says Kim, actually entails the possibility of reducing the supervenient to the subvenient. He thus asserts that "the questions of reducibility are best left out of the concept of supervenience" (Kim 1993, p. 165, fn. 5). The eschewing of the non-reductive character of supervenience deprives it, however, of various functions it was intended to serve. In epistemology, for example, we can no longer appeal to it, as Kim himself once did, to defend the possibility of normative epistemology in the face of calls for its reduction to psychology by the proponents of "naturalized epistemology" (like Quine). While traditional epistemology construes epistemic justification in normative terms, Quine emphasizes the factual and descriptive character of the process of belief formation. It is, thus, normativity that is repudiated in naturalized epistemology. Of course Kim's argument for the reductive character of strong supervenience is very controversial and not everyone has been persuaded by it. It seems to me, however, that what is widely regarded as the most controversial assumption in Kim's argument need not be invoked in the application of that argument to the case of epistemic supervenience.

Suppose we take reduction of one theory to another as consisting of the derivation of the laws of the reduced theory from the laws of the reducer theory with the help of the so-called bridge principles. These principles are usually taken to be biconditionals (of some sort) connecting terms of the reduced theory with those of the reducer. Consider now, as an example, the thesis of mental–physical supervenience which says that whenever a supervening mental property M is instantiated by an object, then there is some physical property P_i in the subvenient set which is also instantiated in the object such that, necessarily, if anything has P_i, then it has M. Kim claims that there is a biconditional, playing the role of a bridge principle, connecting M with the disjunction of the subvenient properties (UP_i). Mental–physical supervenience, thus, entails reduction.

The main objection that has been raised against Kim's claim is that disjunction is not an appropriate mode of property composition, and that, consequently, UP_i in not a genuine property. But this objection does not arise in the case of epistemic supervenience if it is to be grounded, as seems quite natural, in some particular theory of justification. Consider, for example, the reliability theory of justification. On this theory, justification is supervenient on the natural property of "being reliably produced." What it means is that whenever the property of justification is instantiated by a belief, then that belief also has the property of being reliably produced such that, necessarily, if a belief is reliably produced, it is justified. But this is of the form of a biconditional connecting the two properties of "justification" and "being reliably produced." We seem then to have, at our disposal, the required bridge principle to bring about the reduction of epistemology. What distinguishes this case from that of the mental–physical supervenience is that there is no analogue of multiple realizability here. The supervenient base consists only of one property, namely, being reliably produced. The reliability (supervenience) theorist is, surely, not going to tolerate the thought that in some possible worlds a belief's justification is realized in something other than reliability. And that is, indeed, how coherentists and others would feel about their proposed subvenient base. So, in the case of epistemic supervenience, there is no need to construct a disjunctive property to obtain a bridge principle. But, then, if this is the case, those theories of justification which also incorporate the supervenience thesis should find themselves in a rather ironic situation. For, it seems, what the supervenience thesis commits them to in the end is not the normativity of epistemology but its full-blown reduction.

Thus far, I have examined a number of arguments for the supervenience thesis and considered some of the problems that it raises. As noted earlier, none of the points raised here is meant to deny the possibility of epistemic supervenience. They are only intended to show that, being a rich and multi-faceted notion, more needs to be said about the viability and the role that the concept of supervenience is claimed to play in the framework of epistemology. This is particularly important in connection with its alleged role in defusing the problem of how experience can function as reason for the beliefs it gives rise to. Waiving such worries about the thesis of epistemic supervenince itself, I shall now set out to find out of it can discharge that particular function.

5.1.5   Epistemic supervenience and the problem of non-doxastic justification

As noted earlier, Van Cleve has claimed that one can appeal to the supervenience thesis to show how non-doxastic states can confer justification on beliefs they give rise to. To do so, he distinguishes two types of epistemic principles (transmission and generation principles) which are of the form "If . . . . , then S is justified in believing p," and whose consequents refer to the belief's justificatory status. While a transmission principle states a conditional whose antecedent refers to what the subject is already justified in believing, the antecedent of a generation principle specifies relevant circumstances of the subject that are entirely cashed out in non-epistemic terms. The problem of non-doxastic justification arises, says Van Cleve, because it is tacitly assumed that all conferring of justification is of a transmitting sort. But if epistemic justification is supposed to supervene on non-epistemic properties, then the problem would go away, for, given the supervenience thesis, one can say that it is *in virtue of* those non-epistemic (experiential) properties that a belief is justified: "Once we recognize that there must be some states of affairs that confer justification by generating it, the apparently insuperable objection to nondoxastic justification falls aside" (Van Cleve 1985, p. 101).

However, to say that some states of affairs confer justification by generating it can hardly constitute a satisfactory answer to the problem of non-doxastic justification. The problem, we may recall, was to understand how a mental state (experience) that itself lacks positive epistemic status can bestow it on other states (beliefs). The mere claim that epistemic properties supervene on non-epistemic properties hardly addresses this issue. Unless we can *explain* why the supervenience thesis holds, the claim in question merely states that certain variation relation holds between two sets of properties without saying what grounds it. Rather, any respectable theory invoking a supervenience thesis must *explain* why the relevant determination relation obtains, that is, what it actually consists in (Kim 1993, p. xi).

This problem equally afflicts the application of supervenience in resolving the problem of non-doxastic justification. How is the mere postulation of a supervenient dependence relation between justification and non-epistemic properties supposed to *explain* how non-doxastic states can confer something on belief (i.e., justification) which they themselves do not possess. It is very likely that those who find non-doxastic justification a mysterious notion would find the notion of a supervenient dependence relation between epistemic and non-epistemic properties equally mysterious (more on this in the next chapter). In the absence of an explanatory framework, the thesis of epistemic supervenience would merely serve to redress our problem of what it is in virtue of which that states which lack justificatory status can confer justification on the beliefs they give rise to. I conclude therefore that, in the absence of an explanatory framework, the supervenience thesis is unable to show how experience can confer justification on the beliefs it gives rise to. In the second part of this chapter, I shall present a radically different framework in which our problem would receive a more satisfactory treatment.

5.2   Normativity and content: an argument from functional role semantics

To set the stage for discussion, let us begin by reminding ourselves of why epistemic justification is regarded as a normative concept. One may explicate this feature in terms of the ways in which the notion of justification has been conceived. To say that a belief is justified is to appraise it favorably from the epistemic point of view and assign a positive status to it. There are, however, many ways of thinking about this favorable status. One major trend in this area sees epistemic justification as necessarily involving a deontic dimension, thus analyzing the status in question in terms of the fulfillment of an agent's intellectual duties and obligations. This is the so-called "deontological" conception of justification according to which a belief is justified if, in holding the belief, the agent has flouted no epistemic duties and has, thus, behaved in an epistemically responsible manner (see, e.g., BonJour 1985; Chisholm 1987). By contrast, some theorists have proposed an "evaluative" sense of epistemic justification that no longer involves a deontic dimension (e.g., Alston 1988). Roughly put, the latter theory says that an agent is justified in holding a belief p iff the agent's believing that p, as he does, is a good thing from the epistemic point of view of maximizing truth and minimizing falsity. Although the two conceptions may involve important differences, their disagreement will be significantly diminished if one takes one's chief intellectual obligation to consist of believing what is true and avoiding what is false (Chisholm 1987). In any event, on both conceptions epistemic justification is a normative and evaluative concept which pertains to what an agent ought or ought not believe so that to say of an agent that he is justified in holding a belief is to say that there is something alright and satisfactory with the way things are with that agent.

Accordingly, the normativity of justification, being closely tied to the goal of believing truth and avoiding falsehood, turns out to be a semantically sensitive notion. This accords well with how the notion of normativity is generally understood. For example, as we saw in Chapter 1, a number of philosophers conceive of "believing" as an essentially normative act as manifested by the absurdity of asserting the Moorean sentences such as "p & I do not believe that p." Accordingly, the normative aspect of believing is rooted in the fact that to believe a proposition is to be committed to its truth which is why, in contrast to, say, intention, belief is an essentially normative concept. It is perhaps for this reason that some theorists construe normative judgments as involving the concept warrant (rationality) (Gibbard 1994). Thus, to say of a moral term, for example, "good," that it has a normative aspect is to say that to be good is to be desirable, and a thing is desirable if desiring it is warranted. Likewise, to say that logical rules are normative is to say that they lay down prescriptions on how we ought to reason, which inferences are proper and which inferences we should avoid. Now, if responsiveness to truth is to be a salient feature of normativity, this might throw further light on the failure of the aforementioned accounts in reaching their target. For if we seek to show why the process of forming true perceptual beliefs and avoiding false ones has a normative dimension, we need to work with (or invoke) a concept of normativity that is content-sensitive. Experience–belief transition is not just causal but semantic as well in that the content of experience enters into a constitutive relation to the content of the belief it gives rise to.

Accordingly, to show that experience justifies beliefs, one should look for an *appropriate* normative paradigm that would simulate the experience–belief transition. If we can show that such transitions possess content-sensitivity normativity, then we have gone a long way toward establishing why beliefs resulting from non-doxastic states are justified. The sort of approach that I suggest might do the job is one that appeals to a particular theory of content or meaning, namely, the functional role semantics (FRS). So before seeing how this proposal works, we need to highlight certain salient features of FRS that are pertinent to the problem under discussion (see, e.g., Field 1977; Harman 1982; McGinn 1982; Block 1986).

The question about which FRS is intended to provide a response is what it is for a mental state (say, a belief) or a sign to have intentional or semantic content. In other words, we are required to say what it is in virtue of which a particular representation, say, a belief, has this rather than that content, or, alternatively, is about this rather than that object. This problem has been variously called in the literature as the problem of mental representation, the problem of naturalizing the intentional (semantic) content and so on. What is at issue, then, is not just to find a semantic theory that ascribes to each meaningful sentence in a language (mental or public) a meaning but also provide an account of the nature of the ascribed meaning. Put differently, the idea is to explain what determines the meaning a particular expression has or what it supervenes on. (As is customary in these discussions, the terms "meaning" and "semantics" are used in a broad sense applying to both

the expressions in a language and the intentional content of propositional attitudes.) There is, as expected, a heap of material written on
this subject. However, I shall focus on a theory, known as functional
role semantics, that is pertinent to the subject matter of this chapter.

FRS applied to the theory of content is actually functionalism, not
applied to a particular type of mental state, but to the contents of
particular mental representations, for example, the belief that p versus the belief that q. Assuming functionalism, the idea is that while
mental states are individuated functionally certain mental states (viz.,
distinct types of propositional attitudes) are individuated by their contents. It then follows that mental contents are individuated functionally.
Thus, a belief state is said to have a particular content in virtue of its
causal/functional roles. The appeal to causal/functional roles is intended
to reflect the idea behind the so-called "use" theory of meaning according to which the meaning of an expression is determined by its use. It
has, however, proved to be notoriously difficult to say what these roles
are. There are currently two main views on this question, namely, two-
factor and single-factor theories. According to the two-factor theories
there are two components or aspects to the meaning of an expression; a
conceptual role component (entirely "in the head" and usually adverted
to in accounts of the so-called "narrow content"), and an external
component that connects (via a causal theory of reference or a theory of truth-conditions) the internal aspect to the world (see McGinn
1982; Block 1986). Single-factor versions usually take functional roles
to include relations to factors "outside the head" (for example, Sellars
1963; Harman 1982). Thus according to certain two-factor theories,
conceptual roles stop roughly at the skin with outputs construed in
terms of bodily movements and inputs in terms of the proximal stimuli.
Single-factor theories, by contrast, characterize the conceptual role of an
expression by its relation to perception, to other expressions, and to the
behavior.

However, as Block has noted, single-factor and two-factor versions are
actually equivalent for, on a closer inspection, the "long-armed" conceptual role of single-factor theories turns out to consist of an internal,
"short-armed," component and an external component. For our purposes, however, the differences between these versions do not actually
matter (especially in view of the fact that according to certain two-
factor theorists, e.g., McGinn, conceptual roles consist of causal relations
that hold among representational mental states, perceptions and behaviors). So I am going to use the (generic) term "functional roles," rather
than "conceptual roles," intending it to designate relations that include

sensory-input causal relations, behavioral causal relations and causal relations to other mental states. So, applied to a basic perceptual belief p, say, "There is a red book before me," FRS says that p has its particular content in virtue of its causal roles that include causal relations to sensory experience (being appeared to redly), relations to other mental states and to behavior. FRS is specially plausible as an account of the content of logical connectives where the relevant functional roles seem to consist exhaustively of inferential relations. So a certain expression "#" might be taken to mean "and" in virtue of the fact that the thought "p#q" tends to cause the thought "p" and "q" which in turn tend to cause the thought "p#q." Here the relevant functional roles constitute the meaning of "#" which is why logical constants change their meaning when their functional roles are revised as in, say, intuitionistic or quantum logic.[5]

But what is exactly the relation between meaning (content) and functional roles? One way to make sense of this relation is in terms of the relation of individuation. The general idea of FRS is that it is in virtue of its functional roles that an intentional state, such as a particular belief p, has the content it has. That is to say, these roles (e.g., standing in a causal relation to a particular sensory input or experience) determine what the content of p is. They are, in other words, constitutive of the very nature of p such that varying them results in a different belief with a different content. This is not, however, to identify the content of intentional states with the corresponding functional roles. Rather, what is intended is that intentional states are individuated by reference to certain relevant functional roles (in the manner described). Thus, FRS gives the identity or individuation conditions of contentful states.

A useful analogy for the kind of relation suggested is the relation between a set and its members. While a set is individuation-dependent on its members and owes its identity to the identity of its members, it is not identified with either of its members or with their sum. Rather, the members stand in a constitutive relation to the identity of the set such that by varying the members a different set emerges. Thus, one may think of content (meaning)-functional role relation abstractly on the model of the individuation-dependence relation that holds between a set and its members. Just as each member of a set stands in a constitutive relation to the identity of the set to which it belongs, each particular functional role stands in a constitutive relation to the meaning (content) of the particular mental state to which it is related. Thus, reverting to our standard example, being causally dependent on the experience of being appeared to redly is constitutive of the meaning

(content) of the belief state that results from that particular experience (viz., the belief that there is a red book before one). Differently
put, the content or meaning of the belief in question is individuation-
dependent on its being causally related to that particular sensory
experience.

What is the upshot of all this for the problem of non-doxastic justification? Well, to begin with, the functional role singled out above
(standing in a causal relation to a particular sensory experience) is just
another way of describing the already familiar idea of experience–belief
transition. Moreover, assuming FRS, we just noted that this transition
is constitutive of the meaning (content) of the ensuing belief, that is,
the meaning (content) of the belief is individuation-dependent on the
content of the experience to which it is causally related. Thus, the
experience–belief transition is not just causal but semantic as well in
that the content of experience enters into a constitutive relation to the
meaning (content) of the belief it gives rise to. Just as with sets and their
members, varying particular functional roles alters and transforms the
meaning (content) of the corresponding perceptual belief. The main difference between our way of conceiving the experience–belief transition
and the approaches discussed in Chapter 3 lies precisely in the fact that,
in our approach, the transition is question is located in a semantic context where the content of experience stands in a constitutive relation to
the semantic content of the ensuing belief.

The next step on the way of seeing how experience bears a
justification-conferring relation to the ensuing belief is to notice one
important feature of meaning (content) namely, its normativity. Meaning is normative (in the same sense that justification and rationality
are thought to be), or so we are told. One of the main sources of this
thought is Kripke's gloss on Wittgenstein's "rule-following" argument
(Kripke 1982). Normative statements are, roughly speaking, "ought"
statements. A normative judgment, as noted earlier, is one that includes
the concept of warrant (or rationality). As we saw earlier, the normativity of justification was equally construed in terms of what an agent
ought or ought not to believe; that holding a justified belief is a good
thing from the epistemic point of view which ought to be praised. In the
same vein, normative laws of conduct tell us how we ought to regulate
our behavior.

This is the general line of thought along which the normativity
of meaning is also to be understood. Kripke emphasizes this point
in an argument against the dispositional account of the meaning of
expressions like "+."

Suppose I do mean addition by " + ". What is the relation of this supposition to the question of how I will respond to the problem "68 + 57"? The dispositionalist gives a *descriptive* account of this relation: if "+" means addition, then I will answer "125". But this is not the proper account of the relation, which is *normative*, not descriptive. The point is *not* that, if I meant addition by " + ", I *will* answer "125", but that, if I intend to accord with my past meaning of " + ", I should answer "125"... The relation of meaning and intention to future action is *normative*, not descriptive.

(Kripke 1982, p. 37)

Kripke's idea is that if we mean something by a term, this has implications for what we should do when we use the term; it determines what we ought to do. So if we mean addition by "+," it implies that I ought to answer "125" when asked "what is '68 + 57'?" not just that I will answer "125." In this sense the meaning of an expression lays down a normative constraint determining its correct/incorrect uses so that its violation will be deemed as having made an error or mistake, something that ought to have been avoided.

It has, however, been objected that FRS cannot do justice to the normative character of meaning. The reason offered is that, as noted earlier, FRS is actually an extension of the so-called "use" theory of meaning according to which an expression's meaning is its use in communication. If so, then, the objection continues, nothing follows about how an expression ought to be used given the way it is actually used. FRS, thus, fails to account for the normative character of meaning as facts about causal/functional roles are unable to generate normative facts. Applied to the contents of intentional states (beliefs), the objection says that one cannot recover the content of such states by considering the way they are actually used or are disposed to be used because there is always the possibility of misrepresentation affecting the content of the representations, thereby undermining their normative character.[1]

A promising line of response to the normativity challenge has been suggested by Paul Horwich who thinks that use theories of meaning can accommodate the normativity of meaning (Horwich 1998). Although I shall follow Horwich's basic strategy, I think he conflates two distinct issues when trying to account for the normativity of meaning. My qualified version of his account, if successful, has the merit of mapping semantic normativity onto an epistemic plane, thereby bringing us closer to seeing how experience can function as justification-conferring ground. Horwich begins by noting that the normative implications of a property do not necessarily make it intrinsically normative. For example, while "x ought to be treated with respect" follows from "x is a human being," "being a human being" is not an intrinsically normative property. Likewise, while "x ought to be applied to red objects" may follow from "x means red," it does not follow that meaning property is intrinsically normative. Thus, the fact that use properties are not intrinsically normative does not preclude them from grounding meaning facts, or, alternatively, accounting for meaning properties in terms of intrinsically non-normative use properties. In accounting for the normative import of a meaning property, Horwich identifies a fundamental, normative aspect of language, which he calls the "truth norm," as what explains why each predicate ought, in virtue of its meaning, to be applied to certain things and not others.

According to the truth norm one ought to think (believe) what is true. This, Horwich claims, can explain why a meaning property (e.g., "x means RED") has normative implications (such as "x ought to be applied only to red things," or, more formally, "(y)(x ought to be applied to y → y is a red object") (Horwich 1998, ch. 8). The explanation is provided by the schema, "x means F → (y)(x is *true* of y ↔ y is f)," governing our conception of "being *true* of." Consider an instance of this schema: x means RED → (y)(x is *true* of y → y is a red object). It is also uncontroversial, as a general norm, that, (y)(x ought to be applied to y → x is true of y). Then, relative to the "true of" schema, the latter norm implies each particular Kripkean conditional such as "x means RED → (y)(x ought to be applied to y → y is a red object)." Less formally, Horwich's strategy is to appeal to the thesis that having true beliefs is beneficial in that one is more likely to get what one wants by holding such beliefs. Therefore, given the correlation between assenting to certain sentences and believing the propositions they express, then one ought to assent to some sentences and not others (or, equivalently, one ought to apply predicates, in virtue of their meaning, only to particular sets of objects that is, those things of which they are *true*).

Horwich's response in terms of the truth norm seems to explain the normative import of a meaning property without having to assume that the property itself is intrinsically normative. But why accept the truth norm? His response is quite simple: the truth norm has pragmatic value. True beliefs, rather than false ones, facilitate successful behavior, "[t]herefore it is reasonable for us to want all of our beliefs to be true" (Horwich 1998, p. 191). But this explanation is not sufficiently discriminating. Having pragmatic consequences will not distinguish epistemic from, say, prudential justification to claim that only the former is valuable for the attainment of practical goals. Leading to successful actions does not necessarily require beliefs to be true (or likely to be true, viz., epistemically justified). Sometimes it is false beliefs that lead to successful actions. To give a famous example (due to James), suppose someone knows that if he believes he can leap over a big chasm then this will help his jump. Then, all things being equal, it would be practically rational for him to believe that he can make the leap, however inadequate the ground of this belief is (indicating it to be likely false). Thus, if we accept such cases of justified beliefs as genuine, then that would easily result in situations in which, say, our practical reasons for believing a proposition clash with our epistemic reasons for that belief. Indeed such beliefs are deemed as having pragmatic, rather than epistemic, justification precisely because they are not guided by the truth norm. What justifies holding these beliefs is that they lead to successful action. But the justification in question is pragmatic rather than epistemic. In the case of epistemic justification we evaluate our beliefs not from a moral or practical point of view, but, rather, in terms of our concern for believing what is true and not believing what is false.

It seems to me that Horwich's justification of the truth norm suffers from conflating two distinct (though related) issues: the "truth goal" as the goal of epistemic justification and the principle of charity as a constraint on successful interpretation. Let me explain. What Horwich describes as the truth norm (and a normative aspect of language) requiring agents to think (believe) what is true is actually a direct consequence (or identical with some version) of Davidson's principle of charity. As we have seen, Davidson has argued that it is a necessary condition of successful interpretation that the interpreters must assume that the objects of interpretation, by and large, believe what is true. Note, however, that although the principle seems to require only the truth of the interpretee's beliefs, the rationale is quite general for, as both Davidson and Quine have emphasized, charity begins at home. The interpreter's beliefs are as much subject to the constraint of charity as are the beliefs of the interpretee. Moreover, Davidson makes it clear that he does not regard the principle of charity as merely a useful heuristic principle to facilitate the practical process of interpretation. Rather, it is constitutive of the whole process of interpretation. He takes its application as constituting the very notions of rationality and belief such that without it we have no reason to count a creature as rational, as having beliefs, or as saying anything. So Horwich's truth norm according to which people "ought to think what is true" is actually a version of the principle of charity, and, by seeing it in this light, one can make more sense of his claim that the norm in question is a fundamental normative aspect of *language*. It also demystifies the initially puzzling claim that by appealing to a norm of *truth* one can explain the normativity of *meaning*, for, construed as the principle of charity, the truth norm now functions as an adequacy condition on a theory of meaning.

There is, however, another notion in the vicinity which serves a different function (though it is related to the principle of charity in a way to be explained). This is the idea of the so-called "epistemic goal." We have already noted that there is an intimate link between epistemic justification and truth. This is usually construed along the following lines. Epistemic justification, as repeatedly emphasized, is an evaluative concept whose attachment to a belief makes the belief worth having from the epistemic point of view which is, in turn, characterized in terms of a distinct goal, the truth goal, namely, the epistemic goal of believing truth and avoiding falsehood. As Alston has put it, "[e]pistemic evaluation is undertaken from what we might call the 'epistemic point of view.' That point of view is defined by the aim of maximizing truth and minimizing falsity in a large body of beliefs" (Alston 1989, p. 83). So justification is essentially a matter of serving the epistemic goal.

I think this is what Horwich has in mind when he seeks to characterize his "truth norm" as what people should aim at when forming beliefs. This suspicion is confirmed by his subsequent statement that "the truth norm is surely what lies behind norms of epistemic rationality or justification" (Horwich 1998, p. 187). As noted above, however, it is only when construed as the principle of charity that the truth norm can be brought to bear on the normativity of meaning. But Horwich makes no such distinction. This is not, however, to say that the principle of charity and the epistemic goal are unrelated. We have seen that the principle of charity seeks to assigning truth conditions to the interpretee's sentences that make her right when plausibly possible. It demands the interpreter to maximize agreement between himself and the speaker by assigning to her the same type of beliefs as his. It requires, in other words, the maximization of true beliefs (by the interpreter's lights). Now if the process of charitable belief ascription is characterized by the aim of maximizing truth and minimizing falsity in the interpretee's belief system (recall that the interpreter's beliefs are as much subject to the constraint of charity as are the beliefs of the interpretee), the link between charity and the epistemic goal becomes quite transparent. For, as noted above, this is how epistemic justification is generally construed, namely, in terms of the aim of believing truth and avoiding falsehood.

The preceding observations bring us closer to seeing how experience can confer justification on the beliefs it gives rise to. For if both epistemic justification and the principle of charity are constitutively linked via the epistemic goal (in the manner explained above), then epistemic constraints equally count as constraints on possible interpretations. The principle of charity, thus, rules out interpretations that make the people to whom it is applied too irrational (as judged by the commonly accepted norms of rationality). This is in fact how Davidson himself has tended to view the principle in his later writings. Accordingly, if the principle of charity (the truth norm) is seen as what underwrites the normativity of meaning (content), then this would automatically lead to its epistemization giving us the required notion of content-sensitive normativity. This is how I am inclined to interpret and understand Davidson's colorful imagery of "epistemology seen in the mirror of meaning" (Davidson 1984, p. 169). Thus, given the preceding remarks, it is not merely that intentional states like beliefs have both semantic and epistemic normativity; the two are intimately and integrally related. Which proposition constitutes the content of a belief state is constrained by the epistemic status of that state.

We now have the necessary conceptual resources to see how sensory experience can stand in a justification-conferring relation to the ensuing belief states. To give a brief recap of our account, we began by noting that on an FRS approach, the content of a perceptual state stands in an individuation-dependence relation to the content (meaning) of the belief from which it results. Given the normative character of meaning, this showed that the normativity of the experience–belief transition is a semantic property involving the contents of the relata involved. Furthermore, our attempt to account for the content-sensitive normativity of such transitions within the context of an FRS approach culminated in its epistemization by virtue of appealing to the theses of the truth goal and the principle of charity. The normativity of experience–belief transition, thus, turned out to be a semantic/epistemic property.

To complete our account of non-doxastic justification, all that is now needed to show is that, in addition to the normativity constraint, one further desideratum of epistemic justification, namely, the basing relation requirement is also satisfied. I have already alluded to this requirement without saying what it is for a belief to be *based on* experience if experience is to justify it. I shall take up this question in the next chapter.

6
The Problem of the Basing Relation

A complete theory of how experience can justify a belief is both an account of under what conditions the belief is justifiable (rational) and whether it is justified. A justifiable belief is one where an agent is said to have adequate grounds or evidence for the belief in question while a justified belief is one where the agent's belief is based on those adequate grounds. What distinguishes the two cases concerns the obtaining of an epistemic relation, the basing relation whose nature and character are the main concerns of this chapter. To set the stage for discussion, I begin by evaluating two major trends in the basing relation debate, namely, the causal and doxastic theories. My emphasis though will be on causal theories as it is widely believed that some version of the causal theory must be true. There is however disagreement as to how one should account for a major problem with such theories, that is the problem of deviant causal chains. I shall discuss and criticize one recent prominent solution to this problem before proposing my own (Davidsonian) gloss on causal theories. Let us then begin by a brief survey of the current approaches to the question of the basing relation.

6.1 Main approaches to the basing relation: a survey and analysis

The two major theories of the basing relation that have dominated the debate are the so-called causal and doxastic theories. Doxastic theories come in different varieties and strengths. Some hold that the necessary and sufficient conditions for a belief to be based on evidence consist in having a connecting or meta-belief to the effect that the evidence provides adequate support for the belief in question (see, e.g., Tolliver 1981). Others postulate such meta-beliefs only in connection with beliefs whose bases are doxastic rather than experiential (Audi 1993). The doxastic approach is however beset by a number of problems. To begin with, as Alston emphasizes, our beliefs are often based on other beliefs or experiences where no such meta-beliefs are present. This can happen for a number of reasons. Cognizers can have based beliefs even if they lack epistemic concepts. That is, they can form beliefs in response to reasons without yet being able to conceive of those reasons as reasons.

Secondly, beliefs can be unconsciously formed on the basis of the pertinent grounds. Examples abound. Consider, for example, the phenomenon of subliminal cues when our depth perception is dependent on various cues of which we are typically unaware (Alston 2005, p. 87). As Harman puts it:

> [a] man's conscious reasons are those he can tell us about. To equate reasons for which he believes something with reasons he can tell us about is to assume that reasons for which he believes something are conscience reasons. This is a mistake. The reason for which people believe things are rarely conscious. People often believe things for good reasons, which give the knowledge, even though they cannot say what those reasons are.
>
> (Harman 1970, p. 844)

Moreover, an agent, being mistaken about the basis of his belief, would fail to form the appropriate meta-belief even though, intuitively, his belief is based on the evidence at his disposal. These and other problems effectively undermine the prospects of doxastic theories to provide a viable account of the basing relation (see Korcz 1997).

Let us now turn to the causal approach to the basing relation problem that has more or less assumed the status of the standard conception of the relation in question. Very roughly what the causal theory says is that a belief's being based on evidence or a reason involves the belief's being caused or causally sustained by that reason. Let us call this the "simple causal theory" of the basing relation. The causal theory is quite intuitive. If my belief that, say, I will not catch my flight is based on my belief that the traffic on the streets is heavy, then I hold the former belief *because* I hold the latter belief. The same holds for my belief that the traffic is heavy *as a result* of seeing so many cars on the streets. In both cases my reasons causally explain why I hold the beliefs that I do. My reasons, thus, make a difference to what I believe and they could do so, it seems, only if they causally sustain the relevant beliefs: "it is difficult to see how to imagine a difference in the reasons for which people believe as they do without imagining a difference in the explanation of why they believe as they do" (Harman 1973, p. 29).

A long time ago, Davidson argued, on precisely the same grounds, that reasons have to be causes if they are to explain our actions (Davidson 1963). His argument is best explained in terms of an example. Suppose John wants to kill his rich uncle so that he could inherit his wealth. He thus has a reason for killing his uncle. Now suppose John gets involved in a brawl in a Halloween party and accidentally kills a men who later turns out to be his uncle. Consider now another scenario in which John recognizes his uncle in the party and kills him as he had intended to. In both the cases John has the same reason to kill his uncle but only in the second case does he act for that reason and this is because the reason is the cause of his action. Unlike the first scenario, John's reason in the second scenario makes a difference to what he does. It explains why he kills his uncle. What goes for acting on a reason goes for believing for a reason.

There are, however, more sophisticated variants of the causal theory of the basing relation. I briefly mention two versions just to set them aside. On one version of the causal of theory (due to Moser) not only one's belief that q should be causally sustained by his believing that p, if it is to be based on believing p, but the agent must have a *de re* awareness of p's supporting q (Moser 1991). Moser's idea of *de re* awareness seems to be some sort of an internalist constraint where one has a direct, reflective awareness of the grounds of one's belief. But the awareness constraint does not seem to square well with the causal orientation of Moser's theory. If the basing relation is causal in nature, it is difficult to see how one could ever come to know by reflection alone what the relata of a given causal relation are. To identify a causal relation one has to rule out such possibilities as the involvement of common causes, overdetermination, mere correlations and so on. It is difficult to see how on one could ascertain such facts by reflection alone.

Another variant of the causal theory is the counterfactual theory of the basing relation (due to Swain) according to which a belief is based on evidence if the evidence either causes the belief or would have caused it (Swain 1979).[1] That is to say, even if the belief is not originated by the evidence on which it is based, it must be causally sustained by it in the sense that if the agent were not to believe what he does because of what initially gave rise to the belief, but were to continue to believe it nonetheless, then he would believe it as the result of the evidence.

The counterfactual theory is, however, undermined by the following objection which involves basing relations between beliefs that imply each other (Tolliver 1981). Suppose an agent, S, believes p on the basis of some experience e and let us also assume that S believes p if and only if q. It follows from these beliefs that S believes that q. Intuitively, S's belief that q is based on his belief that p but the counterfactual theory falsely implies that it is the belief p that is based on the belief q. For if the belief p had not been caused by e, and S still believed p, then S's belief that q together with the belief that p if and only if q would have caused his belief p.

It thus seems that the more sophisticated versions of the causal theory of the basing relation fail to improve significantly on the simple theory. So we might as well stick with the simple theory and see where it leads. Before turning to what is generally regarded as the standard objection to the simple theory, I would like to evaluate a recent argument that seeks to cast doubt on the causal theory of the basing relation by denying the distinction between being justified in holding a belief and showing that one is so justified. The general view is that the state of being justified should be distinguished from the activity of justifying, that is, one's belief may be justified even if one is incapable of justifying it. This has recently been challenged by Adam Leite (2004). Since the causal theory is committed to the noted distinction, it is worth examining Leite's argument.

He takes the causal theory to be committed to, what it calls, a "spectatorial conception" of the basing relation according to which the justificatory status of an agent's belief is determined by facts that obtain prior to and independently of the activity of justifying the belief in question. Accordingly, the justifying activity itself has no bearing on a belief's justificatory status. This means that all the factors relevant to the justificatory status of a belief, including the basing relations, are already in place and determined independently of the agent's justificatory activity. The activity is then merely a report about these independent relations. The causal theory of the basing relation is certainly committed to such a thesis. Leite, on the other hand, thinks that we should understand the link between one's beliefs and one's reasons as being constituted through one's deliberations and justificatory activities. Perhaps, one way of describing the situation is to think of the causal theory as upholding a realist view of the basing relation, by taking it to obtain independently of our defending our beliefs, while interpreting Leite as advocating a constructivist view of the relation in question much like the way in which mathematical constructivism construes mathematical truths as depending on our activity of proving them with mathematical entities owing their existence to the process in question.

Leite adumbrates a number of arguments for the view he advocates. First he claims that the spectatorial conception does not conform to the phenomenology of the conversational activity of defending our beliefs and our right to hold them in the face of challenge. To answer a challenge, he claims, you do not:

> consider facts about yourself or your psychology, such as how you came to hold the belief, but instead what there is to be said in favor of the belief – whether and why you should hold it. So in many cases, deliberating about whether a consideration represents one of your reasons is a matter of evaluating possible reasons for holding the belief.
>
> (Leite 2004, p. 226)

But it is not obvious that this is at odds with the causal view. We saw that, on that view, one may not be conscious of the reasons on which one has based his beliefs. So, when trying to defend one's beliefs, either one correctly recalls one's reasons in which case one has correctly reported those reasons or one does not in which case, in the face of challenge, one volunteers some possible reasons which may or may not correspond to his actual reasons.

All that the preceding remarks suggest is the possibility of a mismatch between one's suggested reasons and those that actually form the bases of one's beliefs. Is Leite taking such a possibility as counting against the standard account? That this is what drives his argument becomes transparent when he subsequently suggests two basic adequacy conditions for an account of the basing relation: (1) The reasons for which a belief is held can be directly determined; (2) In declaring one's reasons, one directly opens oneself to epistemic evaluation and incur certain obligations like revising one's reasons should they prove to be inadequate and so on. By "directly determining," Leite seems to require some sort of direct or perhaps infallible access to one's reasons as he likens it to establishing our intentions when we sincerely declare "I intend...": "Barring fundamental irrationality, such a declaration of intention precludes one's not so intending unless one changes one's mind" (Leite 2004, p. 228). But the requirement of having infallible access to one's reasons, in the guise of requiring us to be able to directly determine them, is too strong a demand.

After all there is the phenomenon of the so-called "lost justification" (Harman 1986). The idea is that people do not usually keep track of the justification relations among their beliefs. It so happens that many of an agent's beliefs are such that although they were initially based on adequate evidence, and thus justified, the agent subsequently forgets what that evidence was. We have all had experiences in which we justifiably form a belief about something on the authority of some source even though we no longer remember the source despite having retained the belief. This failure to keep track of one's justifications is thought to be a natural consequence of the limitations of our memories and, in general, our brain. Moreover, this is a phenomenon that can also occur in Leite's account of the justificatory status of one's belief. Suppose, following Leite, someone is asked to determine or identify his reasons in the course of justifying his beliefs. After a lapse of some time, however, he forgets how he has justified his belief, and is, once again, taken to task to show that his belief is justified. It is quite possible that this time he comes up with a different defense strategy, thus revising his earlier stance.

As for condition (2), if this is to be an effective requirement yielding the desired result, it should be employed in an epistemic environment where an objective way of determining whether one has based his belief on adequate grounds is available. The epistemic setting must be such that an agent can check if he has gone wrong and this can only be done with the help of another individual. In other words, the environment must be social. This means that one cannot be his own judge. But this is not in accord with Leite's earlier description of the activity of justifying as "often conversational, though it can also take place in private meditation [which] ... if one is taken to have performed successfully, than one's interlocutor (who may be oneself) will conclude that one is justified" (Leite 2004, p. 219, my emphasis). It is also interesting that the combination of (1) and (2), when we are our own interlocutor and "sincerely articulate what we take to be good reasons for our beliefs [and] commit to holding our beliefs for these reasons" (Leite 2004, p. 219), brings Leite's theory close to Richard Foley's well-known theory of egocentric justification according to which it is egocentrically rational for an agent to believe a proposition only if he would think on deep reflection that believing it is conducive to having an accurate and comprehensive belief system (Foley 1987). Foley's conception of rationality is a radically subjective account in that it defines rationality (justification) in terms of the point of view (perspective) of an agent.

Finally, Leite speaks of "adequate reasons" without specifying what counts as adequate as when he proposes his central thesis that if one's belief is justified in virtue of being held for adequate reasons, then one must be able to justify it. Later, however, he introduces some clarifications when he seeks to counter the charge that his proposal has skeptical consequences since it requires one to show the adequacy of one's reasons when this is often beyond the pale of ordinary cognizers. Justifying a perceptual belief, for example, seems to require the impossible task that ordinary cognizers be able to invoke a philosophical theory of perceptual justification. Leite, however, denies that we need to go to such an extent to justify our beliefs. Often, he says, we accept assertions such as "well, I see that it is so" or "there is no reason to doubt it" as quite enough to justify a belief: "In appropriate settings, such considerations can constitute adequate reasons" (Leite 2004, p. 240). One cannot help but feel that such an attenuated sense of "adequacy" makes the justifying activity quite innocuous, thereby rendering the debate whether being justified requires showing that one is justified trivial. I conclude therefore that Leite has failed to show that the causal view is flawed because it heeds the distinction between being justified and the activity of justifying.

As noted earlier, however, the causal theory faces the standard and seemingly intractable objection involving deviant chains that shows that the holding of a causal relation between a belief and a reason is not sufficient for the obtaining of the basing relation between them. Consider a typical example (Pollock 1986, p. 37). John believes that he is going to be late to his class which causes him to run on a slippery pavement, fall down on his back whereupon he finds himself looking at the birds in the tree above him. John's belief that he is going to be late to his class caused him to believe that there are birds in the tree, but he does not believe the latter on the basis of the former. Or, one may consider some of the causal ancestors of a perceptual belief, say, certain neurophysiological states of one's brain. Although the perceptual belief is clearly dependent on the pertinent neural state, it is not based on it. To avoid these problems, it is tempting to want to limit one's reasons for a belief to its proximate mental causes. But this strategy does not work. Sometimes, due to malfunction, a belief may cause and, thereby, ground another belief despite the two beliefs being totally irrelevant. Moreover, such a constraint does not square well with certain characteristics of the basing relation. Unlike the property of "being the proximal mental cause," the basing relation is transitive. In the next section, we shall consider one prominent recent attempt to deal with the problem of the deviant causal chains.

6.2   Alston: basing relation as input to psychologically realized functions

This section deals with Alston's recent work on the basing relation (Alston 1995; 2005). He advocates a broadly causal theory according to which we can think of what a belief is based on as what gives rise to the belief in question. However, in view of the problem of deviant causal chains, the causality involved, says Alston, is not just any form of causality. As he puts it, "[it] is the kind involved in the operation of input-output mechanisms that form and sustains...beliefs" (Alston 2005, p. 84). He does not directly elaborate on this thought but approaches it via the so-called generality problem. So we need to say a few words about the latter problem before considering Alston's proposal to resolve it.

According to the reliability theories of epistemic justification and knowledge, beliefs produced by reliable processes are justified. But how are we to assess a particular belief-forming process for its reliability? A particular process is not the sort of thing that would enjoy a favorable ratio of true beliefs among its products as it occurs just once, and the beliefs it produces are either true or false. Hence it is a type of a process, rather than a particular token of it, that can be assessed for reliability. But, just like any particular item, any particular process is an instance of many types (see, e.g., Feldman 1985). Consider, for example, the visual process that leads me to believe that there is a red book before me. This process can be a token of many different types: the cognitive process, the visual process, the cognitive process occurring on a Thursday, the cognitive process occurring in a middle-aged man and so on. Which is the relevant type? If the relevant type is identified too narrowly, then it will have only one instance, namely, the token itself. This has the absurd consequence that all true beliefs are justified and all false beliefs are unjustified. A very broad identification of the types, on the other hand, leads to the unacceptable conclusion that beliefs produced by the tokens belonging to a broad type are equally well justified (or unjustified). The problem of providing an account of the relevant types between these two extremes is known as the generality problem.

Are there then objective facts that determine a unique type to which a particular token of a belief-forming process belongs? To answer this question, Alston conceives of a process as a psychologically realized function that maps certain features of an input into the outputs which in this case are states of believing with certain contents. We can also think of these psychologically realized belief-forming functions as psychological mechanisms or as habits and dispositions. Alston's idea is that such functions determine the relevant types. Suppose I form the visual belief that a car is parked in front of my house. Spelling out this function in detail is an immense task. Specifying the output side, the belief content, is, however, easy, says Alston, and by using the content of the belief output, we can identify the input side as, say, "my being appeared to car-parked-in-front-of-my-housely" or "an object's looking like a car parked in front of my house." Thus, the type of process the reliability of which determines the epistemic status of the belief in question is the one defined by the function whose input/output have been accordingly specified.

Alston's way of describing the input is by way of his description of the output, namely, the content of the relevant beliefs and thoughts. But what objective criterion can tell us what these thoughts are about? There are potentially many candidates as a thought can be about any of the elements constituting the causal chain that leads to it. Intuitively, the content of a perceptual belief is the usual or normal cause of that belief.[2] For example, the cause of the belief that a cat is present is the past correlations of cats with stimuli similar to the present stimuli. The difficulty with this proposal is that an equally good answer can be that the belief about cats is caused by appropriate stimulation of the same organs, or by the photons streaming from cats to the eye in which case the belief would be about the stimulation or photons. There are endless such causal explanations and each would dictate a different content for the same perceptual belief. There is, thus, as much indeterminacy here as there is with respect to the relevant kind of belief process that Alston's account seeks to identify. Thus, by defining belief-forming processes in terms of functions, Alston is merely replacing one kind of indeterminacy (with respect to process types) with another (regarding belief contents).

The problem is more serious in the case of the basing relation which receives a similar treatment by Alston. For the input to a belief-forming mechanism is just the "ground" on which the belief output is based. For a belief to be based on a certain ground is just for that belief to be the output of a belief-forming mechanism that consists in a realized function of the sort specified in our discussion of the generality problem. Consider, as an example, the formation of the perceptual belief that the object in front of me is a maple tree. What happens here is that an input-output function is activated where the input is a visual experience and the output is a belief that this is a maple tree. The function is one that maps certain features of the visual appearance (VA) into a belief with that content (M): "The ground is again VA and the belief based on VA has the propositional content M. The ground is adequate iff in a large range of (actual and possible) cases of beliefs with content M being based on grounds with experiential content VA, ... the beliefs would be mostly true" (Alston 2005, p. 134).

This treatment of the basing relation inherits the difficulties of the solution to the generality problem. We seem to be, once more, trading one sort of indeterminacy (about the bases) for another (about the content of the belief outputs). Again these beliefs could be about any of the elements in the causal chain leading to them. The indeterminacy at the level of the beliefs, then, mirrors the indeterminacy at the level of the grounds. Moreover, the problem of the deviant causal chains was how to identify the justification-conferring ground of a belief among its causes. But, as Alston's examples show, his description of the input to a belief-forming mechanism is simply derivative of his description of the (belief) output of the process in question – which, as just noted, is, in any case, inadequate. Alston's account fails to establish a conceptual link between the basis of a belief and its content which is why, having decided that the content of a belief output in one of his examples is "there is a car parked in front of my house," he artificially identifies the input as "my being appeared to car-parked-in-front-of-my-housely" (Alston 2005, p. 130). But this cannot be all that there is to the input-output relation for the output of a belief-forming process is obviously affected by, or takes account of, the input to that process.

One may highlight this point, as Alston does, by considering belief-forming process as habits or dispositions. The idea is to see basing relations as manifesting an agent's cognitive dispositions. We habitually take experience at face value (under normal circumstances). We are disposed to believe, for example, that the stick is bent when it looks bent; that there is a maple tree before us when we have an experience as of a maple tree; that it will rain upon seeing the gathering of dark clouds and so on. In such cases, it looks as though the grounds of our beliefs manifest certain of our dispositions. But it seems that all these stable belief-forming capacities are acquired as a result of the obtaining of some sort of law-like connections between our experiences and the pertinent perception-based beliefs they give rise to. These grounds are, in other words, reliable indicators of certain pertinent facts which is why the ensuing beliefs are often true. Again, the capacities-based theory was supposed to identify the grounds of our beliefs from among their causes whereas in describing these capacities we are actually assuming what those ground are. Moreover, such law-like connections exist not only between experiences and the beliefs they give rise to but also between these beliefs and certain neural patterns in our brain that cause them. But, surely, we are disinclined to say that those neural patterns constitute the bases of our beliefs. It is no good to protest that with regard to the latter causes we are unaware of their obtaining for, as we have seen, our (genuine) reasons can be subliminal and unconscious.

Alston himself goes on to admit that, despite his constraints, there are still a large number of possible alternative process-types with respect to which his functional construal of belief-forming processes fails to make a unique choice. He particularly concedes the indeterminacy with regard to the input to the belief-forming processes and the functions themselves. When I look out the window and form the belief that there is a maple tree out there, there are, says Alston, many functions that would yield a belief with that content. Likewise, one may think of the experiential input, he says, as having a "visual presentation with such-and-such features," a "sensory experience," a "visual experience" and the like (Alston 2005, p. 138). In response, he invokes, what he calls, the thesis of "psychological realism" according to which only one way of generalizing from this particular input to the belief output reflects the actual psychological dynamics of the relevant process; that is, of all the possibilities only one of them is realized in this case. But this response falls short of what was promised earlier. What we wished to know was what objective facts determine a unique type to which a particular process belongs. It is no good to be told that *there are* some such facts. Our concern is also epistemic as we want to know how to identify them. To give an analogy, suppose we wish to know which properties of the brain give rise to consciousness. To respond that there are such properties but we may never know them is more an expression of our faith in physicalism than a solution to the mind-body problem. Likewise, Alston's functional account of the basing relation is more an expression of his faith in psychological realism than a solution to the problem of the deviant causal chains.

6.3   Basing relation: triangulation and content

To provide an account of the basing relation, we are not, as repeatedly emphasized, just trying to determine if our beliefs are rational or justifiable. What we are really after is whether those beliefs are justified, that is, if they are based on our adequate reasons or evidence. It is the latter task that requires having a theory of the basing relation. To face up to this challenge, I propose to approach our question indirectly. This is perhaps inevitable in view of the failure of the previous attempts. This is

how we shall proceed. We begin, as our first step, with a functional construal of the basing relation by identifying one of its salient roles in the
context of the epistemic justification of a belief. The claim here is that
we believe for a reason if that reason discharges a certain function. As
for the second step in our argument, we then try to find out if that function has been discharged without relying on assumptions that would
render our account question-begging. Once this has been determined,
we can be confident that our belief is based on a pertinent reason, thus
completing our theory of justified belief.

Let us begin with our first task, namely, providing a functional
analysis of the basing relation.[3] Here I take my cues from some of
Alston's earlier remarks about the basing relation. The problem of casual
deviance, we may recall, was that although the basis or ground of a
belief causally sustains it, not just any kind of causal dependence constitutes the basing relation between the ground and the relevant belief.
The point to note here is that the reason–belief transition is not only
causal but also a contentful one. It is, in other words, in virtue of its content that a reason stands in a basing relation to the belief it causes. This
is quite clear in cases in which the reason–belief transition is inferential,
that is, transitions where, for example, a belief p is derived from another
belief q.[4] Here, not only the belief p is caused by the belief q, its content is also (partially) determined by the content of q. In other words,
the causal transition between p and q tracks the inferential transition
between them. The same, I believe, holds for cases where our beliefs are
based on non-doxastic experiences. The contentful relation between a
reason and what it is a reason for is how I am inclined to interpret the
following remarks of Alston's:

> [wherever] it is clear that a belief is *based on* another belief or on
> an experience, the belief-forming "process" or "mechanism" is *taking
> account* of that ground or features thereof, being *guided* by it even if
> this does not involve the conscious utilization of a belief in a support
> relation.
>
> (Alston 1989, p. 229)

Being guided by the grounds or forming beliefs in the "light of them"
is just another way of saying that our reasons shape or (partially) determine the contents and objects of our beliefs, that is, what the beliefs
are about. It is presumably because of this contentful relation between
beliefs and their grounds that beliefs are sensitive to their evidence. My
belief about, say, the streets being wet is sensitive to the way the streets

look. They are about the streets' conditions. Had they looked differently, I would have formed a different belief taking account of the features of my new experience. So it is only in a content-determining context that the causes of a belief may assume the role of its justifiers. It is for this reason that we are, intuitively speaking, inclined to discount, say, brain states as grounding the beliefs they cause.

Where the grounds of our beliefs are experiences, some distinct arguments have been advanced to show how experience (partially) determines the contents of the beliefs they give rise to (Burge 1986; Brewer 1999). (Here, I shall focus on the most basic perception-based beliefs.) Consider, for example, a class of beliefs about the spatial world whose members have the content that a particular mind-independent thing is determinately thus and so. Consider now a person, S, with a perceptually based belief about a particular object (*a*) and suppose that S actually knows that he is referring to *a*. Let us assume, for reductio, that S's conception of *a* is exhausted by a wholly general description, "The F," that is intended to fix the reference of *a*. Accordingly, S's conception of *a* involves no experience of the object in question. Now, however detailed this conception may be, it is epistemically possible for S that "F" is multiply realized. Thus, "the F" fails to refer which means that S's conception of *a* cannot be purely descriptive. It must, rather, involve some kind of demonstrative component to enable S to grasp the object in question. So the idea is that beliefs cannot be about individual things merely by containing descriptions, but must ultimately inherit the individual components of their contents from perceptual demonstratives, that is, from experience having intentional content of the form "that thing is thus."

Accordingly, perceptual experiences, as intentional states whose objects are aspects of the external reality, give rise to "demonstrative" beliefs with the same or at least overlapping content. They share their objects with the beliefs they give rise to. Note that by narrowing down the range of grounds to those that are both contentful and content-determining (beliefs and experiences), we are still left with the task of determining, in any particular case, what the pertinent beliefs are based on. For, as we saw with Alston's tree example, the particular experience identified as the ground of a perceptual belief can still be a token of many types; visual presentations with such-and-such features, visual experiences, sensory experiences and so on. This concludes the first step of our argument, that is, that reason warrants or justifies a relevant belief if the reason could (partially) determine the content (object) of the belief in question. Thus, unlike Alston's proposal, our account is founded on a conceptual link between the basis of a belief and its content (object).

As for the second step in our argument, it consists, we may recall, of the claim that we can determine what the content of the relevant beliefs are. But, as repeatedly emphasized, this is by no means an easy feat as it is indeterminate, without invoking some independent assumptions, what the content of a belief is. For example, we should allow a sentence reporting the belief that, say, "There is a maple tree in front of me," to be about a maple tree or any causal antecedents leading to the belief in question. It may even turn out to be about certain computer files if we happen to be in fact envatted. It is the burden of a theory of the basing relation that it provide a way of eliminating the relevant indeterminacies without being question-begging. Now since, according to our first premise, a ground determines the content of a perceptual belief as well as causing it, by identifying the belief's content, in a non-question-begging manner, its content we have thereby shown that the basing relation mechanism has been in place, namely, that the perceptual belief in question is epistemically based on a ground with an overlapping content. The crucial question is then whether we can take the second step of our argument without presupposing what we are going to establish.

It seems to me that the best way to meet this requirement is to approach our question by invoking Davidson's idea of triangulation as it would ensure that we will not rely surreptitiously on unwarranted assumptions (see, e.g., Davidson 1984). Before proceeding to explain how this can be done, we may remind ourselves of some of the pertinent points in Davidson's project of radical interpretation where an interpreter seeks to understand the language of an alien community without any antecedent knowledge of their thoughts or what their words mean. As we shall see, the assumptions involved in the Davidsonian project provide an appropriate epistemic setting whereby the question of the basing relation can be pursued without incurring the charge of circularity.

As noted in previous chapters, if, according to Davidson, belief ascription is constrained by the principle of charity, then the ascribed beliefs turn out to be rational. For, as was emphasized, the process of charitable belief ascription is characterized by the aim of maximizing truth and minimizing falsity in the speaker's belief system, which is actually how epistemic justification is generally characterized, namely, in terms of the aim of the maximization of truth and minimization of falsity in an agent's body of belief (Alston 1989). Justification is widely understood as an evaluative concept whose attachment to a belief makes the belief worth having from the epistemic point of view which, as just noted, is, in turn, characterized in terms of a distinct goal, the truth-directed goal, namely, the goal of believing truths and not believing falsehoods, or, alternatively, the aim of maximizing truth and minimizing falsity in a large body of beliefs. So once belief ascription is seen as constrained by the principle of charity, this would render the ascribed beliefs as rational. This is not, however, to say that the imputed beliefs are always true. Rather, what the principle of charity requires is the maximization of truth by the interpreter's own lights and, for all we know, the interpreter's beliefs may be mistaken.

Accordingly, Davidson's project of radical interpretation rests on reflections on what assumptions the interpreter has to make so that he could bring into harmony the concepts of the theory of interpretation with the speaker's behavioral evidence. Adopting the radical interpreter's stance, thus, requires that the meaning of an utterance and the object of a thought depend on how a speaker is embedded in her environment. To identify the meaning of the speaker's utterance, Davidson, as we saw, introduced the principle of charity. The problem is that charity requires only that a speaker's belief about her environment be true. More is needed to ensure that these true beliefs are actually correlated with the conditions that prompt them so that *statements of such conditions can be taken to express the content of her beliefs*. This means that, as a speaker, what her thoughts are about will depend on what the pattern of their typical causes is.

In the case of a single responder, however, what she is responding to is indeterminate. If we take response to be just a causal relation, the production of an effect on an agent by a cause in her environment, then an agent responding to the environment can be regarded as responding to everything along the chain of stimulation. In order to generate a determinate interpretation, therefore, there must be some objective way to select one of the links as the correct one. We could not, for example, decide whether the speaker was responding to a proximal or distal stimulus, or which distal stimulus. So there must be an objective way of narrowing down the choice of the relevant causes of the speaker's thought. What objective criterion can tell us what the thought is about? "If we consider a single creature by itself, its response, no matter how complex, cannot show that it is reacting to, or thinking about, events a certain distance away rather than, say, on its skin" (Davidson 2001, p. 119). The suggestion that Davidson makes here is "triangulation," that is, the idea that what the speaker's thoughts are about makes sense only against the background of a pattern of interaction with other speakers. So we have the interpreter and the speaker triangulating upon a mutually salient stimulus. Otherwise the stimulus is arbitrary and nothing ensures that any of one's thoughts are about the external world as opposed to, say, internal neural firings.

For example, an observer's thoughts about trees are typically caused by trees. However, to determine the typical cause, we need to look at a number of situations in which tree-thoughts are caused and see which elements these situations share. The idea is to "locate" the stimulus typically causing the tree-thoughts. Davidson's proposal is a form of triangulation where one line goes from the first observer in the direction of the tree, another line from the second observer in the tree's direction, and the third line goes between the two observers. Where the lines from the first and second observers to the tree converge, the stimulus is located.

> [U]ntil the triangle is completed connecting two creatures, and each creature with common features of the world, there can be no answer to the question whether a creature, in discriminating between stimuli, is discriminating between stimuli at the sensory surfaces or somewhere further out, or further in. Without this sharing of reactions to common stimuli, thought and speech would have no particular content – that is no content at all.
>
> (Davidson 2001, p. 212)

Note that, thus far, there is no requirement that the observers interact. All that is needed is for one to observe the other. This is actually the form of triangulation that is involved in the very project of radical interpretation where an interpreter seeks to assign truth conditions to the speaker's sentences by identifying correlations between the observable circumstances in the speaker's environment the sentences held true by her in those conditions. One can thus think of the interpreter triangulating the objects of basic perceptual belief by taking the speaker to be reacting to the same features of the world the he would be responding to under similar conditions.[5]

With the help of triangulation, therefore, we identify the content or object of our beliefs without any antecedent knowledge of their grounds. This way, we can escape criticisms that were earlier leveled against Alston. Unlike him, we do not take the content of the pertinent beliefs for granted. Rather, it is identified in a non-question-begging manner via triangulation. Moreover, unlike Alston's account, our proposal is founded on a conceptual connection between the basis of a belief and its content. For, as argued earlier, we believe for a reason if the reason (partially) determines the content of the belief in an epistemic context. Now, having identified the content of a belief, we have thereby shown (indirectly) that it is based on reasons. In particular, the reasons are those causes of the beliefs which (partially or totally) overlap in their contents. The application of the principle of charity, thus, ensures that the associated beliefs are rational placing them in an epistemic context, while, by correlating the beliefs with conditions that prompt them, triangulation locates their content. If our indirect strategy is correct, we have shown that our rational beliefs are based on reasons whose content they inherit.

As we saw in Chapters 4 and 5, experience can confer immediate justification on a belief. On a prominent theory of the structure of justification, the ensuing justified beliefs, called "basic" beliefs, are then standardly taken to constitute the foundation of one's belief system. Given certain plausible assumptions, these basic beliefs give rise to, what is known as, "basic knowledge." It has been argued recently that such a position falls victim to what is known as the problem of easy knowledge, the idea that, on such theories, certain inferences allow us far too easily to acquire knowledge (justification) that seems unlikely under the envisaged circumstances. Moreover, it has been claimed that certain closure inferences involving basic knowledge are actually instances of transmission failure. What has added to the interest in the problem is the claim (made by some philosophers) that answering this question would enable us to explain our felt dissatisfaction with Moore's famous "proof" of the external world and arguments that purportedly share a similar structure. It is to the investigation of these seemingly unpalatable consequences of the evidential sensitivity of beliefs to experiences that I turn in the next chapter.

7
Basic Beliefs, Easy Knowledge and the Problem of Warrant Transfer

In Chapters 4 and 5 we sought to establish that perceptual beliefs are governed by evidential norms, in particular, that experiences can confer justification on the beliefs it gives rise to. These beliefs are regarded as basic because their justification derives not from other justified beliefs, but from the experiences that cause them. On some very plausible assumptions, this leads to the doctrine of basic knowledge (justification), namely, knowledge (justification) that an agent acquires from a certain source, even if he fails to know that the source is reliable. It has, however, been claimed that, on such theories, bootstrapping and closure allow us far too easily to acquire knowledge (justification) that seems unlikely under the envisaged circumstances. It has further been argued that closure arguments exploiting basic knowledge (justification) are not warrant-transmitting. In this chapter, after evaluating some of the well-known solutions to these problems, I offer a mixed view of the legitimacy of basic knowledge inferences while trying to provide novel explanations as to how contrary intuitions arise.

7.1 The problem of easy knowledge

According to a version of the problem of the criterion, to obtain knowledge through cognitive sources we need to know if these sources are reliable. The later kind of knowledge, however, turns out to be dependent and based on the deliverances of the sources themselves. We are thus caught in a circle. The most widely accepted way of breaking out of this circle is to allow that one's belief may count as knowledge even if one does not know that the source is reliable or that one's evidence for the beliefs in question is a reliable indicator of their truth. Adopting this approach commits one to what is known as the "basic knowledge" thesis.

(BK)   A belief source can deliver knowledge (justification) prior to one's knowing that the source is reliable.

Despite its apparent plausibility, the doctrine of basic knowledge seems to have some untoward consequences. Stewart Cohen has recently argued that, once basic knowledge is allowed, it provides too easy a route to certain cases of knowledge that seem unlikely under the envisioned circumstances (Cohen 2002). This is the problem of easy knowledge and it arises most fundamentally via the following inferential routes (henceforth, EK-inferences).

(a)   Epistemic Closure

Given (BK), I can know that, say, the table before me is red on the basis of its looking red without knowing that the table's looking red is a reliable indication of its being red. According to the principle of closure, on the other hand, if I know that the table is red and I competently deduce from it the proposition that the table is not white with red lights shining on it, I know that the table is not white but illuminated by red lights. This is implausible for it seems that I have acquired this knowledge much too easily.

b)   Bootstrapping

Again, assuming (BK), we can know that (p), "The table is red" prior to having evidence for the reliability of our sense perception. We can also know, via introspection, that we believe that the table is red. This gives us the conjunction $< p_1 \,\&\, Bp_1 >$. By repeating this process enough times with respect to similar propositions, I could then amass, what Alston calls, "track-record" evidence of the form $< p_1 \,\&\, Bp_1, p_2 \,\&\, Bp_2, \ldots, p_n \,\&\, Bp_n >$ to bootstrap up to the knowledge that my color perception is reliable, something which we did not know before (see Fumerton 1995; Vogel 2000). Again, it seems such knowledge has been acquired too easily. Cohen's main concern is how to deal with the problem of EK-inferences without giving up either of the basis knowledge or closure principles. Before evaluating the proposed solutions, however, let us get clearer about the reasons underlying the claim that easy knowledge is problematic.

7.2 What is wrong with easy knowledge?

Thus far we have merely characterized EK-inferences as those providing too easy routes to certain cases of knowledge. Why is it implausible to think that we can gain such knowledge through these inferences? Cohen himself tries to bring out the problematic nature of EK-inferences through the supposedly unsatisfying nature of the following kind of dialogue. Consider, for example, the case of closure and the example involving the red table.

> It's counterintuitive to say we could in this way know the falsity of even the *alternative* that the table is white but illuminated by red lights. Suppose my son wants to buy a red table for his room. We go in the sore and I say, "That table is red. I'll buy it for you." Having inherited his father's obsessive personality, he worries, "Daddy, what if it's white with red lights shining on it?" I reply, " Don't worry – you see, it looks red, so it is red, so it's not white but illuminated by red lights." Surely he should not be satisfied with this response.
>
> (Cohen 2002, p. 314)

A similar illustration is provided for the bootstrapping case where the son now wonders if his father's vision is really reliable. Under such circumstances, the father's attempt to go through the bootstrapping reasoning to convince his suspicious son would be futile, says Cohen. In a recent response to Cohen, Peter Markie has claimed that we can in fact gain knowledge through EK-inferences and the problem with the father–son dialogue is simply that it is question-begging (Markie 2005). For while the son wants a reason to believe that the table is not white but illuminated by red lights, his father gives him as a reason the very point about which he is suspicious. Cohen has, in turn, replied that nowhere in the dialogue does the father assume that the table is red but infers it, rather, from the fact that it looks red (Cohen 2005). So the father has begged no question against his son in the way suggested by Markie. To elaborate, Cohen goes on to remove the son from the story and considers the father *himself* as trying to buy a table while being anxious to avoid buying a white table that looks red. However, going through the closure reasoning, says Cohen, the exercise would hardly bolster the father's confidence that he is not buying a white table that looks red (because illuminated by red lights):

> Presumably, the intuition remains that there is something wrong with my having reasoned this way. Can we appeal to the dialectical context to explain why? Of course here there is only one reasoner ... But again, surely there is something unsatisfactory about the way I have convinced myself that the table is not deceptively illuminated. Again, the appeal to dialectical context cannot explain our intuitions.
>
> (Cohen 2005, pp. 419–20)

Although Cohen has a point here, we still need to be clearer about what underlies our dissatisfaction with EK-inferences. With the dialectical context rendered ineffective through Cohen's modification of the story, his remarks seem to be simply inviting us back to consult our brute intuitions about the defective nature of such inferences something which the father–son dialogue was supposed to bring out. But this is puzzling. For if the premises of the obviously valid EK-inferences are assumed to be true, then what explains our skeptical intuitions, and how are the latter related to the unsatisfying nature of the father–son dialogue? Perhaps the key to demystifying the situation is to make a sharper distinction between our doubts about the legitimacy of EK-inferences and our dissatisfaction with the dialectical context of the father–son dialogue. It seems that what underpins our contrary intuitions in the case of an EK-inference has to do with facts involving the strength of the pertinent evidence in such cases. For if, as in the table example, *all* one has to go on is that the table looks red, then one is hardly in a position to gain the knowledge that the table is not white but illuminated by red lights. In other words, while the evidence (the table's looking redly) is strong enough to justify the belief that the table is red, it does not seem to be strong enough to justify the belief that the table is not white but lit by red lights. This seems to be consonant with Cohen's elaboration of his views in response to Markie's objections (more about this point later).

What seems, on the other hand, to underlie the unsatisfying nature of the reasoning embedded in the father–son dialogue has to do with the dialectical effectiveness of EK-inferences, namely, the fact that such arguments are unable to convince those who are already skeptical of their conclusions. That is why the father's attempt to infer that the table is red from the fact that it looks red could hardly impress his obsessive son (reflecting the strength of his evidence). To get a better grip on the points just raised, we may distinguish the (epistemic) *legitimacy* of such inferences from their (dialectical) *effectiveness*. For an inference to be legitimate is for it to transmit warrant so that if one is justified in believing its premises, one is *thereby* justified in believing its conclusion. Legitimacy is, thus, a fundamentally epistemic notion. Accordingly, those who regard EK-inferences as legitimate think that basic knowledge can be inferentially expanded (by closure) to yield knowledge of their pertinent conclusions. Being a legitimate inference is not, however, the same thing as being an effective one. The latter is a context-dependent notion which is a function of the assumptions that are embedded in the context in which the argument is applied. The concept of dialectical effectiveness is thus supposed to apply to inferences in terms of their ability to modify one's epistemic state in a context.

Take, for instance, a paradigmatic form of a valid inference in logic text books.

(V)   All men are mortal
      Dalai Lama is a man
So,   Dalai Lama is mortal

I do not think anybody would doubt the legitimacy of (V). However, for all its logical perfection, if (V) is tried on someone who already doubts its conclusion (on, say, religious grounds), he would hardly be rationally convinced by the argument that Dalai Lama is mortal. Rather, given his grounds for skepticism about its conclusion, he would refuse to go along with its major premise that *all* men are mortal. But this is a point about the dialectical effectiveness of (V) rather than its legitimacy. The same holds for EK-inferences. Doubts about the legitimacy of such inferences ought to be distinguished from doubts about their effectiveness. Accordingly, the point brought out by the father–son style of dialogue is not really what marks EK-inferences but a general point that applies to all arguments across the board.

7.2.1 Responses to the problem of EK-inferences: a survey and critique

I shall now turn to some of the responses that have been offered to the problem of easy knowledge. These reactions can be classified as falling into one of the following groups: rejecting EK-inferences as illegitimate, that is, as failing to transmit warrant; regarding them as legitimate in some contexts but illegitimate in others; and accepting them as legitimate while seeking to explain away the contrary intuitions. My own proposal is a mixed view that significantly differs from most such accounts while sharing some grounds with some. Let us, however, start with the first group of such responses.

7.3 EK-Inferences as illegitimate

The rejection of EK-inferences as illegitimate has been upheld most notably by Cohen. We shall now look at how he proposes to block them. Earlier we saw Cohen offering the father–son dialogue as a way of highlighting the problematic nature of EK-inferences. However, because of the problems highlighted in Section 7.2, he also proceeds to provide some "independent considerations in support of our skeptical intuitions" (Cohen 2005, p. 424) in the case of the closure inferences. It would thus be prudent to begin by evaluating this new argument before attending to how he seeks to block EK-inferences (he qualifies his earlier proposals in the course of elaborating his stance).

Cohen claims that there is something special about the nature of evidence in the closure version of EK-inferences that renders them illegitimate. Consider the table example again where our evidence (e) for the belief in the proposition (p) that the table is red consists of its looking red. Before looking at the table, the probability of both e and $\neg$e is 0.5. On the other hand, $Pr(p/e) = 0.5$ as is the conditional probability of (q) "The table is white but illuminated by red lights" given that it appears red (e). Since $Pr(e/q) = 1$, it follows that $Pr(q) = Pr(e) \times Pr(q/e) = 0.25$. But, after looking at the table, $Pr(e)$ will be 1 in which case $Pr(q) = 1 \times 0.5 = 0.5$. This, says Cohen, is a strange result because, before observing the table, I did *not* know $\neg$q but, after seeing it and using the closure inference, I come to know that $\neg$q despite the fact the probability of q is raised by 0.25 during the process. This conception of evidence, says Cohen, is untenable for it means that acquiring evidence which raises the probability that the table is white but red appearing provides a basis for coming to know that the table is not white but red appearing.

But this argument is not effective as it cuts both ways. For although the acquiring of evidence (e) raises the probability of p from 0.25 to 0.5, thus providing the ground for claiming to know p, it equally raises the probability of q by the same amount, thus allowing us to claim to know q (recall that $Pr(p/e) = Pr(q/e) = 0.5$). One could then reason in the reverse order to argue that since q entails $\neg$p, then, by closure, one can come to know that $\neg$p contradicting the assumption that we have basic knowledge of p. Cohen's crucial assumption (A) in his argument comes in when he declares that although acquiring the evidence that the table looks red naturally "counts in favor of the table's being red, it is not clear why it does not also count in favor of the table's being non-red but deceptively illuminated to appear red" (Cohen 2005, p. 424).

Though initially plausible, this assumption turns out to undermine Cohen's argument. To see this, recall that Cohen's argument was set up with the sole purpose of explaining our skeptical intuitions in the case of the closure argument, namely, to explain why knowledge of propositions like ¬q seems problematic under the described circumstances. However, given (A) that p and q are equally supported by e, there is no reason why one could not claim to know q on the basis of e, and, then, since q entails ¬p, to argue (through closure) that one knows ¬p, thus contradicting the claim that we know that p. The only way out of this impasse is for Cohen to claim that, despite (A), we cannot have knowledge of propositions of the type q under the envisaged circumstances (he may even concoct an appropriate father–son dialogue to support this claim). But to resort to this measure is to move in full circle, for the whole point of the exercise was to "support . . . our skeptical intuitions" in the closure case, that is, that knowing propositions as complex as ¬q (or q) is implausible under the circumstances described. Cohen's appeal to assumption (A) is actually reminiscent of the so-called underdetermination principle (UP) according to which if S's evidence for believing that φ does not favor φ over some incompatible hypothesis ψ, then S's evidence does not justify φ. In fact Cohen has argued elsewhere that the principle of closure entails (UP) (Cohen 1998). Since he accepts closure here, it would only be a short step to conclude, via the conjoining of (A) and (UP), that one does not know that p; a conclusion that was drawn earlier in a more long winded manner.

In any case, since Cohen wants to allow for basic knowledge while denying the legitimacy of EK-inferences, he must find ways of blocking them. This he does by suggesting that the premises of, say, closure inferences involve different conceptions of knowledge. He proposes to adopt Sosa's distinction between animal knowledge which requires only that one track reality and reflective knowledge which, in addition, demands precluding the unreliability of one's faculties (Sosa 1991, pp. 225–44). He proposes to identify basic knowledge with animal knowledge and then to prohibit the application of closure to animal knowledge. However, this solution seems rather ad hoc, not least because Cohen, acknowledging an objection of Markie's according to which even reflective knowledge can yield easy knowledge, goes on to suggest a contextualist solution for dealing with these species of easy knowledge. Moreover, one could, as we did, rewrite the closure version of EK-inferences in terms of justification rather than knowledge. It would then be quite obscure what one could intend by identifying basic justification with "animal" justification especially if one is following Sosa's lead here. As for blocking the bootstrapping reasoning, Cohen's initial suggestion was to deny the ability of basic (animal) knowledge to combine with self-knowledge to yield the required conclusion. However, following an objection of Markie's, he tries a different tack by appealing to the so-called "independent principle," which he takes to govern animal knowledge, and according to which one cannot appeal to knowledge produced from a particular faculty to gain knowledge of the reliability of that faculty. However, Cohen candidly admits that "this proposal is ad hoc. [But] at present, it is the best [he] can do" (Cohen 2005, p. 424). I conclude therefore that Cohen has neither succeeded to prove the illegitimacy of EK-inferences nor provided viable means of blocking them.

A different account to deny the legitimacy of EK-inferences has been suggested by Crispin Wright who approaches the problem via the question of whether warrant transmits across the entailment from premises to conclusions of a wide variety of EK-inferences. This question has commanded much attention in the recent epistemological thought. What has added to the interest in the problem is the claim that answering this question would enable us to explain our felt dissatisfaction with Moore's famous "proof" of the external world and other arguments that purportedly share a similar structure. To examine Wright's reasons for the denying the legitimacy of EK-inferences, a few remarks are in order.

Looking at his hands, Moore famously suggested the following argument for the existence of the world.

Moore-I   Having a visual experience as of two hands.
Moore-II   Here are two hands.
Moore-III Therefore, there is an external world.

There is no denying that this argument hardly strikes one as a satisfying "proof" of the external world even though it has proved to be quite difficult to put one's finger at where it goes wrong. It seems quite plausible to take Moore-I as providing warrant or justification for believing Moore-II, and, given the fact that Moore-II entails Moore-III, to conclude that one's belief in Moore-III is also justified. Some philosophers, most notably, Crispin Wright, have however claimed that **Moore** is actually an example of transmission failure (see, e.g., Wright

2002; 2003; 2004). He thinks that such arguments possess a certain justificational architecture, which he labels "disjunctive template," that renders them epistemically impotent. The idea, in a nutshell, is that warrant fails to be transmitted from the premises of a valid argument to its conclusion if having justified belief in one of its premises requires having antecedent justification to believe its conclusion. This, says Wright, is how the epistemic status of perceptual beliefs such as the belief in Moore-II should to be understood, namely, as having its justification dependent on the justification of the belief in Moore-III. Such a view has been termed "conservatism" (Pryor 2000; 2004).

Wright illustrates his point by offering further examples that are supposedly obvious cases of transmission failure.

Soccer-I	John has just kicked the ball between the white posts.
Soccer-II	John has just scored a goal.
Soccer-III	Therefore, a game of soccer is in progress.

Election-I	John has just written an X on a ballot paper.
Election-II	John has just voted.
Election-III	Therefore, an election is taking place.

It is clear, says Wright, that the warrant provided by Soccer-I/Election-I for the beliefs in Soccer-II/Election-II is not transmissible to their conclusions for the former confers justification on the latter only if one already has antecedent or independent reason to accept that a game of soccer or an election is taking place. Other examples (known for their epistemic significance) that are said to share the same template are as follows.

Table-I	Having a visual experience as of a red table.
Table-II	The table is red.
Table-III	Therefore, this is not a white table lit by red lights.

Zebra-I	Having a visual experience as of a striped horse-like animal.
Zebra-II	That animal is a zebra.
Zebra-III	Therefore, that animal is not a cleverly disguised mule.

BIV-I	Having a visual experience as of two hands.
BIV-II	Here are two hands.
BIV-III	Therefore, I am not a BIV.

Wright himself does not dispute the claim that type-I propositions (conceived as propositional evidence) provide support for type-II beliefs which is why he goes on to suggest that we enjoy some sort of default justification (warrant) to accept type-III propositions such as "There is an external world" or "I am not a BIV." This default justification or warrant, which he calls "entitlement," need not be something that the agent does anything to earn. I shall discuss the thesis of entitlement more fully below, but, even with entitlement in place, Wright thinks that no additional support for type-III beliefs is thereby gained through a I–II–III type of inference. Before proceeding to criticize Wright, it is obvious that I–II–III-style arguments are typical cases of easy knowledge inferences. Given (BK), one can know, for example, that the table is red on the basis of its looking red and thereby come to know that Table-III (The table is not white but illuminated by red lights). Knowledge of Table-III is said to be implausible for it seems that one acquires it much too easily. Table-I does not constitute a strong enough evidence to support Table-III.

7.3.1 Negative and positive epistemic dependence: criticizing Wright

Wright provides no direct argument for his conservative claim that type-I propositions provide warrant for believing type-II propositions only if one has antecedent warrant for believing type-III propositions. The closest we get, by way of an argument, are the remarks he makes in regard to the **Election/Soccer** examples. Suppose, he says, you live in a society where electoral drills are held as frequently as real elections. Being in possession of such information, however, would undercut the justification that Election-I would otherwise have provided for believing Election-II. Under these circumstances, John's writing an X on a piece of paper is no longer a reason that he has voted. From this he concludes that "[i]t is only if you already have grounds for [Election-III]…that [Election-I] gives you reason to believe [Election-II]" (Wright 2002, p. 334). And so "the ground provided by [Election-I] for believing [Election-II] is *not* transmissible across the entailment from [Election-II] to [Election-III]" (Wright 2002, p. 334).

Wright's thesis of warrant transmission has prompted a number of responses prominent among which is the "dogmatist" view according to which having justification for believing type-II propositions does not require antecedent justification for believing type-III propositions. Pryor, for example, delineates a number of ways that the premises of an argument might be said to epistemically depend on its conclusion (Pryor 2004). According to, what he calls, a "type-4" dependence, evidence against the conclusion of an argument would undermine one's purported justification for its premise(s). This type of dependence, says

Pryor, does not undercut an argument's legitimacy. A different type of dependence, "type-5", on the other hand, is when one's warrant for the premises of an argument depends on having antecedent warrant to believe its conclusion. This, he says, is precisely the type of dependence that renders an argument an instance of transmission failure (in Wright's sense). Although Pryor thinks that arguments with such justificational architecture are epistemically defective, he goes on to show, by way of examples, that the two types of dependence are distinct. Thus, although **Moore** displays a type-4 of dependence, it is an epistemically respectable argument, he concludes.

While I am in full agreement with Pryor's assessment of Wright's argument, there is, I think, a more principled way of responding to the argument that does not rely heavily on examples. Recall that Wright's argument begins by observing that having reasons to doubt type-III propositions would undercut one's justification for believing type-II propositions (as provided by type-I propositions). This is a correct observation, but all it shows is that one's justification for believing a type-II proposition is *negatively* dependent on our justification for believing a type-III propositions. It does not follow from this that it is also *positively* dependent. While positive dependence is a kind of foundational dependence and looks backward to a source of justification, negative dependence is a forward-looking dependence and some kind of vulnerability. To use an analogy by Audi, "[i]f my garden is my source of food, I (positively) depend on it. The fact that people could poison the soil does not make their non-malevolence part of my food source or imply a (positive) dependence on them ... Negative dependence does not imply positive dependence" (Audi 1993, p. 144).

This observation has ramifications for a number of epistemological controversies. In the foundationalism/coherentism debate, for example, a foundationalist need not deny that a belief's justification can be defeated by incoherence (or, negatively depend on coherence); she only needs to deny that the belief owes its justification to coherence. Likewise, in discussions about the nature of a priori justification, an a priorist can maintain that a priori justification only requires that a belief be positively dependent on no experience and empirical beliefs while acknowledging that it may, nonetheless, be negatively dependent on experiences and empirical beliefs in the sense that their occurrence could undermine its justification in counterfactual circumstances. Given the fact that neither kind of dependence entails the other, a priorists are able to claim that the vulnerability of a priori beliefs to empirical defeaters (i.e., their negative dependence on experience) need not upset their a priori status (see, e.g., Summerfield 1991). I conclude therefore that Wright's suggested reasons fail to make good his claim that Moore-type arguments are cases of transmission failure.

Secondly, the idea of positive epistemic dependence is not all that there is to the idea of the disjunctive template. Rather, it seems to me that Wright's guiding thought is founded on a substantial theory of justification. To see this, let us look more closely at the properties of the disjunctive template. An argument of the form "A, if A then B, therefore B" fits the template, says Wright, if (i) A entails B; (ii) there is a proposition C incompatible with A; (iii) my warrant for A consists in my being in a state which is subjectively indistinguishable form a state in which C could be true and (iv) C would be true if B were false (Wright 2002, p. 343). To give an example, consider how **Zebra** fits the template. A = That animal is a zebra; B = That animal is not a disguised mule and C = That animal is a disguised mule. **Zebra** satisfies the above conditions and is therefore an example of transmission failure. The crucial condition is (iii): My warrant for A (that animal is a zebra) is my experience as of a striped horse-like animal which is indistinguishable from what I would experience if C were true (the animal was a disguised mule). So "in treating my state as being a perception of zebras... I implicitly *discount* the uncongenial, deceptive alternatives C. And now, whatever my warrant for doing so, it has to be there *already*" (Wright 2002, p. 343, my emphasis).

What this means is that only if my perceptual experience could favor A over C, would it warrant my belief in A, otherwise independent warrant would be needed to discount the alternative C. What seems to underlie this claim is the so-called underdetermination thesis (UJ) according to which if one's evidence for believing that ϕ does not favor ϕ over some incompatible hypothesis ψ, then the evidence in question does not justify ϕ. I do not wish to examine the credentials of (UJ) here sufficing to say that, with (UJ) in force, the question of whether warrant transmits across entailment from the premises of an argument to its conclusion becomes redundant for one can now apply (UJ) directly to type-III beliefs (conclusions) themselves to determine their epistemic worth.

Let us now turn to Wright's thesis of entitlement. According to Wright, we may recall only if we are antecedently justified in believing a type-III proposition that a type-II proposition can be said to be supported by a type-I proposition. However, since an antecedent (evidential) justification is not available, skepticism would ensue. To meet the skeptic's requirement, Wright introduces a notion of rational warrant, "entitlement," that one does not have any specific evidential work to do to earn: "If I am entitled to accept P, then my doing so is beyond rational reproach even though I can point to no cognitive accomplishment in my life" (Wright 2004, p. 75). Wright seems to think that we enjoy some sort of a default justification with respect to certain beliefs though he does not say where this comes from. Neither does he say much about the *epistemic* standing of his notion of entitlement. If it is not evidential, is it deontological? If so, in what sense? Does he take deontological justification to be truth-conducive? We are eventually told that this is not an evidential warrant to *believe* a proposition P but to "accept" it, something like a warrant to "act on the assumption that P, take it for granted that P or (rational trust) that P" (Wright 2004, p. 176). Wright does not quite explicitly address the question of how a non-evidential notion of warrant involving a weaker attitude than belief can provide an epistemic context whereby a type-I proposition can confer justification on a type-II belief. But this is not the question that I wish to pursue here. Rather, I want to highlight the non-epistemic nature of Wright's notion of entitlement as the sort of reasons that he adduces in its favor seem to be entirely non-epistemic.

Wright invites us to consider a cognitive project that is indispensable for us such that we cannot lose and may gain by doing it. We are thereby rationally entitled to it and may take for granted its presuppositions. Suppose, for example, that Crusoe is starving on his island where the only available food are plenty of colored fruits all strange to him and none being eaten by the birds visiting the island. He has no reason to believe that the fruits are safe for consumption. Nevertheless, says Wright, assuming an interest in survival, he is warranted in eating the fruits. For they either turn out to be edible which would be fine or not edible in which case the outcome would be no worse than the alternative of starvation. But this situation is best described as one where our reasons for believing that the fruits are safe are pragmatic rather than epistemic, thus not truth-conducive, and not as reasons for taking the weaker attitude of acceptance toward the proposition in question.

Wright cites van Fraassen's work in this connection but, perhaps, a better example would be Bratman whose claim is that there are practical pressures for accepting a given proposition in the background of one's deliberation (Bratman 1999). These pressures are context-relative in the sense that they apply in only some of the practical contexts, thus requiring us to distinguish between a context-relative attitude of acceptance and belief. But, as we saw, in Chapter 1, Bratman's argument foundered on equivocating the epistemic and pragmatic senses of reasonableness, thus undermining his claim that the reasonability of what one accepts changes as one moves from one context to another. And, once the equivocation is noted, one is longer bound to introduce a different type of attitude (acceptance). For even a *belief* can be practically reasonable in one context but epistemically unreasonable in another involving different concerns. Thus, one could recast Wright's point about entitlement or rational acceptance in terms of the distinction between pragmatic reasons for believing and epistemic reasons for believing. Given the pragmatic, non-epistemic sense of entitlement, it is perhaps no wonder that Wright subsequently claims that his proposal at most delivers a *skeptical solution* to the skeptic's challenge in the sense of conceding its basic point, namely, that "we do indeed have no claim to know, in any sense involving possession of evidence for their likely truth, that certain [presuppositions] of what we take to be procedures yielding knowledge and justified belief hold good" (Wright 2004, p. 206).[1]

7.4   Dogmatism: EK-inferences as legitimate

I shall now turn to the views that take the I–II–III arguments as generally cogent. Pryor, for example, thinks that **Moore** is particularly immune to Wright's objections. His position is, however, rather curious in that while he regards **BIV** and **Table**, along with **Moore**, as warrant transmitting, he thinks that **Zebra** is an instance of transmission failure for he concurs with Wright that our justification for believing Zebra-II ("That animal is a zebra") requires us to have antecedent justification in believing Zebra-III ("That animal is not a disguised mule"). His reason for not taking a dogmatist position in this case is that, unlike Zebra-II, Moore-II ("Here is a hand") is a perceptually basic proposition. Zebra-II goes beyond what is given to us in our experience: "If it turned out that the animal in the pen *is* a cleverly-disguised mule, or a fur-covered robot, we wouldn't say that you've mis-seen it. The error wasn't in what vision represented to you, but in what you went on to believe" (Pryor Manuscript, p. 11, fn. 13). It is, however, difficult to see how this observation could support Pryor's case for discriminating between **Zebra** and **Moore** in terms of the idea of warrant transmission for what he says about **Zebras** seems to be equally true of **Moore**: Moore-II goes beyond what is represented in one's experience. If it turned out that the object is a cleverly disguised mechanical hand, we would not say that you have mis-seen it. The error was not in what vision represented to you, but in what you went on to believe.

Pryor's position can be further challenged by considering a different version of **Table** which he regards as legitimate.

Table*-I   Having a visual experience as of a red table.
Table*-II   The table is red.
Table*-III   Therefore, this is not a white cleverly disguised card-board lit by red lights.

Table* is more similar to **Zebra** than **Table** is, as both Table*-III and Zebra-III are similarly structured. **Table*** raises the following dilemma for Pryor. Either he is willing to count **Table*** and **Zebra** as being epistemically on the same footing (i.e., failing to transmit warrant) in which case he should also take a *conservative* stance toward believing Table*-II, that is, to accept that Table*-I (i.e., Table-I) does not justify the belief in Table*-II (i.e., Table-II) unless one has antecedent justification to believe Table*-III. But this would contradict his dogmatist attitude in the case of **Table** where he denies his "perceptual justification for believing [Table-II] requires [him] to have antecedent justification for believing *anything* like [Table-III]" (Pryor Manuscript, p. 17). Or, he might stick to his guns and take a similar *dogmatist* attitude with regard to Table*-II (after all Table*-II and Table-II are identical). But then he should allow **Table*** to be a case where warrant is transmitted across the entailment to Table*-III. But this would, once again, be incompatible with his official position. For Table*-I stands to Table*-III as Zebra-I stands to Zebra-III, and Pryor claims that **Zebra** is an example of transmission failure: "[Zebra-I] doesn't seem to be good enough to *know* that the animal in the pen is not a cleverly-disguised mule. You haven't made any special tests, or anything like that" (Pryor Manuscript, p. 1).

Moreover, Pryor is inclined to take a dogmatist (liberal) stance toward BIV-II, that is, he thinks that BIV-I provides justification for believing BIV-II without requiring antecedent justification to believe BIV-III ("I am not a BIV"). On the other hand, what he says about **Table** and **Moore** seems to suggest that he does not even think that, what he calls, an "intermediate" view is correct in the case of **BIV**, where the view in question differs from dogmatism by additionally requiring that BIV-III be at least true if BIV-I is to justify BIV-II. But if Pryor does not even require the truth of BIV-III for the obtaining of perceptual justification, then this means that beliefs in a vat world can also be justified. This has some untoward consequences. To begin with, with the beliefs in the vat world being systematically false, our senses are unreliable in that world. Accordingly, even the truth of "Our senses are reliable" is not required for the justification of our perceptual beliefs. This is not only an implausible result, it also fails to square with Pryor's earlier approval of an externalist reliability theory of justification regarding our perceptual beliefs (Pryor Manuscript, p. 9). Moreover, the view has the consequence that a brain in a vat can construct a version of **BIV** to argue that he is not a BIV. This would deprive the I–II–III arguments of their anti-skeptical potentials.

Finally, Pryor's account seems too close to Cohen's despite holding apparently different stances toward EK-inferences. To elaborate, we may recall, Cohen denies the legitimacy of such inferences proposing to identify basic knowledge with animal knowledge and then to prohibit the application of closure to animal knowledge. By contrast, Pryor thinks that some of these inferences are legitimate and so feels compelled to explain why they seem to be nonetheless useless to convince anyone who has doubts about their conclusions. Pryor's explanation consists of distinguishing between having justification to believe something and being rationally committed to believe something by beliefs one already has. The former is understood standardly in terms of having adequate grounds for a particular belief while the latter is intended to explain how having mere doubts might negatively affect the epistemic status of the belief in question without having the power to defeat its justifier.

According to Pryor, a belief is rational "when it's a belief that none of your other beliefs or doubts rationally oppose or rationally obstruct from believing" (Pryor 2004, p. 364). This is hardly a satisfactory explication of "rationality" as the notion appears again in its own definition. One gets the impression, however, that it is intended to mean something like "holistic coherence or consistency" (henceforth, P-rationality). Pryor, on the other hand, is quite clear about the concept of justification construing it as "the quality that hypotheses possess for you when they're epistemically likely for you to be true" (Pryor 2004, p. 352) (henceforth, P-justification). He maintains that, thus understood, justification does not require the agent to be blameless, or have reflective access to the grounds of his belief, and so on. To put a more familiar gloss on Pryor's terminology, one may take P-justification as being roughly equivalent to what Sosa calls "aptness" (see various articles in Sosa 1991). An apt belief is one that is produced by a reliable faculty in the environment in which it is operating. On Sosa'a account, aptness is of an entirely external character.

There is also a notion of justification that Sosa invokes (henceforth, S-justification). S-justification is essentially internal: "[J]ustification amounts to a sort of inner coherence... [where] the justification of a belief B requires that B have a basis in its inference or coherence relations to other beliefs in the believer's mind" (Sosa 1991, p. 289). It would not be unfair to say that P-rationality and S-justification are also roughly equivalent. Moreover, commensurate with aptness and S-justification, Sosa, as noted earlier, also distinguishes between animal and reflective knowledge. While animal knowledge requires only apt belief, reflective knowledge requires a belief to be both apt and S-justified. We may now reformulate Pryor's explanation of our contrary intuitions in the case of the closure version of easy knowledge inferences in Sosa's terminology. Accordingly, while the belief in Table-II would be apt (thus, a candidate for animal knowledge), it is not S-justified (thus, not a candidate for reflective knowledge). Viewed thus, Pryor's response is not too different from Cohen's since he, too, views a belief like Table-II as a candidate for animal, not reflective, knowledge. It is thus rather mystifying how, despite sharing Cohen's epistemological framework, Pryor thinks himself entitled to rule in such inferences as legitimate. In the next section, I shall turn to a different approach to EK-inferences.

7.5 The legitimacy of EK-inferences as context-dependent

I shall now discuss two rather similar approaches which hold that EK-inferences are legitimate in some contexts but illegitimate in others. These accounts take, in their own different ways, the epistemic relations obtaining between the premises and the conclusion of an EK-inference to vary with context. One such account is due to Bergmann who thinks that, *pace* Cohen, such inferences can be legitimate (though his target is actually epistemically circular arguments) (Bergmann 2004). He distinguishes between two contexts in which such inferences are or are not legitimate. Consider, for example, the bootstrapping argument. If someone who has no doubts about the reliability of her sense perception comes to believe that it is reliable by means of that argument, then her belief is justified and the reasoning is legitimate. This would be an example of, what Bergmann calls, an "unquestioned source context." Suppose, however, that the agent is doubtful about the reliability of her sense perception because, say, someone recently "persuaded [her], by some skeptical argument that her perception is unreliable... If she [is offered a bootstrapping-type of argument], she will (if she's sensible) consider it to be useless as means to help her regain her confidence in perception. The reason is simple. She does not trust perception" (Bergmann 2004, p. 717). This would be an example of a "questioned source context" where EK-inferences are illegitimate. Bergmann explains the difference between the two cases by noting that since in a questioned source context the subject "questions [her source's] trustworthiness, the subject has an *undercutter defeater* for all her beliefs produced (even in part) by [that] source" (Bergmann 2004, p. 719).

If an inference is legitimate, it follows that whenever one is justified in believing its premises one is thereby justified in believing its conclusion. How could then EK-inferences be legitimate in some contexts but illegitimate in others when both the epistemic status of their premises and their logical form are supposed to remain intact across those contexts? I think the best way of making sense of Bergmann's claim that legitimate EK-inferences may be illegitimate in some contexts is to see it as addressing the issue of the dialectical potentials of such inferences. His "questioned source" contexts are precisely those in which one seeks to rationally convince, by means of an EK-inference, those who are wary of its conclusion. Moreover, while one might go along with Bergmann's explanation in cases in which an agent has a defeater for, say, her beliefs produced by perception, that does not seem to hold for all cases of a questioned-source-context variety. It is not clear at all that when an agent merely "thinks [her perception] is unreliable, or, at the very least, … is uncertain about whether it is reliable" (Bergmann 2004, p. 418) constitutes a cases where the agent has a *defeater* for her beliefs produced by perception.

A similar response has been advanced by Neta (2005). While Bergmann is concerned with the use of EK-inferences in different contexts, Neta, following the lead of contextualism, takes context into the truth-conditions of knowledge claims, thereby making the truth value of knowledge/justification attributions dependent on context-sensitive standards. According to Neta, while the basic knowledge that the table is red can be inferentially expanded (by closure) to yield knowledge that the table is not white, it cannot be so expanded to achieve the knowledge that the table is not white with red lights shining on it. For once the skeptical hypothesis that the table is white but lit by red lights is considered, we move into a context in which we can no longer claim to know that the table is red. That is why when the possibility of the skeptical hypothesis becomes salient, thereby generating a context shift, then the closure inference from "The table is red" to "The table is not white but lit by red lights" becomes worthless. Again, as in Bergmann's account, the distinction between legitimacy and effectiveness of EK-inferences should facilitate a better understanding of Neta's explanation of how skeptical scenarios can undermine our claim to having the basic knowledge in question. The question, however, is whether we need to go as far as making the truth value of our knowledge attributions dependent on context-sensitive standards in order to account for our contrary intuitions in the case EK-inferences.[2] I shall return to this point later on in the chapter.

Finally, both Bergmann's and Neta's accounts are faced with a problem which may be called the problem of "easy ignorance." Recall that on, say, Bergmann's account, when an agent harbors no doubts about the reliability of her sense perception, she can come to justifiably believe that, say, her perception is reliable by inferring it from the relevant basic knowledge she possesses. However, as we have seen, on both Bergmann's and Neta's accounts, the mere entertaining of skeptical hypothesis is able to generate a "questioned source context" or a "context shift" rendering the EK-inference in question illegitimate and, in turn, undermining the basic knowledge itself. If so, then, for every piece of basic knowledge, one can *easily* bring about a situation where one is no longer entitled to that knowledge. All one has to do is to conceive of an alternative skeptical scenario to that described by the basic knowledge in question. The routes to easy ignorance would thus be as "easy" as the routes to easy knowledge, as in both cases we help ourselves with the same resources (the ability to conceive of alternative skeptical possibilities and logic). So in the cases of easy ignorance we have the exact converse of the easy knowledge problem. The difference is that in such cases we seem to be provided with an easy route to losing our knowledge, thus, the name "easy ignorance." It is ironic that attempts aimed at preserving basic knowledge, in the face of the problem easy knowledge, would also provide an easy way of moving from that state of knowledge to a corresponding state of ignorance. I shall now proceed with presenting my own solution to the problem of easy knowledge which, though different from the accounts discussed so far, has affinities with some. It will be claimed that EK-inferences do not admit of a uniform treatment. In all cases, however, I shall maintain, as I have done, a sharp distinction between the legitimacy and effectiveness of such inferences.

7.6 Strength of evidence and epistemic distance: varieties of transmission failure

Appearances notwithstanding, the differences between Wright's conservative and Pryor's dogmatist do not seem to be really substantial. For while they disagree about the extension of the concept of "transmission failure," they seem to agree about its intension. Pryor follows Wright in thinking that inferences which display, what we called, positive epistemic dependence fail to transmit warrant across entailment to their conclusions. He only challenges Wright's claim that inferences such as **Moore** and **Table** are instances of transmission failure.

I do not, however, think that the putative features of positive epistemic dependence really mark out transmission-failure inferences. First of all, as argued earlier, the I–II–III arguments do not necessarily exhibit such characteristics. Moreover, the thesis of positive epistemic dependence does not seem to be anything other than an extension of an internalist requirement on the justification-conferring *grounds* of our one's beliefs to the *background conditions* of their justification. According to an externalist, beliefs are justified if they are produced by reliable faculties. Thus, for an externalist, the truth of (R) "Our faculties are functioning properly" is necessary if our, say, perceptual beliefs are to be justified. An internalist, by contrast, demands that we have some sort of (strong) epistemic access to the grounds of such beliefs. A conservative, as depicted here, is someone who extends this strong internalist attitude to the background assumptions (understood non-attitudinally) that are required for the justification of one's beliefs.[3] It is difficult to specify exactly how these background assumptions are to be understood. They have been variously described as "background conditions" (BonJour 1998, p. 137), "presuppositions" (Burge 2003) and "cornerstones" (Wright 2004). Cornerstones for a region of thought are those propositions such that a warranted doubt about them would defeat or undermine a putative justification for any belief in the corresponding region. In the context of our current discussion, however, these are taken to be propositions of type-III variety like BIV-III, Moore-III and so on. So the conservative gloss on why the I–II–III arguments form a special category says more about their underlying conception of justification rather their epistemic import.

This is not very satisfying for such arguments seem to strike all theorists, even those who reject the conservative treatment of perceptual judgments, as being odd. That is, there is some sort of a felt dissatisfaction with such inferences that leaves its mark on epistemologists regardless of their conservative or dogmatist allegiances. I think this common impact stems from the fact that such inferences impart, what was earlier described as, easy knowledge. They provide, it seems, too easy a route to pieces of knowledge that appear unlikely in the relevant circumstances. **Zebra**, for example, appears, on all accounts, to provide too easy a route to having knowledge or justified belief in Zebra-III.

Ditto for other type-I/III propositions. For precisely this reason, however, I am disinclined to count **Moore** and **Election/Soccer** as instances of transmission failure. Such inferences do not seem to display the easy knowledge symptom. Our felt dissatisfaction with these arguments needs to be handled differently, as I shall explain later.

How are we then to explain why inferences like **Zebra**, **Table** and **BIV** are not warrant transmitting now that we have rejected Wright's argument for such a failing? Let us begin by reminding ourselves of the fact it is only in the context of a background theory that observations have evidential meaning or confirm a hypothesis (see Sober 1994, p. 171). The same is true of differential support: observations support one hypothesis better than another only relative to a set of background assumptions. Couched in epistemological jargon, the idea is that our evidence (say, perceptual experience) justifies a belief only against a set of background conditions of the agent. Thus, Table-I (seeing a red table) justifies believing Table-II (this is a red table) only against the backdrop of a certain set of assumptions like "perceptual conditions are normal," "my senses are reliable" and so on. It is evident that if, say, our perceptual circumstances are abnormal, seeing a red table cannot justify the belief that there is a red table before us. Incidentally, this point is in accord with our earlier observation that yielding easy knowledge is what marks out the I–II–III inferences since, as noted then, the problem in question stems from the strength (or its lack) of the pertinent evidence which is, in turn, a function of what background assumptions are in force.

Let us then proceed by assuming that type-I propositions justify type-II beliefs in an appropriate context (call this a "p-context" referring to the justification context of the relevant premise). After all, what is at issue is whether if one *has* warrant for a premise in an inference, one is thereby warranted to believe its conclusion. The question is therefore whether a type-I warrant can transmit across the entailment from type-II premises to a type-III conclusion. To take a concrete example, consider **Zebra**. Does Zebra-I justify Zebra-III *given* that it justifies Zebra-II? The short answer is that it depends. For whether Zebra-I can justify a Zebra-III belief depends on the context in which it is expected to discharge its warranting function. Consonant with what was said earlier, this function cannot be discharged in a vacuum. Now either this context is identical to (or includes) the relevant p-context or it is not. Suppose it is identical to the p-context (where this consists of a set of presuppositions, the most pertinent of which are the likes of "perceptual conditions are normal" or "there is no deception," etc.). This means that, once we move across the entailment we let the p-context to fix the epistemic context of the conclusion. With the justification context of the conclusion so fixed, the question whether seeing zebra-like animals justifies the belief that the animals are not disguised mules will have to be answered in the positive as the "no-deception" presupposition would automatically rule out the possibility of our being deceived by disguised mules.

But although **Zebra** is rendered legitimate under these conditions, the presumed epistemic situation is unrealistic. For by deriving Zebra-III from Zebra-II and raising the question whether believing such a proposition is justified we are automatically entertaining the falsity of Zebra-III as an open possibility. Unlike the conservative approach, such an objection is not dictated by an underlying theory of justification like the relevant alternatives theory, contextualism and the like. It is rather the dynamics of the argumentative context that demands we treat the conclusion as an open question; something whose status ought to be decided on the basis of the epistemic strength of the pertinent premises (evidence). This is not only true of the I–II–III inferences but also applies to all *argu*ments across the board. Accordingly, we can no longer let the p-context spill over, so to speak, once we move across the entailment to the conclusion. Rather, we need to adjust and qualify the p-context to accommodate the possibilities raised by the conclusion (Zebra-III) – which means, among other things, not retaining the "no deception" presupposition. Within this qualified context, it would be an open question whether Zebra-I justifies the belief in Zebra-III. It is evident that, under these circumstances, seeing a striped horse-like animal is incapable of conferring justification on the belief that the animals are not disguised mules. Our warrant is simply not strong enough to be transmissible across the entailment from Zebra-II to Zebra-III. The same moral holds good in the cases of **Table** and **BIV**.[4]

It was pointed out that it is unrealistic to ignore the possibilities raised by type-III propositions once they are derived from type-II propositions in the context of the I–II–III arguments. It will be instructive to compare an analogous case which involves similar issues. The case concerns what is known as the "ravens paradox" (due to Hempel), which in its simple form has the following structure. Observations of black ravens confirm the proposition "All ravens are black" while observations of black pens, white swans and so on are neutral to it. But the proposition "All non-black things are non-ravens" is equivalent to (and, *a fortiori*, entails) "All ravens are black" and since a white swan confirms the former it should also confirm the latter which seems paradoxical. To resolve the paradox a number of solutions have been proposed. The difference between these solutions can be traced to the amount of background information that is taken into consideration. I believe lessons drawn from the paradox can be used to account for the conflicting intuitions in the cases of transmission failure.

One early solution to the paradox was proposed by Hempel himself (1965). Consider the proposition (p) "All sodium salts burn yellow." Suppose we hold a piece of ice into a colourless flame and it does not turn the flame yellow. This confirms the proposition (q) "Whatever does not burn yellow contains no sodium salt" and because the two propositions are equivalent it also confirms p which is paradoxical. But, Hempel argues, the paradox is only apparent. For if we take an object whose chemical structure we do not know and hold it into a flame and it fails to burn yellow and subsequent investigation proves that it contains no sodium salt, then this observation would confirm p. The difference between the two cases is only that in the first one we already knew that the substance is ice and ice contains no sodium salt whereas in the second case we did not know this. So, Hempel concludes, the seemingly paradoxical nature of the first case is only due to our allowing the additional information that the object is ice.

So as long as we ignore any additional information we can solve the paradox in the way Hempel suggests. If we completely ignore the background knowledge we can follow Hempel and say that the observation of black pens and white swans confirms "All ravens are black." But Hempel's solution is unrealistic for it requires the theorist to ignore much of what he knows and regard the evidence ("This thing is non-black and non-raven") as all the information that is available. This is very odd for it involves a concept of confirmation which is totally at odds with how this concept is understood in ordinary contexts. The situation is analogous to the case of warrant transmission across the I–II–III inferences. Here, too, if we ignore the information raised by the conclusion and fix the context accordingly, type-I propositions would justify type-III beliefs in as trivial and unrealistic a sense as that which Hempel claimed holding a piece ice into a flame confirms "All sodium salts burn yellow."

The question of warrant transmission is thus inextricably linked to the strength of one's evidence in a given context. To get a better grip on this issue, we may think of evidence as having something like an epistemic momentum aiming at a target proposition representing a region of epistemic space such that if the evidence can cover that space, then believing the proposition in question would be epistemically commendable (just as we may wonder if a bullet has enough momentum to hit a target occupying part of the physical space). To see if Zebra-I, thought of as evidence, has enough epistemic momentum to reach the region of epistemic space represented by "That animal is not a disguised mule," it is helpful to consider first those regions of epistemic space represented by the more mundane consequences of Zebra-II like Zebra-IIIa, "That animal is not a raven"; Zebra-IIIb, "That animal is not a dog" and Zebra-IIIc, "That animal is not a mule." It is quite clear that Zebra-I has enough epistemic potentials to reach the regions of space represented by the first two propositions though it can more easily cover the region represented by Zebra-IIIa than it could with regard to Zebra-IIIb. As we move along through the epistemic spaces represented by Zebra-IIIa, Zebra-IIIb and Zebra-IIIc, the epistemic momentum of the evidence decreases commensurate with the decrease in the degrees of justification of the corresponding beliefs until it fails to reach the region of epistemic space represented by Zebra-III. That is, Zebra-I fails to justify Zebra-III.

These observations are confirmed by considering the degree of the intrusion of error when forming beliefs about those particular propositions on the basis of Zebra-I. It is highly unlikely that what we see as a striped horse-like animal is a raven, very unlikely that it is a dog, rather unlikely that it is a mule and quite likely that it is a cleverly disguised mule. There is thus a negative correlation between the justification of the pertinent beliefs and the possibility of error. The preceding observations, I believe, are also true of **Table** and **BIV**. These arguments are all instances of transmission failure. It is worth noting that **BIV** is a special case in that BIV-III represents the farthest region of epistemic space that perceptual evidence might ever reach. It is in fact unreachable by any type of perceptual evidence. This observation is attested to by the fact that no amount of strengthening of our evidence could ever endow it with enough epistemic momentum to reach that region of space. That is, however we may strengthen our perceptual evidence, the result would still be compatible with the hypothesis that one is not a brain in a vat.

7.6.1   What is wrong with Moore's argument

These conclusions do not, however, hold good in inferences of **Moore** or **Election/Soccer** variety. And indeed such inferences were earlier differentiated from the rest of the I–II–III batch for not displaying the easy knowledge symptom. So let us see why they are not instances of transmission failure. I start with **Election**. Either Election-I warrants

Election-II or it does not. If the latter, then the question of warrant transmission does not arise at all, for there would be nothing to be transmissible. And, indeed, our main concern has all along been that if type-I propositions warrant type-II beliefs, will type-III beliefs be thereby warranted. So we may start by assuming that Election-I does justify Election-II. As we saw, however, Wright claims that it is only if one is antecedently justified in believing Election-III ("An election is in process") that Election-I (John's writing an X on a ballot paper) can justify Election-II ("John has just voted") and so **Election** is an instance of transmission failure. We did, however, reject Wright's claim and the reasoning behind it. It seems uncontroversial, however, that Election-III has, at least, to be true if Election-I is to justify Election-II. What are we then to say about **Election**? If it is not a case of transmission failure, how are we to explain our felt dissatisfaction with it as there is, I believe, a widely shared antipathy toward perceiving such inferences as **Election** and **Moore** as *arguments* for their respective conclusions.

It seems to me what makes these arguments rather odd is that their job in "establishing their conclusion" is already done by the time we get to their second premise. Consider **Election** again. One cannot believe Election-II without believing Election-III. Grasping the concept of "voting" presupposes having the concept of an "election." That is, anyone who believes that John has *voted* (and not just written an X on a piece of paper), also believes that a voting process (i.e., an election) is taking place. When I believe that I have just deposited money in my savings account, then I also believe that there are banks. The question that arises now is whether someone can be justified (or be in a position to be justified) in believing Election-II without being justified in believing Election-III at the same time?

To answer this question, we should take note of one the particular features of the case, namely that Election-III is entailed by Election-II. This means that it is impossible for Election-II to be true while Election-III is false. Now combining the assumption that epistemic justification is a truth-conducive concept, that is, that a justified belief is more likely to be true than when it is not justified, with the fact one cannot believe Election-II without believing its consequence (Election-III), it follows that if some evidence justifies Election-II, it would, *ipso facto*, justify Election-III. In other words, Election-II and Election-III stand or fall together in the epistemic space.[5] That is, given their close epistemic proximity, anything that tends to boost Election-II in epistemic space would also boost Election-III which is why, while, unlike **Zebra**, **Election** is not a case of transmission failure, it is nonetheless unsatisfying as an *argument*. The reason, as noted earlier, is that the argument's epistemic job is over and done at its second line (Election-II).

In the preceding paragraph, I referred to the "close epistemic proximity" of Election-II and Election-III in view of their conceptual and logical interconnections. The idea is not merely a metaphor. There is actually a way of substantiating this notion. The idea involves a version of the so-called Moore's paradox. As we saw in Chapter 2, Moore observed that there is something odd or defective about sentences of the form "P but I do not believe that P," or < P & ~IBP > for short. For although such sentences can be true, they cannot be sensibly asserted. For example, while one may countenance situations where it is raining but one happens not to believe it, one cannot properly assert the corresponding sentence. It is absurd to assert that it is raining but then go on to deny that one believes that it is.

Some philosophers have claimed that the same sort of oddity is present in sentences of the form "P but I have no reason to believe that P," that is, while they have coherent truth conditions they cannot be coherently asserted (de Almedia 2001). I think Moorean sentences of the latter kind can be used as a way of measuring up the epistemic proximity between two sentences where one is entailed by the other. Any sentence is obviously the closest sentence to itself (epistemically speaking) and it trivially passes our test – if we agree that the sentence (schema) mentioned above is Moore-paradoxical. I believe Election-II and (its consequence) Election-III also pass this test. Not only "John has voted but I have no reason to think that he has voted" is Moore-paradoxical, but so is, "John has voted but I have no reason to believe that an election is in process." The same is true of "John has scored a goal but I have no reason to believe that a soccer match is in progress." All these sentences can be true but cannot be coherently asserted. I take the absurdity of asserting these sentences as showing their close epistemic proximity.[6]

I think the same diagnosis holds of **Moore**. But there are some complications here. Unlike the case of **Election**, some philosophers believe that the truth of Moore-III, "There is an external world," is not necessary if Moore-I were to justify Moore-II. Since the claim is controversial, we shall consider both alternatives. Suppose the truth of Moore-III is not necessary. This means, as we saw before, that our beliefs are justified in a vat world despite being systematically false, and despite our senses constantly playing tricks on us. There is, of course, a perfect sense in which our beliefs are justified under such circumstances. They can be said to be deontologically justified in that in forming the beliefs in question the agent has flouted no intellectual obligations and has been epistemically responsible. He cannot thus be blamed for the beliefs he has formed. This is a perfectly respectable, though a non-truth-conducive, conception of justification. But it is quite contentious whether this is the sense that is relevant to the context of the question of warrant transmission which, as we have seen, is tightly connected with such truth-related properties as the strength of evidence and the like.

Consider now the alternative scenario where the truth of "There is an external world" is necessary for Moore-I to confer justification on Moore-II. In this case, **Moore** would resemble **Election** as Moore-II and Moore-III are epistemically too close. To see this, we need to have a more fine-grained description of their contents. When Moore-II says that there are hands, it is clearly referring to hands as mind-independent objects. What it intends to state is certainly not the existence of mind-dependent objects like hand sense-data and the like, otherwise Moore's project of proving the existence of the world by means of **Moore** would be in tatters. Moore-III, on the other hand, is about the existence of a world of mind-independent object. Thus understood, "These are mind-independent objects that look like hands" and "There is a world of mind-independent objects" would turn out to be epistemically close propositions (in our sense). The latter is a consequence of the former and the assertion of "These are two mind-independent hand-like objects but I have no reason to think that there are mind-independent objects" is Moore-paradoxical. Accordingly, Moore-II and Moore-III stand and fall together in the epistemic space. One cannot be justified in believing Moore-II without being justified in believing Moore-III.

This is not to deny that there is a I–II–III inference in the case of **Moore**, and this is in accord with our account of epistemic the closeness of Moore-II and, its consequence, Moore-III. One can view **Moore** as a "normal" argument where, by being derived from the justified premise Moore-II, the conclusion Moore-III is also justified. But Moore-II and Moore-III are not just any two propositions with one being a consequence of the other. Rather, they are also related to one another in such a way that one cannot believe Moore-II without believing Moore-III so that when some evidence e makes the former more likely true (justified), it will also justify the latter. Accordingly, given the epistemic closeness of Moore-II and Moore-III, the argument's job is already done by the time we get to its second premise. So while **Moore** can be seen as a "normal," sound argument, it is only so in a trivial sense, for, unlike substantial arguments, its dialectical function has already been discharged by the time we get to one of its premises – although we may proceed to derive and thereby "establish" its conclusion in a trivial sense pretty much like establishing "there is an election in process" by deriving it from the proposition that John has just voted when our belief in the latter happens to be justified. This explains why **Moore** strikes philosophers as being rather "disingenuous." For it is not in virtue of standing as the conclusion of **Moore** that we become convinced that there is an external world, but because the argument's dialectical function has been discharged by the time we get to its second premise.

7.6.2   Bootstrapping inferences

Finally, turning to the bootstrapping version of EK-inferences, I think such inferences are illegitimate because bootstrapping is not a reliable enough method. To see this, suppose an agent (S) sets up a bootstrapping argument in the familiar manner by forming premises of the form $< p_i \ \& \ Bp_i >$. The first conjunct is true (or likely to be true) because S is assumed to have basic knowledge/justification while the truth of the second conjunct follows from the assumption that introspection is a reliable process. Suppose, however, that, unbeknownst to S, he is envatted by a neuroscientist who continues to feed him with the same true beliefs (and experiences) about his environment that S would have formed (and received) had he continued his normal life. S's phenomenological life, thus, does not undergo any change. We had assumed that S's justified beliefs in the normal period of his life were basic in the sense that the beliefs were formed on the basis of his experience without him being required to know the reliability of his source and that they were true (or likely to be true). He was thus able to assert truly each p_i.

It would be fair to assume that S's beliefs still remain justified (as beliefs in a vat world are generally thought to be justified). In any case, what *is* important for a successful setting up of the bootstrapping argument is for the agent to be able to truly assert both p and that he believes that p in order to amass sufficient number of true premises of the type $< p_i \ \& \ Bp_i >$. Such features of S's epistemic life, however, remain intact when he is envatted. True, S's beliefs are no longer caused by his environment. But as Markie says, and Cohen concurs, if a belief is an instance of knowledge (or justified belief), then its evidential value should not be affected by its source "just as money, however gained, still spends the same, so too reasonable beliefs, however gained still epistemically support the same beliefs" (Markie 2005, p. 428). Our envatted agent would still be able to assert truly (and unreflectively) both p_i (the scientist sees to it that the assertions are true) and Bp_i (S's introspective beliefs are, despite being a BIV, still justified). Thus, there is nothing to prevent S from setting up a bootstrapping argument along the lines he used to when he was a normal being (with $< p_i \& Bp_i >$ as its premises) to conclude that his sense perception is reliable. (The agent himself does not notice any change in his circumstances.) But this conclusion is surely false in S's new circumstances.

Note that our argument is not really about the legitimacy of (enumerative) induction. It rather concerns a specific type of bootstrapping inference whose input consists of sentences of the form $< p \& Bp >$ and whose output pertains to the reliability of the relevant belief-forming process. Our target is therefore the legitimacy of a very particular type of inductive method or algorithm (an echo of the generality problem). Moreover, the failure highlighted above is not just a one-off. We can set up similar arguments for any proposition and for any belief source whose deliverances satisfy the basic knowledge requirement (BK). Given such massive failings, bootstrapping turns out to be not a reliable enough method to yield justified results. The bootstrapping argument is therefore illegitimate.

Having investigated some of the consequences of forming basic beliefs, I shall now turn to a further epistemic feature of such beliefs, namely, the kind of justification these beliefs enjoy. Some traditional epistemologists certainly seemed to think that basic beliefs are none other than beliefs that are infallible where a belief that p is said to be infallible when an agent's believing that p entails that p is true. But this reply is no longer upheld by the majority of contemporary epistemologists who claim that basic beliefs are fallible. However, exactly how the fallible/infallible divide is to be understood is quite controversial not least because there is as yet no consensus as to how belief in necessary propositions can be accommodated within a fallibilist framework. This is the topic of the next chapter.

8
Belief, Justification and Fallibility

Fallibilism has assumed the status of the default position in the contemporary theories of knowledge. Although it has been used to characterize belief or justified belief, it is fallibilism about knowledge that has been the central theme throughout the history of epistemological thought with theorists being in dispute with one another over the extension of fallible/infallible knowledge as well as ways of accommodating knowledge of necessary truths. Despite enjoying wide currency, however, there is surprisingly no consensus as to how the notion of fallibility is to be understood.

In this chapter, after criticizing a number of recent accounts of fallible knowledge, I argue that the problems stem from the very coherence of that notion. It will then be claimed that the fallible/infallible divide in the domain of knowledge is best understood in terms of the externalist/internalist conceptions of knowledge (justification). The idea is that when a belief is maximally justified, it is infallible on an internalist conception of justification and fallible on an externalist conception. The very concept of fallibilism is necessarily bound up with externalist assumptions. In other words, fallibilism cannot be coherently construed within an internalist framework. I end by highlighting some of the consequences of the thesis which include, among other things, its surprising bearing on the recent controversy over the question whether internalism in the theory of justification is compatible with externalism in the theory of content.

Much has been made in the history of epistemology of the fallibility of cognitive agents. This has been understood as highlighting either the fragility of human cognitive faculties (such as memory, perception and the like) or their outputs like belief and knowledge. In either case fallibility is understood to be conceptually linked to the possibility of being mistaken. It is, however, with the second way of using the term that we will be concerned in this chapter. Almost all contemporary theories of knowledge claim to be fallibilist. It has, however, proved to be notoriously difficult to explain how fallible knowledge is to be understood. Standardly, fallibilism has been understood as the view that, although we have quite a bit of knowledge, our beliefs may well have been mistaken. However, since fallibilists tend to claim that almost all knowledge is fallible, the standard account runs into difficulty in accommodating knowledge of necessary truths. For if a proposition is necessarily true, there is no way that a belief with that content could have been mistaken. Thus one of the main tasks of the existing theories of fallible knowledge has been to bring knowledge of necessary truths within the sphere of fallibility. As I shall explain shortly, however, these attempts are all unsuccessful.

The problem, as I see it, is not just the usual problem of accommodating a counterexample to a theory about the nature of a concept by elaborating on the necessary and sufficient conditions of its applications. Rather, it seems to me that it is the very notion of "fallible knowledge" that is problematic bordering on incoherence. It is the burden of this chapter to show that if we are to make sense of the fallible/infallible divide in the theory of knowledge, we ought to rethink it in radically different terms. Before embarking on this task, however, we need to get a clearer insight into how the issue has been traditionally conceived.

It is widely acknowledged that a great chunk of our knowledge, namely, knowledge gained through sense experience, is fallible in the sense outlined above. We could easily go astray in regard to the subject maters that constitute the domain of perceptual knowledge. However, fallibilists' claim notwithstanding, it is by no means obvious that *all* human knowledge is fallible as there are instances of knowledge that seem to be infallible. It is nonetheless true that the domain of infallible knowledge, as it was traditionally conceived, has significantly shrunk. For example, it is now widely believed that not every instance of knowledge of our mental states is infallible. This is especially true of the so-called intentional, contentful states like beliefs and desires where there are good reasons to be suspicious of their infallibility. To begin with, it is often difficult to identify one's beliefs or desires because they may be unconscious or subconscious despite influencing our behavior. Sometimes it is simply difficult to be sure what it is that one believes or desires. And then there is the widespread phenomenon of self-deception where people deceive themselves about what they truly believe or desire. Moreover, scientific investigation has shown that, in identifying one's beliefs or desires, one systematically but sincerely reports attitudes one thinks rational to hold under those circumstances despite actually lacking them.

The preceding observations do not, however, entail that the domain of infallible knowledge is empty. For there is still our knowledge of our phenomenal states like sensations, feelings and experiences that seem to possess an infallible character. This is certainly both a traditionally respectable position as well as a view held by many contemporary theorists. To mention but a few examples, while admitting that one may doubt nearly everything, Descartes claimed that "it is at least quite certain that it seems to me that I see light, that I hear noise, and that I feel heat. That cannot be false" (*Meditations*, II quoted in Alston 1989, p. 251). Brentano, on the other hand, took our mode of access to mental phenomena as their distinguishing character noting that, in addition to the special nature of its object, inner perception is distinguished by "that immediate, infallible self-evidence, which pertains to it alone among all cases in which we know objects of experience" (*Psychology From An Empirical Standpoint*, quoted in Alston 1989, p. 252). And, referring to the possibility of identifying a class of statements which would be logically immune from doubt, Ayer focused on statements that report the content of one's experiences: "I cannot . . . be in any doubt or in any way mistaken about [them]. I cannot be unsure whether I feel a headache, nor can I think that I feel a headache when I do not" (Ayer 1956, p. 55).

More recently, and in a similar vein, theorists such as Shoemaker have singled out statements about private experiences and mental events as being incorrigible in the sense that "if a person sincerely asserts such a statement it does not make sense to suppose, and nothing could be accepted as showing that he is mistaken, that is, that what he says is false" (Shoemaker 1963, p. 216). Finally, referring to the platitudes that constitute a relevant mental theory, David Lewis makes the following pointed observations.

> [A] belief that one is in pain never occurs unless pain occurs . . . Then the necessary infallibility of introspection is assured . . . The state that *usually* occupies the role of belief that one is in pain may, of course, occur without the state that *usually* occupies the role of pain; but in that case . . . the former no longer is the state of belief that one is in pain, and the latter no longer is pain . . . Therefore it is impossible to believe that one is in pain and not be in pain.
>
> (Lewis 1980, p. 214)

The idea, then, is that, in regard to phenomenal states, one can determine with certainty whether the pertinent belief about the state has justification and consequently whether it qualifies as knowledge. It is therefore implausible to claim, initially at least, that all knowledge is fallible. (Later we shall see how these observations bear on the central claim of this chapter.) For now, however, let us go along with that claim and see if the fallibilists have succeeded in providing a viable account of fallible knowledge on their own terms.

Earlier we presented the standard account of fallible knowledge in a rather informal and intuitive manner. Here is a more rigorous presentation (for similar formulations see, e.g., Ayer 1956; BonJour 1985; Cohen 1988; Fogelin 1994; Audi 1993).

(Falk) S fallibly knows that $p =_{df}$ (1) S knows that p on the basis of justification j and (2) S's belief that p on the basis of j could have been false.

It was noted, however, that the account runs into difficulty in accommodating knowledge of necessary truths. In the following sections, I shall critically examine two recent attempts to patch up the problem and show why they fail. Their failure, I shall suggest, is not just a technical hitch in accommodating a counterexample, but, rather, an indication of the problematic nature of the very idea of fallible knowledge.

8.1 Fallibility as the possibility of falsity or accidental truth

The first account that I wish to examine is due to Reed who seeks to improve on the standard account through the following proposal (Reed 2002).

(Falk') S fallibly knows that $p =_{df}$ (1) S knows that p on the basis of justification j and yet (2) S's belief that p on the basis of j could have been either (i) false or (ii) accidentally true.

This, he thinks, takes care of the problem of knowledge of necessary truths by illustrating it through the following example. A student, Seth, has very good reason to trust Linda, his logic instructor, who has so far provided him with only justified true beliefs. Now Linda presents Seth with a valid argument. Although Seth does not follow all the intricacies of the proof, he gains a good sense of how it works, and, assuming Linda's reliability, he comes to know that the conclusion follows from the premises. Compatibly with this, however, Linda could have made two errors with negations that cancel each other out. In that case, Seth would have come to form the same true belief "with the same justification," but, says Reed, "it would not have been knowledge. Despite holding the belief with considerable justification, the justification for it would not have been connected to the truth in the right sort of way to count as knowledge" (2002, p. 149). So since the justification of Seth's belief could have failed to be appropriately linked with the truth, that is, the belief could have been accidentally true, knowledge of necessary truths is also fallible.

But this example does not really support Reed's claim that (Falk') can accommodate knowledge of necessary truths. An initial problem concerns his analysis of accidental truth in terms of the justification of a belief failing to be appropriately linked with its truth. Consider the well-known barn example where an agent points in the direction of a real barn in an area which is, unbeknown to him, infested with fake barns. Under such circumstances, the agent's reasons for his belief that he is seeing a barn is appropriately linked with its truth (i.e., there is no deviant link in the process leading to the belief), but the belief is nevertheless accidentally true and, thus, not an instance of knowledge. Or consider cases involving misleading evidence one does not possess (Harman 1973, ch. 9). Suppose one has formed a justified true belief about an event, but, because he has failed to read an inaccurate report of that incident in a well-known newspaper, the belief does not amount to knowledge. Under these conditions, although the belief's justification is appropriately liked with its truth, it is still accidentally true.

Admittedly, we still lack an adequate account of the notion of accidental truth, but since Reed fails to give it much substance beyond using the blanket term "appropriate link," his example does not show that Seth's necessarily true and "justified" belief could have been accidentally true. Rather, the appropriate moral to draw from the example is that the agent's belief is not justified at all. To see this, consider the epistemic status of Seth's belief under hypothetical circumstances. While one may grant that Seth's reasons are *relevantly* connected to the truth of his belief, the connection does not seem to be of an *appropriate* sort. This is because the type of process through which Linda arrives at the conclusion under these circumstances is unreliable. Linda's reasoning is defective and it is only by chance that she arrives at the truth. She could have easily gone astray. If so, *pace* Reed, the resulting belief is not justified but accidentally true, rather, it is simply unjustified. The same would be true of Seth's belief which derives from Linda's. This would, in turn, affect the status of Seth's belief in the actual scenario. For, if what we have said is correct, it would follow that even in the actual scenario Seth's belief is unjustified, since, according to Reed, Seth has the *same* justification in both actual and counterfactual cases.[1]

Reed further remarks that (Falk′) is equally plausible for empirical knowledge.

> My knowledge that I am seeing a barn is fallible in spite of justifica-tion – because the belief could have been false ... but the knowledge is also fallible – in spite of justification – because the belief could have been accidentally true: I could have been looking at a real barn but one that is in an area filled with lots of barn facades and no real barns.
> (Reed 2002, p. 150)

But this reasoning is fallacious. To begin with, why should the fact that the belief "I am seeing a barn" could have been false make the corre-sponding *knowledge* fallible? All it shows is that the belief itself is fallible (more on this point later). As for the subsequent argument that since the belief "I am seeing a barn" could have been accidentally true, so the corresponding knowledge is fallible, it is too quick. Reed fails to notice that the first conjunct (1) of (Falk′) constrains the second (2). He agrees that a proper analysis of knowledge needs to go beyond the standard JTB account by postulating a fourth condition to ensure that the agent's belief is not accidentally true. Since we do not yet know how to unpack this requirement, let us label it "G" (for "Gettierized" as it was Gettier who first highlighted "resistance to luck" as an adequacy condition on a proper analysis of knowledge). Now, when Reed assumes that S *knows* that he is seeing a barn, this means that S's corresponding belief pos-sesses the property G. But then it would be difficult to see how this very belief could have been accidentally true for the very function of possessing G is to safeguard against its being accidentally true.

Finally, and this related to the preceding objection, why should one take (Falk′) as providing a definition of "fallible *knowledge*"? If (Falk′) is to be an analysis of "fallible knowledge," its two conjuncts should bear on one another rather than form independent clauses. But that is not the impression that (Falk′) imparts, for while its first conjunct refers to knowledge, the second is intended to characterize fallibility without indicating how it is supposed to bear on or qualify *knowledge*. One might as well see it as an account of "knowing a proposition with fallible *jus-tification*." That the knowledge and fallibility definans of (Falk′) should *directly* bear on one another is also evident in Reed's own critique of a proposal that interprets the notion of possibility that figures in the standard account (Falk) as having an epistemic rather a logical character. This suggests reading the second conjunct of (Falk) as saying that "for all S knows ~p." However, as Read rightly objects, given the first conjunct, we are committed to the fact that S knows that p and this automatically rules out ~p as being epistemically possible.

A further reason for the claim that the fallibility definans in the analysis of fallible knowledge should be seen as qualifying *knowledge*, rather than one of its constituents like justification, is that the structure of (Falk') may be radically affected by the conception of knowledge that it incorporates. For example, on Nozick's tracking theory of knowledge, granting knowledge in the first conjunct of (Falk') automatically rules out the second conjunct. For, on Nozick's account, to know that p it must be the case that if p were false the agent would not believe it. So, having granted the obtaining of knowledge in the first conjunct, the scenario countenanced in the second conjunct of (Falk') would no longer be possible. I conclude therefore that Reed's attempt to improve on the standard account is unsuccessful. Let us now turn to a more sophisticated proposal (due to Hetherington).

8.2   Fallibility as failable knowledge

Hetherington acknowledges that the standard account runs into problem when applied to knowledge of necessary truths (Hetherington 1999). He thinks however that by exclusively tying fallibility to the possibility of being mistaken, philosophers have lost sight of a more general kind of epistemic failing that, he claims, not only "underlies the traditional concept of knowing fallibly" (Hetherington 1999, p. 565) but also has far-reaching consequences for understanding the nature of knowledge and the function of Gettier cases. He calls this phenomenon "epistemic failability."

(Failk)   S knows failably that p =$_{df}$ (1) S knows that p but (2) S might have failed to do so.

Now, assuming that knowing that p involves at least having a well-justified true belief that p, there are three possible ways to fail to have that knowledge: (i) when truth is absent, (ii) when the belief that p is absent and (iii) when the justification for that belief is missing. This gives us the following account of failable knowledge.

(Failk') S knows failably that p = $_{df}$ (1) S knows that p and (2) there is an accessible possible world where (i) p is false (but S believes that p with j), or (ii) S fails to believe that p (though p is true and S has j), or (iii) S fails to have justification for p (but S has true belief that p).

Hetherington calls these worlds "epistemic-failure" worlds. Put differently, failable knowledge is knowledge with which one can associate a possible epistemic-failure world and it comes in degrees.

Now to the consequences of (Failk'). First, Hetherington claims that it takes care of knowledge of necessary truths (like $7 + 5 = 12$). This knowledge, too, is failable because one can associate with it two epistemic-failure worlds (belief-failure worlds and justification-failure worlds) where one (consequently) fails to know that $7 + 5 = 12$. The fact that failability is a matter of degree also explains why knowledge of contingent propositions differs from knowledge of necessary ones, for there is an additional epistemic-failure world (truth-failure world) associated with the former species of knowledge. Hetherington further suggests that the phenomenon of failable knowledge radically transforms our understanding of Gettier cases and their function. His thesis is that, current orthodoxy notwithstanding, not only is the JTB account of knowledge correct but also there is knowledge in each Gettier case albeit a very failable one (Hetherington 1999, fn.6). Gettier cases are cases where the agent is lucky. Hetherington traces this fact to the presence of, what he terms, "strange" occurrences in such cases. These come in two different varieties: (1) helpful strange occurrences and (2) dangerous strange occurrences. Consider, for example, Chisholm's Sheep Case. Here the agent has good but misleading evidence that leads him to believe he is seeing a sheep (but the animal is a disguised dog) and concludes that there is sheep in the field. Hidden from his view, however, there is in fact a sheep in the area. This is a case where the strange occurrence functions helpfully. If it had been absent, the agent's belief would not have been true.

Now recall the fake barn example. Here the subject's justified belief is true, but the strange occurrence (the nearby fake barns) functions as unseen threat to the subject's justified true belief. And there are close possible worlds where it does interfere (e.g., a close possible world where the agent is deceived by a fake barn): "In each Gettier case, therefore, the strange occurrence brings it about that the epistemic subject almost fails to have his well-justified true belief" (Hetherington 1999, p. 573). But, says Hetherington, this should not lead us to conclude that in the

Gettier cases the subject lacks the pertinent knowledge. Rather, the right conclusion to draw is that knowledge in such cases is very failable as there are close possible worlds where at least either the belief, its truth or justification is missing. Thus, Gettier cases turn what would otherwise be some distant epistemic-failure worlds into close ones, and this is precisely what misleads people into thinking that the subject lacks knowledge in those cases.

It does not seem to me however that, either as a way of identifying what underlies the traditional concept of fallible knowledge or as an explanation of the function of the Gettier cases, Hetherington's account of failable knowledge is successful. Let us start with the latter contention. He claims that "a Gettier situation turns what would otherwise be some distinctive and *distant* epistemic-failure worlds into *close* ones" (Hetherington 1999, p. 575). This may be true about Gettier cases involving dangerous strange occurrences, but that is surely not the case with those involving helpful occurrences. For in the latter cases the strange occurrence has, as it were, already kicked in, that is, it has been allowed to influence the status of the agent's belief in the actual world. Indeed, if it had not actually obtained, the belief in question would not have been true. So, unlike cases involving dangerous occurrences (as in the fake barn example), helpful occurrences do not turn a distant epistemic-failure world into a close one. On the contrary, their presence turns a close epistemic-failure world (where the belief is false) into a distant one. It is, thus, their absence, rather than their presence, that creates an epistemic-failure world. Strangely enough, Hetherington fails to notice the asymmetry and, thus, goes on to make inconsistent remarks. First, as noted above, he says that "[i]n *each* Gettier case ... the strange occurrence brings about that the epistemic subject almost fails to have his well-justified true belief" (Hetherington 1999, p. 575). This fits Gettier cases involving dangerous occurrences like the fake barn example. But in cases involving helpful occurrences (like the Sheep Case), it is when such occurrences *fail* to obtain (as when there is no real sheep in the field) that we get epistemic-failure worlds (i.e., where the agent no longer knows the relevant proposition).

A more substantial problem with Hetherington's failability account is that, far from illuminating the Gettier phenomenon, it completely neutralizes its force and function. For Gettier cases were introduced with a view to adjudicate between competing theories of knowledge by ruling out those that allow knowledge by luck. As we have seen, however, Hetherington claims that the JTB account fully captures the nature of knowledge, and that, far from undermining this account, the relevant Gettier cases actually highlight the failability of knowledge in those scenarios rather than its absence. But note that one can deploy Hetherington's strategy with regard to *any* (XYZ) account of knowledge (e.g., true belief caused by the relevant facts, etc.), and equally claim that, far from undermining that account, potential Gettier counterexamples only turn distant epistemic-failure worlds into close ones: So the XYZ account of knowledge is correct and the agents have knowledge in the relevant Gettier cases though the knowledge in question is very failable. I take this to be a *reductio* of the failability account.

Moreover, the failability account also fails to identify what is so distinctive about Gettier cases for its fails to discriminate between those cases and cases of simple knowledge-failure. Consider a simple (non-Gettier) knowledge-failure case. Smith is looking at his newly decorated wall of his office where a Van Gogh is hanging, and thus comes to form the belief that there is a Van Gogh painting on his wall. It so happens, however, that his secretary, not knowing anything about painting, had randomly picked up that painting from a box containing a number of paintings by Monet and only one by Van Gogh. She could have easily picked up a Monet. This would then be a case of failable knowledge as there is a nearby epistemic-failure world where Smith's belief is false and instead the belief that there is a Monet on his wall is true. We could make such cases as failable as we wish (to the degree that Hetherington attaches to Gettier cases), but in Gettier cases knowledge fails to obtain (or is failable, on Hetherington's account) for entirely different reasons whereas Hetherington's account treats them all along the same lines.

Finally, if Hetherington's strategy is viable, there is no reason why one should not adopt it to identify the nature of other epistemic concepts such as justification. Suppose we wish to say that S is justified in believing that p iff the belief in question is adequately grounded. We then run into counterexamples where although one's belief is adequately grounded, it would be implausible to regard it as justified. Consider, for example, cases involving defeaters, say, of an undercutter variety. Suppose we are looking at a red book and accordingly form the true belief that the book is red. However, we learn later that the room is lit by red light. The orthodoxy quite plausibly regards the belief under these circumstances as unjustified. But, by helping ourselves with Hetherington's strategy, we can offer the following unpalatable re-interpretation of the epistemic standing of such cases: Such defeaters do not actually undermine the justification of beliefs in question. Rather, they highlight the failable character of epistemic justification. Of course even in normal circumstances one's justification *is* failable (or fallible), but, in cases involving defeaters, the relevant justification is of a *very* failable sort.

In the light of the preceding problems with Hetherington's failability account, and given his claim that the phenomenon of failability is actually what underlies fallibility, I conclude that he has failed to cast any light on the nature of fallible knowledge. All he has shown is the simple truth that a conceptual compound (knowledge) fails to obtain if any of its constituents fails to materialize. This is just another way of saying that "knowledge" is a contingent property. This is not what theorists are inclined to take as the salient feature of fallibility.

8.3   Analyzing fallible knowledge

Recall how fallible knowledge was analyzed according to (Falk').

(Falk')   S fallibly knows that $p =_{df}$ (1) S knows that p on the basis of justification j and yet (2) S's belief that p on the basis of j could have been either (i) false or (ii) accidentally true.

To see why (Falk') is incoherent, let us begin by noting how two *unproblematic* epistemic notions involving fallibility, namely, fallible (true) belief and fallible justified (true) belief, may be analyzed.

(I) Fallible (true) belief that $p =_{df} T(B_p) \,\&\, \Diamond \sim T(B_p)$

(II) Fallible justified belief that $p =_{df} T(JB_p) \,\&\, \Diamond \sim T(JB_p)$

(I) only says that a true belief can be false while (II) says that a justified belief can be false. What is however important to note is that in both (I) and (II) it is the same entity, that is, (B_p) and (JB_p) respectively, that possesses possible truth-values in the relevant definans. But this is not the case with (Falk'). To see why let us assume that knowledge is a belief that has the following properties: being true (T), being justified (J) and being Gettierized (G). (The presence of the last property, we may recall, is to safeguard against the possibility of the belief being accidentally true.) Then while the first conjunct of (Falk') attributes a truth-value to a *Gettierized justified belief*, it is only *justified belief* that is taken to be the bearer of possible truth-values in the second conjunct (however one construes "accidental truth"). Accordingly, the bearers of possible truth-values in the definans are different which is why it is difficult to see how fallibility (as represented by the second conjunct) can be seen as qualifying *knowledge* (represented by the first conjunct). This problem is absent in (I) and (II) because here there is an "it" (namely, (B_p) and (JB_p) respectively) that possesses possibly different truth-values which is why the possibility of being mistaken (fallibility) can be said to attach to (or qualify) a belief (or justified belief).

One might respond to this objection by invoking, what may be called, the thesis of property transfer, according to which a conceptual whole automatically inherits the properties of its constituents. So suppose we take knowledge to be a belief that is true, justified and Gettierized. We have just seen that a belief (or justified belief) has the property of being fallible. By the thesis of property transfer, knowledge, too, inherits this property. However, without further qualifications, this argument is obviously invalid. For if a justified belief is fallible, that is, could have been false, it can also have the property of being accidentally true. The idea is that if a false belief could be warranted, it would be possible for the belief to be accidentally true. To see this, suppose that in the actual world a certain belief, for example, that Smith owns is Ford is justified but false. Now consider a possible world identical to the actual world except for some remote incident that makes the belief true (e.g., Smith's uncle dies bequeathing him a Ford). Now, assuming that a justified belief has the property of being fallible, it would, by the above argument, also have the property of being possibly true by accident. By the thesis of property transfer, knowledge would automatically inherit the latter property. But this is absurd. Every possible world where a belief is knowledge, it is non-accidentally true: "Infallibility in the sense of *cannot be mistaken* is a feature necessarily possessed by every piece of *knowledge* in a strong sense of 'knowledge'" (Alston 1989, p. 259). Incidentally, the preceding observations also show that the problem of knowledge of necessary truths is a red herring in so far as it is the fallibility of *knowledge* that is at issue.

We could equally pose the problem using the narrative of radical interpretation. We have seen that, for Davidson, an adequate semantic theory for a language should enable a person who learns the theory to partially understand the language. This involves a Tarski-style characterization of the truth of the speaker's language, and a theory of his beliefs (see various articles in Davidson 1984). The evidence for such a semantic theory consists in the conditions under which the speakers hold sentences true. As noted before, to break into the closed circle of meaning and belief, Davidson introduces the principle of charity which suggests the holding of belief constant (as far as possible) while solving for meaning. Understood thus, charity is forced on us, says Davidson, if we wish to understand others.

Davidson's initial characterization of charity construes it in terms of the maximization of truth (by the interpreter's own lights). As we saw in Chapter 1, this leaves room for the skeptical possibility of most of one's beliefs being false, for both the speaker and the interpreter might understand one another on the basis of shared but false beliefs. Subsequently Davidson adds further constraints on the principle of charity to endow it with epistemic bite. This he proceeds to do in two, not quite related, ways (Davidson 1986). We may either imagine an omniscient interpreter trying to interpret the language of a fallible speaker. This ensures the beliefs of the speaker to be mostly correct (by objective standards). Alternatively, we may wish to rule out the skeptical possibilities by saddling the principle of charity with – what Davidson calls – the thesis of the inseparability of the speaker's environment from her utterances and her beliefs, and to identify beliefs by matching them with the facts in the world that prompt them. By allowing us to identify the objects of beliefs with their causes, the principle of charity rules out widespread fallibility: "Belief is in its nature veridical" (Davidson 1986, p. 314) and non-accidentally so. This means that one has to interpret the utterances of, say, a brain in a vat, as referring to the brain's virtual environment. Given the preceding constraint on the principle of charity, one can view it as attributing knowledge to the speakers in the process of interpretation. We may thus see Davidson as moving from a truth–maximizing principle of charity (where fallibility or the possibility of being mistaken is a serious possibility) to a knowledge-maximizing principle of charity where beliefs are held to be essentially and non-accidentally veridical. It is not my aim here to decide which of these principles is necessary for the possibility of interpretation but only to provide further support for our earlier claim that the notions of fallibility and knowledge (as opposed to, say, fallibility and justification) do not sit well together.

8.4 Fallible knowledge as externalist knowledge

It is now time to see if we can present a coherent picture of the distinction between fallible and infallible knowledge, one that is immune to the problems facing the accounts examined thus far. To set the stage for the forthcoming analysis, it would be helpful to start with *in*fallibility first. We may recall that the paradigm cases of the infallible knowledge included knowledge of phenomenal states like feeling pain or having perceptual experiences. What do we exactly have in mind when we assert that we know we are in pain (i.e. in the clear cases of such states)? The concept that is more often associated with our beliefs about such states is certainty and absence of doubt. We saw Descartes, Brentano, Lewis and others talking about one's beliefs about such states as exhibiting the highest degree of certainty. That is to say, it seems that when one is in such states one cannot be in doubt as to whether one is. As Malcolm says, "you can be *in doubt* as to whether I am in pain, but I can not; ... You can be mistaken as to whether I am in pain, but I cannot" ("The Privacy of Experience," quoted in Alston 1989, p. 253). In the same vein, Ewing states, "I cannot help being ... absolutely certain of the truth of these propositions [concerning phenomenal states] and I do not think that I ought to be otherwise" (*The Fundamental Questions of Philosophy*, quoted in Alston 1989, p. 253). This is not just a mere psychological phenomenon. Rather, it is a reflection of certainty in the normative sense of the word as lacking any ground for doubt. It is true, of course, that a general identification of the concepts of certainty, infallibility or indubitability is implausible, but as Alston says, "the degree of certainty typically ascribed to one's belief about one's own mental states amounts either to infallibility or indubitability" (Alston 1989, p. 258).

In any case, regardless of how tight the connection between these concepts is, it is quite palatable, I believe, to see infallibility as, at least, involving certainty. The impression that, however, one gets from discussions of the latter concept is one that depicts certainty as being a second-order concept. For example, when delineating the concept, Alston says that "to be certain in this [normative] sense is to be justified in feeling complete assurance" where "[t]o feel complete [assurance] that one is correct is to entertain no doubts about the matter" (Alston 1989, p. 258). Carrier, too, declares that in his view "epistemic certainty is expressed by saying that one knows that one is not mistaken" (Carrier 1993, p. 367). This is also the sort of picture that emerges from Klein's study of the concept of certainty (see Klein 1981; 1992). He presents a broadly Cartesian characterization of the concept. To say that a belief p is certain is to say that "we have a guarantee of its truth" (Klein 1992, p. 62) where this is, in turn, analyzed in terms of the agent's "belief system [containing] adequate grounds for *assuring* [the agent] that p is true because his belief system would warrant the denial of every proposition that would lower the warrant of p" (Klein 1992, p. 63).

Klein also adds a further condition to ensure objective immunity to doubt. However, it is clear from his analysis that he takes certainty as involving a second-order belief. For to say that an agent is certain that p is not only to say that he is warranted in believing that p but also that, in Klein's words, his belief system contains enough epistemic resources to rule out any potential defeaters. The reference to the agent's belief system containing adequate grounds to *assure* him that his belief p is true clearly indicates that in addition to the agent's first-order belief p, he has a second-order (dispositional) belief to the effect that his first-order belief is true. His belief system provides him with enough justification (assurance) that his belief p will not be undermined. Since, according to Klein, a proposition that is certain in this sense "is indubitable and guaranteed both subjectively and objectively to be true," one might say that if a proposition p is certain for an agent, then not only does he know p but also justifiably believes (knows) that the belief p is true.

We might then take the preceding observations as suggesting that we should go for second-order if we wish to define "infallible" knowledge.

(Infalk*)   S infallibly knows that $p =_{df}$ (1) S knows that p on the basis of justification j and (2) S knows that the belief p is true.

Having got a grip on the notion of infallibility, fallible knowledge can be construed in a contrasting manner as follows.

(Falk*)   S fallibly knows that $p =_{df}$ (1) S knows that p on the basis of justification j and (2) S does not know that the belief p is true.[2]

The question that arises now is how the second conjunct in (Infalk*) and (Falk*) may obtain. We have already schematically defined knowledge as Gettierized justified true belief. There are, however, differing views as to how the Getterization condition could be best secured. For our purpose here, I shall focus on one proposal which is widely held and, though incomplete, contains an important grain of truth about the nature of knowledge. This idea has appeared in different guises. Thus, Pollock speaks of objective justification as what turns true belief into knowledge (Pollock 1986). It requires that the agent be not only subjectively justified but also that the belief in question will be ultimately undefeated. This is also, roughly, what Lehrer and Dretske call "undefeated justified acceptance" and "conclusive justification" respectively (Dretske 1971; Lehrer 1989; see also Sturgeon 1993 and Tomberlin 1980, who use the terms "fully justified" and "completely justified" respectively to refer to roughly the same property).

Objective or full justification is intended to convey the thought that the kind of justification needed to turn a true belief into knowledge should be maximal and undefeated. Indeed, on many accounts of this notion, full justification entails truth. Now, assuming that something as strong as objective justification is needed for knowledge, it is only a small step to see how the second conjunct in (Infalk*) and (Falk*) might obtain. The issue actually hinges on whether it is an internalist or externalist conception of epistemic justification (knowledge) that is being employed. Epistemic internalism is usually presented as the view that imposes an accessibility constraint (AC) on the justifiers of a belief (i.e. the grounds that confer justification on that belief). Justification has, accordingly, a pronounced internalist character in the sense that one must be able to tell whether one's beliefs are justified.

(AC)   The only facts that qualify as justifiers of a cognizer's believing p at time t are facts that are accessible to him in the sense that he can readily know, at t, whether they obtain (see, for example, Goldman 1999).

By contrast, epistemic externalism denies that the justifiers of a belief need to be accessible to those who hold it. Reliabilism is a paradigm case of an externalist theory that takes the mere reliability of a belief-forming process to be sufficient for the justification of the beliefs it gives rise to. Internalism, of course, comes in different strengths depending on the relevant mode of access (justified belief, knowledge, etc.) as well as whether it is required that one also know (justifiably believe) that the grounds of one's beliefs are adequate. Most internalists, however, hold that the only interesting form of internalism is one which not only requires a cognizer to know (justifiably believe) that the grounds of his belief p obtain, but also know (justifiably believe) that they are adequate.

Going back to the requirement of objective or full justification for knowledge, suppose we take it to involve an internalist conception of justification. Now, given that an internalist conception of justification requires access to (knowledge of) both the grounds of a belief p and their adequacy, then if S knows that p, it would follow that S knows that those grounds adequately support the belief in question. Furthermore, since the justification in question is assumed to be maximal or conclusive, it would follow that S also knows that his belief p is true. Ignoring the accessibility constraint, on the other hand, that is, adopting an externalist stance, would imply that the agent need not be aware of the obtaining of the grounds of his belief or their adequacy in order to know that p. This means that knowing that p is quite compatible with the agent not knowing that p is true. Thus, depending on whether one adopts an internalist or externalist stance in justification theory, we arrive at either infallible or fallible species of knowledge (in line with (Infalk*) and (Falk*)) when the justification in question is assumed to be maximal or full. When a belief is maximally justified, we get an infallible species of knowledge on an internalist conception of justification and a fallible one when the notion of justification is assumed to be externalist. The concept of fallibilism is thus inextricably linked with externalist assumptions and it is incoherent on internalist assumptions. This means that the fallible/infallible distinction in the theory of knowledge is best understood in terms of the externalist/internalist conceptions of knowledge.

8.5   Consequences and confirmations

This is the radical gloss on the fallibility/infallibility controversy that was earlier said is needed if the notion of fallible knowledge is to make sense at all. I have already argued directly for the plausibility of this thesis by noting how it retains the intended functions of the fallible/infallible distinction while avoiding its problems. In this section, I am going to highlight some of the consequences of our proposal which would, in turn, lend indirect support to it.

To begin with, the type of beliefs that fallibilists usually regard as paradigm cases of fallible knowledge, namely, empirical beliefs about objects in the world, are also the type of beliefs that externalists usually refer to when defending their conception of knowledge. Externalists are usually on strong grounds when they claim that our every day, empirical knowledge is typically externalist. The normal cognizers often lack, they say, the sort of sophistication that internalists require if one is to have perceptual knowledge. But those unsophisticated human agents are surely often justified in what they take their environment to be like despite not being in a position to even raise the problem of the adequacy of the grounds of their beliefs.

> Do I have evidence it would take to adequately support a belief that my present perceptual grounds for believing that there is a maple tree near my study window are adequate? I very much doubt it ... [I]t seems very dubious that we store enough observational evidence to constitute evidence for the thesis that normal sensory experience is an adequate ground for our beliefs about the physical environment.
> (Alston 1989, p. 241; see also Goldman 1999)

Internalists, on the other hand, are equally fond of pointing out that our knowledge of our phenomenal states is typically internalist since, by being aware of such states, agents are *ipso facto* aware of their grounds and adequacy. These instances of knowledge, as we have seen, also constitute the entire extension of infallible knowledge.

The thesis also appears to have surprising consequences for a seemingly remote and distant controversy involving issues in the philosophy of mind and epistemology. It seems that it can be invoked to adjudicate between the two sides of the recent controversy over the question whether justification internalism (externalism) is compatible with content or semantic externalism (internalism). Content externalism is the view that facts about social and physical environments affect the individuation conditions of the contents of certain of our thoughts. It implies that certain thought contents of an individual fail to supervene on her intrinsic physical properties. A recent question that has vexed philosophers is how the internalism/externalism distinction in justification theory stands vis-à-vis the internalist/externalist divide within the theory of content.

A number of theorists have argued that justification internalism (externalism) and content externalism (internalism) are incompatible (call this the "incompatibility thesis"). I shall not examine these arguments here as I am only concerned to see what consequences, if any, our proposed analysis of fallible knowledge has for the incompatibility thesis.[3] What is surprising is that the proposal propounded in this chapter seems to lend some support to the incompatibility thesis. To see this, let us recall our discussion of the purported extension of fallible/infallible knowledge. We found out that while knowledge of empirical propositions and the content of our propositional attitudes (like beliefs and desires) seem to count as instances of fallible knowledge, our knowledge of our phenomenal states (like pain and experiences) is typically thought to be infallible. Since content externalism is about the individuation conditions of the content of certain of our mental states, one way to test the incompatibility thesis is to try to refute it by coming up with instances of knowledge of our mental states that are either of an internalist character but whose mental states have externalist content, or are species of externalist knowledge but with the mental states involved having internalist content.

Are there such cases? If our *knowledge of our mental states* is to be of an internalist nature, one must not only know that one is in such state but also know that the grounds of the relevant belief obtain and are adequate. Given our assumption that knowledge involves objective or full justification, the internalist character of knowledge (justification), as we saw, entails that one also knows that one is in the mental state in question. As noted earlier, this is precisely how the notion of infallible knowledge was eventually analyzed. We found out that our concept of infallible knowledge is best understood as knowledge that is internalist (when the pertinent belief is fully justified). On the other hand, it was argued that the only viable instances of such knowledge involve knowledge of our phenomenal states (like pain, experiences, etc.). So the conclusion is that the internalist (infallible) species of knowledge of our mental states only involve phenomenal states such as sensations, experiences and the like. Interestingly, these are precisely the states of which content externalism is not true. Such states include sensations which, being non-representational, lack semantic content. In addition to bodily sensations, perceptual seemings (like seeing a red book or hearing a loud noise) are also thought to be not subject to content externalism. What distinguishes the case of perceptual content from that of the content of natural kind thoughts is that in the former, unlike the latter, there is no conflict between how things seem and how they are. In other words, in the case of perceptual seemings, as McGinn remarks, there is no room for an is/seems distinction (McGinn 1989). They are, thus, exempt from Twin earth arguments for content externalism. Their content is therefore not externalist. So mental states the knowledge of which is of an internalist character include only those that have internalist content.[4]

On the other hand, we saw that the concept of fallible knowledge is best understood as expressing an externalist conception of knowledge, that is, that it is bound up with externalist assumptions. It was further discovered that the class of fallible knowledge include, among other things, knowledge of mental states such as beliefs, desires, and propositional attitudes in general, namely, mental states that have semantic or intentional content. But these states are precisely those whose content is externalist. So, once again, mental states the knowledge of which is of an externalist character are confined only to those that have externalist content. We thus seem to have failed to refute the incompatibility thesis. If anything, these observations go a long way to corroborate (what some theorists regard as) the independently plausible claim that justification internalism (externalism) and content externalism (internalism) are incompatible. Moreover, I am inclined to think that such potential consequences of our account of fallible/infallible knowledge turn it into a so-called "progressive research program" infusing it with further plausibility beyond that already advertised.

Finally, it is time to look at one further feature of our beliefs, namely, the epistemic significance of our knowledge of their contents. Each of us easily knows an enormous amount about our thoughts, attitudes, sensations, emotions and so on. True, we also know a lot about others and their mental lives. But self-knowledge, unlike our knowledge of others, is immediate, at least, in basic cases. This has nothing to do with the fact that in the case of self-knowledge we are concerned with knowledge of properties that are ours. It takes some empirical investigation to find out about our weight or our height. But this is not how we proceed with respect to our psychological attributes. Our knowledge of such properties is not usually founded on evidence. There is no other thing that one knows or has observed from which one infers that one is experiencing, say, a particular sensation. It is such epistemic features of self-knowledge, namely, immediacy, authority and so on, that require a different treatment of such a species of knowledge – we shall only be concerned, however, with knowledge of our thoughts and beliefs.

In the case of self-knowledge one is the sole subject of both one's first-order and second-order states. As Burge observes, this gives a subject a single perspective on his states (Burge 1988). It is this unified perspective that underlies the epistemic directness of our knowledge of the content of our thoughts. And it is precisely this feature that seems to pose problems for such widely shared views as content externalism. Externalism is the view that the content of some of our mental states is an extrinsic, relational property of a person. What makes, say, beliefs to be about something, that is, to have intentional content are the relations in which these internal states stand to external affairs. This seems to be incompatible with our privileged knowledge of what is going on in one's own mind. Whether this is the case is the subject of our investigation in the next chapter.

9
Knowledge of our Beliefs and Privileged Access

A number of recent discussions of externalism have claimed that it undermines the traditional doctrine according to which cognizers enjoy some kind of privileged access to their own intentional states. There have been two lines of argument in support of this claim. The first, which is primarily an epistemic argument, exploits the so-called "slow switching" cases to argue that, if externalism is true, one could discover the contents of one's thoughts only after investigating the physical and/or social environment in which one exists (Boghossian 1989). It is then concluded that externalism is not compatible with the doctrine of privileged access (call this "the incompatibility thesis"). The second line of argument, due to McKinsey, draws attention to the absurd consequence of there being a non-empirical route to knowledge of empirical facts that seems to follow from the combined theses of externalism and privileged access (McKinsey 1991).

In this chapter, in line with the general drift of this book, I shall focus only on the first, epistemological, line of argument (see, e.g., McLaughlin and Tye 1998 on the second line of argument).[1] After examining various responses that have been made to the slow switching argument and finding them wanting, I set out to explain why the argument fails. It will be suggested that the argument trades on an ambiguity when claiming that our knowledge of our thoughts is susceptible to empirical contingencies. I shall try to show that it is only by relying on certain controversial assumptions about the concepts of justification and a priority that this claim, however construed, can stand a chance of establishing the incompatibility thesis. Finally, drawing on an analogy with Benacerraf's argument against Platonism, I will offer some reasons as to why the switching argument fails to bring out the real source of tension between externalism and privileged self-knowledge.

9.1 The slow switching argument explained

According to externalist theories of content the contents of an individual's thoughts do not supervene on her intrinsic properties. Rather, facts about the social and physical environments enter into the individuation of her mental contents. This means that two individuals could be indiscernible as far as their intrinsic physical properties are concerned, and yet differ in respect of the contents of certain of their thoughts. The externalist thesis is motivated by the well-known Twin Earth thought experiments due to Putnam and Burge (Putnam 1975; Burge 1988). Consider two individuals, Oscar and Toscar, who are molecular duplicates. Oscar lives on Earth while Toscar lives on Twin Earth, a planet which is an exact duplicate of Earth except for the fact that the liquid that the Twin Earthians call "water" and fills their lakes and falls from the sky and so on and is superficially indistinguishable from water is not H_2O but has a different chemical composition, XYZ. Now, the widespread intuition is that when both Oscar and Toscar utter the words "Water is wet" they express different thoughts, for "water" in their mouths refers to different entities. While Oscar is expressing the thought that water is wet, Toscar expresses the thought that twater – translating his word "water" into Oscar's language – is wet. This difference, according to the externalist, reflects the difference in their environments.

But content externalism seems to undermine the intuitively plausible thesis of privileged access according to which we enjoy a direct and authoritative access to the contents of our mental states. For, if externalism is true, to know whether we are thinking about water or twater, we should investigate our environment to see if it contains H_2O or XYZ. This means that we do not have the kind of immediate and direct access to the contents of our thoughts that the thesis of privileged access claims we have. It might be protested, however, that in order for us to know something our evidence need not rule out *all* the alternatives to what is known but only those that are *relevant*, and, under ordinary circumstances, the twater hypothesis is not a relevant alternative. So the fact that we do not seem to be able to rule out the twater hypothesis does not undermine our claim to know that we are thinking about water.

Following Burge's lead, Paul Boghossian has suggested that it is easy to describe scenarios in which the twater hypothesis is a relevant alternative. Suppose, unbeknownst to Oscar, he is switched back and forth between Earth and Twin Earth, remaining on each planet long enough to acquire the concepts appropriate to the respective environments.[2]

Suppose, having returned from Twin Earth, Oscar is now on earth expressing the thought that water is wet. Does he know that he is thinking about water? Well, given his circumstances, one can attribute such knowledge to him if he is able to rule out the relevant hypothesis that he is thinking about twater. But this would require Oscar to investigate his environment first in order to find what he thinks, which is precisely what the thesis of privileged access denies. Externalism is thus incompatible with self-knowledge.

9.2   Some responses to the slow switching argument

There are currently, at least, two types of responses to the switching argument. I will not dwell very much on the first response (due to Warfield) as I do not think it addresses what is really at issue here (Warfield 1992). Warfield points out that all that the argument can be taken to show is that, given externalism, *if* the switching case is actual, then the subject does not know the contents of his thoughts by introspection. This shows, at most, the consistency of externalism and lack of self-knowledge; it does not show that externalism is incompatible with self-knowledge. In reply, Peter Ludlow has claimed that slow switching cases are not mere possibilities, but that, for the Burgian brand of social externalism, they are in fact quite common (Ludlow 1995; see also Butler 1997). Such cases happen, says Ludlow, when one unknowingly moves across language communities. Warfield, however, insists that even if we grant all the assumptions underlying Ludlow's claim, we have still not been given any reason to think that externalism *implies* a lack of self-knowledge.

But the question is not so much about whether an entailment relation holds between the theses of externalism and content skepticism as about whether the traditional doctrine of privileged access is flawed. Ordinarily, self-knowledge is understood as involving some sort of privileged access to the contents of one's thoughts in the sense that the justification of the resulting second-order beliefs obtains independently of experience. But the slow switching cases are precisely cases where the justification-conferring grounds (however construed) appear to involve experience. Under such circumstances we seem to have to investigate our environment first in order to know what the contents of our thoughts are. And this threatens the privileged status of self-knowledge, for it seems that it is, after all, vulnerable to empirical considerations. Warfield does not address the substantive questions associated with the incompatibility thesis and treats it in a purely formal manner. For example, he is willing to grant that in the switching cases the subject might fail to have introspective knowledge of his thought contents without launching an investigation into the grounds of such failure. But, as we shall see below, this is precisely what gets denied in the second response to the switching argument whose approach to the problem is substantive rather than formal.

The second response to the slow switching argument was initiated by Burge himself, and has since been emphasized by a number of other theorists who deny the incompatibility thesis (Burge 1988; Heil 1992, Ch. 6; Falvey and Owens 1994; Gibbons 1996). Let us call this, following Butler, "the standard strategy" (Butler 1997). The idea is that the contents of our second-order thoughts are determined by the contents of our first-order thoughts. And since, according to externalism, the latter are environmentally determined, our second-order thoughts turn out to be about the very same objects and stuff that our first-order thoughts are. In other words, our first-order and second-order thoughts involve the same concepts. This means that when, during the switching process, Oscar is transported to Twin Earth, his belief that he is thinking that the liquid falling from the sky is wet involves the very same (Twin Earthian) concepts that his first-order belief does. They both involve "twater," and, consequently, Oscar cannot be wrong about the contents of his first-order thoughts. Now, how does this bear on the slow switching argument? To get a better grip on the standard strategy, let us examine some of the attempts that have been made to spell out the connection.

Falvey and Owens, for example, believe that what underlies the slow switching argument is the following principle (Falvey and Owens 1994).

(RA′) If (i) q is a relevant alternative to p, and (ii) S's justification for his belief that p is such that, if q were true, then S would still believe that p, then S does not know that p.

Now consider again the case of Oscar who undergoes a series of switches and is now on Earth thinking that water is wet. Under such circumstances the hypothesis that he is thinking about twater is a relevant alternative. Does he then fail to know that he is thinking about water? No, because the antecedent (the appropriate instance) of (RA′) fails to be satisfied in this case. For if externalism is true, Oscar's environment determines the contents of his second-order thoughts just as it determines those of his first-order thoughts. If Oscar were on Twin Earth he could not believe that he was thinking that water is wet any more than he could think that water is wet. So, *contra* Boghossian, externalism is compatible with self-knowledge when "knowledge" is understood along the lines of the relevant alternatives theory. Before turning to what, I believe, cripples the standard strategy, it would be instructive to examine one detailed response to it by Anthony Brueckner (Brueckner 1994).

Brueckner does not directly address the question whether the standard strategy is able to neutralize the switching argument. Rather, he seeks to defend an argument of his (for content skepticism) against the claim (made by Falvey and Owens) that it too is undermined by the standard strategy. Brueckner's initial supposition was that an argument, analogous to that used by the Cartesian skeptic to undermine our claim to know the external world, can be set up to undermine our claim to know the contents of our thoughts. Suppose I claim to know that I am thinking that water is wet. Appealing to the principle of Closure, the content-skeptic would then say that if I know that I am thinking that water is wet, then I know that I am not thinking that twater is wet. But, he says, I do not know that I am not thinking that twater is wet. Therefore, I do not know that I am thinking that water is wet. But, as we saw, for reasons involving (RA'), it is not true that, under these circumstances, I do not know that I am not thinking that twater is wet, and, so Falvey and Owens conclude, Brueckner's argument fails to establish content-skepticism.

In response, Brueckner claims that by relying on (RA') we deprive the skeptic of appealing to Closure when trying to establish his skeptical claims, particularly, about the external world. To be more concrete, let us go through the example that Brueckner presents in support of this claim. Consider Fred Flintstone who, inhabiting a normal world, comes to believe that, for example, he is holding a rock. Does he know this proposition? Brueckner says yes, for such an attribution is quite compatible with all the constraints, including (RA'), that Falvey and Owens seem to impose on the concept of knowledge. The only way that (RA') might preclude knowledge in this case is if we take such alternatives as Fred's being a brain in a vat as relevant. But, "relative to Fred's humdrum's Bedrock context," says Brueckner, this alternative is not relevant. The alternatives that are relevant in this context include cases like Fred's holding his pet dinosaur. Now if Fred knows that he is holding a rock, he knows, by Closure, that he is not a brain in a vat. But, by (RA'), he does not know that he is not a brain in a vat, and so Fred constitutes a counterexample to Closure: "It is therefore uncharitable to interpret the Cartesian skeptic as employing (RA') in his reasoning, since this would rob him of the Closure principle on which that reasoning depends" (Brueckner 1994, pp. 332–3). By contrast, Brueckner offers the following "underdetermination principle" as what actually underpins the skeptic's argument to undermine our knowledge of our thoughts and of the external world.

(U) Suppose I am considering a hypothesis H and a competing incompatible skeptical hypothesis SK. If my evidence and reasons (and whatever other considerations are available) do not favor H over SK, then I do not have justification for rejecting SK; hence I do not know that not-SK.

There is no conflict, he says, between (U) and Closure. The content-skeptic can thus utilize (U) to argue that I do not know that I am not thinking that twater is wet and, relying on Closure, conclude that I do not know that I am thinking that water is wet.

Apart from the fact that Brueckner's remarks do not have a direct bearing on the question of the anti-skeptical potentials of the standard strategy, it is interesting to note that his own appeal to (U) puts him in a similar sort of dilemma vis-à-vis the principle of Closure. To see this let us consider how (U) itself handles the example of Fred. (U) describes a situation in which someone is considering a hypothesis H and a competing incompatible skeptical hypothesis SK, but is silent over the range of the skeptical hypotheses that can be considered alongside H (whether they are relevant alternatives to H or just any sort of competing hypotheses). In view of this ambiguity we need to consider two versions of the example: A case where Fred believes he is holding a rock in his hand, and a competing skeptical hypothesis SK (e.g., that he is a brain in a vat) is being considered, and a case where no such hypothesis is being entertained. In the latter case Fred can be said to know that he is holding a rock. But then, by Closure, he can also be said to know that he is not a brain in vat. But, as Brueckner admits, Fred does not know the proposition that he is not a brain in a vat. The reason being that, with respect to this latter proposition, he is placed in a context where a skeptical hypothesis (Fred is a brain in a vat) is also being considered, and so, by (U), Fred does not know that he is not a brain in a vat. Fred would thus constitute a counterexample to Closure.

What about the case where a skeptical hypothesis (SK) is being considered alongside the common sense hypothesis about the rock? Does Fred know that he is holding a rock? Well, by (U), he may be justified in believing that he is holding a rock (and equally justified in believing SK), but this would not be a case of knowledge. This is because anything that can be said about the common sense hypothesis (as far as Fred's epistemic perspective is concerned) can also be said about SK. In particular, SK is equally justified for Fred since, by hypothesis, Fred's evidence does not favor the common sense proposition over SK. Now since these two hypotheses are incompatible Fred cannot claim to know either on the basis of the evidence available to him. There would, thus, be no need to invoke the principle of Closure as (U) would directly deliver the skeptical conclusion. So Brueckner's reconstruction of the skeptical argument in terms of (U) forces him to face a dilemma in regard to Closure; the principle is either invalid or not needed. Let us now return to the standard strategy and see if it really succeeds in neutralizing the slow switching argument.[3]

9.3   The standard strategy: a critique

The main problem with the standard strategy is that although it makes the cognizer always *right* about what she thinks, it does not furnish us with enough grounds to attribute *knowledge* to her. To see what motivates this problem let us consider John Gibbon's construal of the standard strategy (Gibbons 1996). Like Falvey and Owens he thinks that the externalist thesis that the contents of our second-order thoughts are environmentally determined blocks the derivation of a skeptical conclusion about knowledge of content from the premises of the slow switching argument. To explain this he compares a knowledge-precluding relevant alternative situation with a knowledge-consistent relevant alternative situation. Suppose, for example, you are sitting by a lake and see a duck which you can easily identify as duck. Unbeknownst to you, however, there are a number of decoy ducks in your vicinity. Assuming a relevant alternatives account of knowledge, a knowledge-precluding situation is one where the following counterfactual is true.

(P)   If a decoy duck had been in front of you, you would have falsely believed that it was a duck.

Consider now a situation where decoy ducks are not particularly life-like. In that case (P) would be false and the following counterfactual (C) is true.

(C)   If a decoy duck had been in front of you, you would have correctly believed that it was a decoy duck.

This is a knowledge-consistent relevant alternative situation. Gibbons then asks whether the switching case is more like the knowledge-precluding situation or the knowledge-consistent one. The relevant counterfactuals are as follows.

(P') If Oscar had thought about twater, he would have falsely believed that he was thinking about water.

(C') If Oscar had thought about twater, he would have correctly believed that he was thinking about twater.

Now, given the externalist thesis according to which second-order thoughts inherit their contents from first-order thoughts, (P') is false and (C') is true: "This makes the switching case a knowledge-consistent situation" (Gibbons 1996, p. 298). But there is an important difference between the epistemic situations of the cognizers in the cases of (C) and (C') despite the counterfactuals sharing the same truth value. Under the circumstances associated with (C), ducks and decoy ducks are not evidentially identical for the cognizer. He can effectively discriminate between them and is aware of their differences. But this is not true of the cognizer's epistemic situation in the case of (C'). Oscar cannot, by hypothesis, discriminate between water and twater-thoughts. Phenomenologically they are indistinguishable. What this difference highlights is that (C), unlike (C'), describes the agent as having performed a cognitive task. By discriminating between ducks and decoy ducks the agent is aware of what grounds his belief that he is seeing a duck. By contrast, the cognitive task reported in (C') is performed automatically and unconsciously with Oscar exercising none of his discriminating abilities. Oscar may always get the contents of his thoughts right, but that does not seem to warrant attributing knowledge to him.

Oscar's epistemic situation is, in fact, more similar to that of the agent in the knowledge-precluding case (P) than in the knowledge-consistent case (C). They are both incapable of discriminating between the competing relevant alternatives. The fact that, unlike the agent in (P), Oscar always ends up with a true belief, in virtue of the holding of an entirely independent determination relationship between his thought contents and the environment, does nothing to enhance his status as an epistemic agent. I think this is what lies behind a question that Falvey and Owens raise but leave unanswered. Having argued for the compatibility of externalism and self-knowledge in accordance with the standard strategy, they ask, "How can it be that the subject is always right about contents of her beliefs, despite the fact that the introspective evidence in her possession underdetermines their contents?" (Falvey and Owens 1994, p. 118). The underdetermination of alternative hypotheses by evidence is, as was noted, precisely what distinguishes the circumstances depicted in (C) and (C'). In (C'), unlike (C), evidence underdetermines the alternative hypotheses.

There is, however, a sense of "know" in which Oscar can be described as knowing the contents of his thoughts in (C'), but it seems unlikely that it would be endorsed by the parties involved in the debate. This is the conception of knowledge that has been defended by William Alston among others. According to this account, knowledge is a "true belief that is formed and/or sustained under the effective control of the fact believed" (Alston 1989, p. 181). As long as a true belief satisfies this constraint, the believer has knowledge regardless of whether he is justified or not. Consider, for example, the case of an *idiot savant* who regularly comes up with correct answers to complex arithmetical questions that normally require calculation in writing. Suppose the person also believes these answers. There is a sense in which his ability to deliver correct answers is not accidental. According to Alston, he can be said to have knowledge despite lacking justification. (He might be described as having "natural knowledge" (see Audi 1988, Ch. 7).) This situation seems to be epistemically analogous to that depicted in (C') where the cognizer is always right about the content of his thoughts despite his total ignorance of what grounds it. But natural knowledge cannot be what the parties to the dispute have in mind when they speak about self-knowledge. Boghossian explicitly says that "by self-knowledge I shall mean not just a *true* belief about one's own thoughts, but a *justified* one" (Boghossian 1989, p. 6). And Falvey and Owens construe the principle (RA') in terms of justification. Proponents of the standard strategy, thus, still owe us an explanation of why Oscar's second-order beliefs count as knowledge.[4]

9.4 Examining the switching argument

By highlighting cases where we seem to have to investigate our environment in order to know what we think, the slow switching argument seeks to show that our purported privileged knowledge of our thoughts can be vulnerable to empirical contingencies. As Gibbons has pointed out what the slow switching argument aspires to show is that "[o]ne consequence of externalism is that our knowledge of our own thoughts is more susceptible to empirical contingencies than we may have believed" (Gibbons 1996, p. 294). From this it is concluded that we lack the sort of privileged access we are supposed to have to our thought contents. But the claim that our knowledge of our thoughts is susceptible to empirical contingencies is ambiguous depending on how "susceptibility to empirical contingencies" is to be understood. One can understand the claim as saying that self-knowledge is *positively* dependent on experience of the environment or that it is only *negatively* dependent on experience of the environment. However, as was emphasized above, in speaking about self-knowledge, the disputants do not mean a merely true belief about one's thoughts but a justified one. After all you can have an infallible belief but not be justified in holding it. So, in the end, it all comes down to the question whether the cognizer's belief is justified if it is to count as knowledge.

Moreover, the issue here is not whether one can know what thought one is having, if the thought is individuated by environmental factors. The issue is whether one can know in a *privileged* way if the thought is individuated by environmental factors.[5] And it is here that the negative/positive dependence distinction becomes prominent. Let us, then, say that a belief is positively dependent for its justification on experience of the environment if and only if that experience plays an appropriate role in producing or sustaining that justification. A belief's justification, on the other hand, is said to be negatively dependent on experience if and only if it is undermined by the empirical evidence the cognizer comes to possess.

We might, thus, construe the (alleged) susceptibility of self-knowledge to empirical contingencies as either saying that the resulting second-order beliefs are positively dependent on experience of their environment for their justification, or that their justification is only negatively so dependent (empirical incorrigibility, in other words). To evaluate the switching argument, we must, therefore, consider it in two cases commensurate with the interpretation of its moral, namely, the susceptibility claim. In what follows I will try to show that, however the claim is construed, the argument does not stand any chance of establishing its conclusion.[6]

Let us start with positive dependence. If our second-order beliefs are positively dependent on experience of the environment for their justification, then the incompatibility thesis would be immediately established. But does the switching argument prove the claim of positive dependence? Before answering this question, let us first be a bit more precise about what the thesis of privileged access involves. Normally, the thesis that we have privileged access to the contents of our thoughts is formulated in terms of the a priori, non-empirical character of the justification of the resulting second-order beliefs. Here is a typical statement of the thesis of privileged access (PA) (due to McLaughlin and Tye) according to which what is distinctive of self-knowledge is that the self-ascriptive beliefs involved are not justificatorily based on the empirical investigation of the environment.

(PA)   It is conceptually necessary that if we are able to exercise our actual normal capacity to have beliefs about our occurrent thoughts, then if we are able to occurrently think that p, we are able to know that we are thinking that p without our knowledge being justificatorily based on empirical investigation of our environment (McLaughlin and Tye 1998, p. 286; see also Heil 1992, p. 158; Alston 1971).

Now consider Oscar's story again. Suppose he is on Earth thinking and believing that water is wet (under normal conditions). His first-order belief is justified because the liquid that has filled his cup has all the superficial characteristics of water. Suppose further that he takes himself to be thinking that water is wet. Since the circumstances under which Oscar forms this second-order belief are normal, and there are no defeaters (indicating, e.g., that his cognitive powers are impaired) the belief that he is having a water-thought is justified. Moreover, since the belief is the result of a process of reflective thought, it is justified non-empirically. It, thus, seems plausible to say that he is directly and immediately justified in believing himself to have the thought in question as the warrant he possesses for his second-order belief does not involve any empirical information at all. No further question needs to be addressed for as Heil says, "[i]n the case of my belief about [say] Clara's thought, you might reasonably ask *why* I believe what I do. In the case of my self-assessment, such a request seems out of place" (Heil 1992, p. 158; see also Alston 1971). This shows that the justification of our second-order self-ascriptive beliefs is not positively dependent on experience of the environment, as empirical contingencies do not seem to be playing any role in producing or sustaining that justification.[7]

Let us now consider the susceptibility claim as construed in terms of negative dependence. Although Oscar's belief is not positively dependent on experience of the environment, it may nonetheless be negatively dependent on such an experience. And this possibility, the incompatibilist might say, is enough to undermine the (alleged) privileged character of self-knowledge by showing that knowledge of our thoughts is, after all, susceptible to empirical contingencies. One straightforward way of illustrating this possibility is by supposing Oscar coming to possess a misleading evidence for his belief that he is having a water-thought. Suppose some reputable philosophers of Oscar's acquaintance perversely persuade him that he is wrong in believing that he is having a water-thought. They base their claim on the electroencephlographic readings of his brain. Under these circumstances, Oscar's new evidence (involving the readings) will override his introspective evidence, defeating the initial justification of his second-order belief.[8] His justification is undercut by learning about the new evidence vindicating the incompatibilist's claim that our knowledge of our thoughts is vulnerable to empirical contingencies (in the negative sense). But does this undermine its privileged, a priori character? No, for Oscar's case is just an instance of a much larger question about whether a priori justification can be revisable. Two species of revisability should, however, be distinguished; revisability in the light of experiential evidence and revisability on the basis of non-experiential evidence. The latter kind of revisability seems compatible with a priori justification for, intuitively speaking, a belief is said to be justified a priori if experiential evidence plays no role either in the original justification or in its subsequent revision. It is, thus, revision on the basis of experiential considerations that seems to be incompatible with a priori justification.

But even that has been challenged by the proponents of a priori justification (who call their position "modest a priorism"). According to modest a priorists, a priori justification is compatible with infallibility and revisability. To explain this, they distinguish between positive and negative dependence on experience (in the way already described) (Edidin 1984; Summerfield 1991; Vahid 1999). What modest a priorists, thus, maintain is that a priori justification only requires that a belief be positively dependent on no experience and empirical beliefs. It may, nonetheless, be negatively dependent on experiences and empirical beliefs in the sense that their occurrence could undermine its justification in counterfactual circumstances. Given the fact that neither kind of dependence entails the other, modest a priorists are able to claim that the vulnerability of a priori beliefs to empirical defeaters (i.e., their negative dependence on experience) need not upset their a priori status.

To conclude, it seems by claiming to have shown that our access to our thoughts are susceptible to empirical contingencies, the defenders of the slow switching argument have confused between positive and negative dependence on experience of the environment. Our privileged knowledge of our thoughts only requires that our second-order beliefs be positively dependent for their justification on no experience or empirical contingency. As we saw, however, it is very implausible to claim that such beliefs positively depend on experience of the environment for their justification. And as far as the negative dependence claim is concerned, we can say (with modest a priorists) that this need not upset the privileged status of self-knowledge.

9.5   Externalism and privileged self-knowledge: a diagnosis

The switching argument was intended to illustrate how externalism can undermine the privileged status of self-knowledge. But as the preceding remarks show, the argument fails to deliver the goods. What can be said as a diagnosis of the failure of the switching argument? It seems to me what actually underlies its shortcoming is its failure to properly depict the problem situation. And the reason for the latter failing is that it makes the problem too dependent on the particular theory of knowledge (relevant alternatives) in terms of which it is formulated. This makes judgments about the epistemic achievements of Oscar vary greatly depending on which version of this theory or other theories of knowledge are invoked in assessing those achievements. To see this, consider how the adoption of a slightly different variant of the relevant alternatives theory might result in a different conclusion.

The relevant alternatives theory of knowledge was initially proposed by Dretske and Goldman. Goldman's account was developed, however, within a reliability theory based on the notion of discrimination (Goldman 1976). The idea is that, according to one sense of "know," knowing something involves discriminating or distinguishing it from relevant alternatives. More formally the theory says that "a true belief (p) fails to be knowledge if there are any relevant alternative situations in which the proposition p would be false, but the process used would cause S to believe p anyway" (Goldman 1986, p. 46). If this happens to be the case, then the utilized process fails to discriminate the truth of p from those alternatives, and the subject would fail to know p. Falvey and Owens's principle (RA′) was meant to capture the idea expressed in the above definition.

What is important to note, however, is that, for Goldman, the alternatives are *counterfactual* alternatives. For there is another version of the discrimination account of knowledge where this feature is missing (McGinn 1984). McGinn, too, states that knowledge involves the exercise of a capacity to discriminate truth from falsehood within some relevant class of propositions. A discriminative capacity is "a capacity to *tell the difference* between true propositions and false ones within some given class of propositions" (McGinn 1984, p. 536). But he explicitly refrains from using counterfactuals in the manner of Goldman. For him if the cognizer is unable to discriminate the truth with respect to a range of distinct relevant propositions, his true belief fails to be knowledge. McGinn's dismissal of counterfactual conditionals is partly rooted in his belief that it is the categorical facts about a believer that ground certain counterfactuals about him. Counterfactuals are true in virtue of categorical propositions. They should not be employed in a primitive way. It is because a cognizer possesses certain capacities that he would behave thus and so under the relevant circumstances.

On McGinn's version of the discrimination approach, knowledge requires global reliability with respect to a range of propositions. To say that a cognizer is globally reliable is just to say that he can discriminate truth from falsehood within a certain range of propositions. It is to impute to him a capacity to tell the difference between true and false propositions within some given class. According to McGinn, nothing in the discrimination approach requires us to consider only counterfactual situations, that is, what would the cognizer's belief be if the associated propositions were true or false. What is required for knowledge is the possession of a propensity by the cognizer to form true beliefs across a range of propositions whose truth values are taken as fixed in the actual world. To give an example, suppose you visit a country whose inhabitants have the custom of simulating being in pain, but you do not know this, and, consequently, form many false beliefs. One person (N), however, is an exception, and, being constantly in pain, shows it in her behavior. You thus come to believe that N is in pain. Your true belief, however, is not knowledge because, in these circumstances, you cannot *tell* a real pain feeler from a simulator.

Regardless of the details of McGinn's reasons for his version of the relevant alternative approach, what is important for our purpose is that his theory delivers a different verdict in regard to Oscar's epistemic achievement in the slow switching scenario.[9] Suppose, after returning from Twin earth, Oscar is now on Earth thinking that water is wet. On McGinn's account, if Oscar is to know the content of this thought, he must be able to tell the difference between his water-thought and, its relevant alternative, his twater-thought. But he lacks this discriminative capacity. For to be able to tell the difference between the two thoughts, he must have the concept of twater and, by hypothesis, Oscar cannot think in terms of concepts that are not hooked up to his environment (on Earth). Since Oscar cannot discriminate between the propositions that he is thinking that water is wet and its relevant alternative (that he is thinking that twater is wet), he does not know that he is thinking that water is wet. The externalist idea (behind the standard strategy) according to which second-order thoughts inherit their contents from first-order thoughts is of no help to Oscar when his epistemic status is judged in accordance with McGinn's version of the relevant alternatives approach which involve no counterfactuals.

McGinn's version of the relevant alternatives theory also undermines another step in the argument that Falvey and Owens offer for the compatibility of self-knowledge and externalism (Falvey and Owens 1994). They distinguish between two versions of the idea that we enjoy a direct and authoritative access to the content of thoughts. There is, on the one hand, the familiar idea of introspective knowledge of content according to which each individual knows the contents of his thoughts directly and authoritatively. There is, on the other hand, the idea (that they call "knowledge of comparative content") which says that with regard to any two thoughts or beliefs one can know whether their contents are the same or different. They admit that externalism is incompatible with introspective knowledge of comparative content, but point out that this does not raise any problem for externalism since there are strong reasons, independently of externalism, that the thesis of introspective knowledge of comparative content is false anyway. They then go on to claim that many of the current attempts at proving the incompatibility thesis suffer from failure to recognize this distinction.

But this is an unwarranted generalization, for the ability to distinguish between the two versions of the idea of knowledge of content depends very much on the type of the theory of knowledge that is in force. Falvey and Owens do not spell out how their adopted theory of knowledge sustains such a distinction, but there may be theories which leave no room for such a distinction. Indeed, McGinn's version of the relevant alternatives approach is one such theory. As we saw McGinn requires the knower to have a discriminative capacity to tell true from false within some relevant (non-counterfactual) class of propositions. This makes the capacity to attain knowledge of comparative content a prerequisite for attaining knowledge of content. Thus, contrary to what Falvey and Owens claim, the rejection of the distinction between these two versions of knowledge of content can be quite legitimate if, as is the case here, there is an account of knowledge that sustains that rejection.

What the preceding remarks bring out is that by relying on a particular theory of knowledge, both the switching argument and the standard strategy fail to address the source of the tension that allegedly exits between the theses of privileged self-knowledge and externalism. They

make the fate of the incompatibility thesis too dependent on a particular theory of knowledge, leaving room for other theories to deliver
different verdicts about the thesis. This would make the problem look
more like a challenge to show whether the subject of the switching scenario has knowledge, prompting theorists to examine various accounts
of knowledge to see which one fits the bill. But the problem is really
independent of any particular theory. In this respect it resembles a more
famous dilemma in philosophy namely, Benacerraf's claim that there is
a tension between our best semantic theory (due to Tarski) and our best
theory of knowledge (the causal theory) in the case of mathematical
statements (Benacerraf 1973). The tension arises because the standard
semantic theory seems to commit us to the existence of mathematical
entities which are traditionally thought of as being abstract. But this
makes mathematical knowledge impossible since we cannot enter into
causal interaction with abstract entities.

Although Benacerraf formulates the problem in terms of the causal
theory of knowledge, this theory has long since fallen into disrepute.
But there is an almost general consensus that, although Benacerraf
was wrong to tie his argument to the causal theory of knowledge, the
Benacerraf-style challenge against Platonism is really independent of
any particular theory of knowledge. The problem, in other words, is
not resolved by attacking the causal theory of knowledge or suggesting
a different account in its place. For it still leaves us with a how-question:
"[H]ow our beliefs about these remote entities can so well reflect the
facts about them" (Field 1989, p. 26). It is this striking correlation
between mathematicians' belief states and the postulated mathematical facts that requires an explanation. So the challenge is not simply
about finding some way of justifying mathematical beliefs involving
abstract objects. Even if it turns out that none of the existing theories of
knowledge work, there will still remain the problem of explaining the
mathematicians' reliability about their field of expertise. One can also
describe the challenge, equally effectively, in terms of an unacceptable
situation (for the Platonist) in which a false consequence seems to follow from two plausible theses. From the two seemingly plausible claims
that (1) we have mathematical knowledge, and (2) human beings exist
entirely within spacetime, it follows that (3) mathematical entities have
spatio-temporal locations. The Platonist is required to explain what has
gone wrong.

The same, I believe, is true about the question of the compatibility
of the theses of privileged self-knowledge and externalism. Again, the
problem is really independent of any particular theory of knowledge.

Even if a compatibilist can argue for his position by invoking the distinction between positive versus negative dependence on experience, the tension still remains unresolved. For, just as with Benacerraf's dilemma, the problem would not go away by appealing to a theory of knowledge (justification) that might restore consistency to an apparently inconsistent set of premises. The problem is, rather, that the compatibilist owes us an answer to a certain how-question: How is it that our knowledge of what we are thinking is merely negatively dependent on experience and not positively dependent on experience, given that the type of thought in question may be individuated by environmental factors? We need, in other words, an explanation of how it is that I know what I am thinking otherwise than on the basis of empirical evidence, given that what I am thinking depends on environmental factors.

So the problem is to explain how privileged knowledge of content is possible if our concepts are environmentally determined (just as Benacerraf's problem was to explain how mathematical knowledge is possible if mathematical entities are abstract). The problem can also be described in terms of an unacceptable situation (for the externalist) in which a false consequence seems to follow from two plausible theses. From the claims that (1) we have privileged (a priori) knowledge of the contents of our thoughts, and (2) our thoughts are environmentally determined, it follows that (3) we can know a priori certain substantial facts about our environment. The externalist is required to explain what has gone wrong.[10] It is this explanatory requirement rather than the theory-of-knowledge oriented scenario of the switching argument that underlies the incompatibility thesis.

Notes

1 Truth and the aim of belief

1. Perhaps what Wedgwood has in mind is that, since decisions or choices can be correct but not true, "true" and "correct" are not identical. But one should, in general, be suspicious of arguments that rely exclusively on linguistic intuitions to derive metaphysical conclusions. This is rather like rejecting the identity theory in the philosophy of mind solely on the ground that, say, while we can ascribe truth to a particular thought, we do not normally, on pain of violating our linguistic intuitions, say of a particular neural firing (deemed as being identical with that thought by the identity theorist) that it is true.
2. This is not of course to say that the norm of correctness is either trivial or circular. In fact, as mentioned earlier, the normativity of content is something that is supposed to be explained by the aim-of-belief thesis. My claim is only that Wedgwood's arguments fail to show this.
3. Another example of Bratman's involves the attitude of someone driving down a narrow, winding mountain road. He says that, while it is wise to assume that a car is coming up on the opposite side, the driver may actually not believe it. But surely it is more plausible to say that the driver *assumes*, rather than accepts, the proposition that a car is coming up.
4. Note that I am not arguing that acceptance-in-a-context is never a different attitude from belief. I take no position on the general question whether acceptance can be a different attitude from belief. My only concern here is with the viability of Velleman's analysis of "belief" where he appeals to Bratman to claim that acceptance is a non-doxastic attitude different from belief which is why I seek to find out whether Bratman's arguments deliver the goods.
5. It is a matter of controversy though whether the epistemic goal should be interpreted diachronically or synchronically. But I need not decide this question here (for an overview, see David 2001).
6. This is not, however, a universal position. As we shall see, Velleman, for one, claims that a cognitive module can "[regulate] the cognitions for truth ... [regardless of whether the agent] is oblivious to it, or he disapproves of it" (Velleman 2000, p. 253).
7. Nowhere in his article does Wedgwood give any specific account of the norm of rationality beyond saying that "only beliefs that have property R are rational." It is, thus, quite mystifying how the norm of correctness is intended to explain the norm of rational belief whose content is left unspecified.

2 Belief, interpretation and Moore's paradox

1. So, according to Wittgenstein, these are in fact the same assertions. However, since I think the approaches discussed in this chapter all share a common

ground, I shall, for reasons that will become clear later, focus on the principle that to assert P is to assert IBP (see also Heal 1994).

2. In the other case, if I assert that <p & IB~p>, then since assertion distributes over conjunction, I assert that IB~p and so by Wittgenstein's thesis, I assert that ~p. But since assertion distributes over conjunction I also assert that ~IBp.

3. It might be worth noting that this claim holds for <p & ~IBp> but not for <p & IB~p>. If I believe that <p & ~IBp>, then assuming that belief distributes over conjunction, IBp, so the content of my original conjunctive belief is false, because its second conjunct is false. By contrast, if I believe that <p & IB~p>, then assuming that belief distributes over conjunction, again IBp. But the content of my original conjunctive belief is still true, provided I hold a pair of contradictory beliefs, that is IBp & IB~p (see Williams 1994).

4. "xBx*Bp" is to be read as "x believes of x himself, that he (self-consciously) believes that p" (see Casteñeda 1963).

5. This is how the derivation goes.

$$\text{HOT) } xB^c p \to (xBp \ \& \ xBxBp)$$

$$B^c \text{Dist } xB^c(p \ \& \ q) \to (xB^c p \ \& \ xB^c q)$$

1. IB^c<p &~IBp>	Assumption
2. $IB^c p$ & IB^c~IBp	1, B^cDist
3. $IB^c p$	2, &-elimination
4. IBp & IBIBp	3, HOT
5. IBIBp	4, &-elimination
6. IB^c~IBp	2, &-elimination
7. IBIBp & IB^c~IBp	5, 6, &-introduction

We get a different result for <P & IB~P>.

6. This is how the derivation goes.

B^{con}) If x considers whether she believes that (p & q) then she considers whether she believes that p, and she considers whether she believes that q

$$xB^{con}(p \ \& \ q) \to (xB^{con} p \ \& \ xB^{con} q)$$

Bdis) If x believes that (p & q) then x believes that p, and x believes that q

$$xB(p \ \& \ q) \to (xBp \ \& \ xBq)$$

SI) If x believes that p, then if x considers whether she believes that p then x believes that she believes that p

$$xBp \to (xB^{con} p \to xBxBp)$$

1. IB(p & ~Bp) & IB^{con}(p & ~Bp)	Suppose
2. IB(p & ~Bp)	1, &-elimination
3. IB^{con}(p & ~Bp)	1, &-elimination

4. IBp & IB~Bp   2, Bdis
5. IBp   4, &-elimination
6. IB^{con}p   3, B^{con}
7. IB^{con}p → IBIBp   5, SI, MP
8. IBIBp   6, 7, MP
9. IB~Bp   4, &-elimination
10. IBIBp & IB~IBp 8, 9, &-introduction

7. For the other type of Moorean sentences, suppose I am justified in believing "P & IB~P". Then I am justified in believing P. By an analogue of (EA), JBP → JB~B~P. It follows that I have the same justification for both BB~P and B~B~P which is logically impossible.
8. Consider a non-conjunctive Moorean sentence like "I have no beliefs." When a speaker utters this sentence, our default position is to interpret is as meaning that "I have no beliefs", and, invoking charity, infer that the speaker *believes* that she has *no beliefs*. But to be a speaker is to exhibit a large degree of rationality which, in turn, requires the consistency of attitudes as well as their rational integration.

3   Belief, sensitivity and safety

1. It is true that we are often inclined to attribute knowledge even to animals. But it is the propositional sense of knowledge that we are concerned with here. The "animal" sense of knowledge is best construed as a discriminative capacity that need not require even belief as a constitutive element (see McGinn 1984).
2. Safety$_d$ is not the same as sensitivity. Both Sosa and Williamson deny that subjunctive conditionals contrapose.
3. Note that our account does not have the false consequence that belief q, "I am not a BIV" is sensitive. For although q follows from, say, p, "I have two hands," ~q does not follow from ~p; just as ~s, "These animals are disguised mules," does not follow from ~r, "These animals are not zebras," despite r entailing s.

4   Basic beliefs and the problem of non-doxastic justification

1. Here, I shall ignore the controversial issue of the psychological reality of such beliefs.
2. Heck's invoking of appearance judgments also renders his account susceptible to the objection I raised earlier against McDowell's account, for now such judgments might be thought to be better placed to play the role of justifiers.
3. There also seems to be a further disanalogy between perceptual skills and such purportedly rule-governed practices like playing the piano or the game of chess. Unlike the latter activities, forming a perceptual belief (on the basis of experience) is not something one does. Belief formation is not under one's control. I will come back to this point at the end of the chapter.

5 Experience as reason for beliefs

1. It is interesting that when introducing the three constitutive features of supervenience, namely, covariance, dependence and non-reducibility, Kim, too, takes Hare's remarks as only establishing the covariance of moral and natural properties: "The basic idea of supervenience we find in Sidgewick, Moore, and Hare, therefore, has to do with property covariation" (Kim 1990, p. 137).

2. Not all coherentists agree that "coherence" is a non-epistemic property. Lehrer, for example, has claimed that, at least in his version of coherentism, an adequate account of coherence must involve epistemic notions. He, thus, rejects the supervenience thesis (Lehrer 1995).

3. Here I am not making the strong claim that no theory of justification could ever work. I am only saying that arguments for the supervenience thesis from particular theories of justification stand or fall with those theories themselves, even though, judging by the history of the subject, I am not sanguine about a successful outcome.

4. Note that even if N_1 is taken to be logically supervenient on N_2, it would still imply the weaker claim that it is also naturally supervenient on N_2.

5. FRS, especially its two-factor version, is explanatorily quite rich. It can explain some of the most intractable problems involving meaning, for example, the Frege puzzle, Twin-earth cases and so on. While it has a hard time to explain phenomena such as compositionality or intersubjective synonymity (Fodor and LePore 1991), it is fair to say that some of the criticisms of FRS almost entirely rest on certain dogmas of recent philosophy such as Quine's repudiation of the analytic/synthetic distinction. (For a perceptive assessment of the Quinean case, see Sober 2000). In any event, all the current theories of content have their own problems and FRS is no exception. But one has to start from somewhere.

6. It is worth noting that the objection, if genuine, afflicts almost all the existing theories of content such as the information-theoretic account and the like. This has prompted the proponents of these theories to wonder if the problem of normativity presents anything over and above the problems that naturalistic accounts of content usually have to grapple with. Thus Fodor has claimed that the problem of normativity is nothing other than the problem of misrepresentation. Once naturalized theories of semantics have done their job, he says, no further question about why it is correct to apply a term to a certain set of objects is left to answer.

6 The problem of the basing relation

1. The counterfactual theory was specifically designed to take care of the so-called gypsy-lawyer-style counter-examples (due to Lehrer 1971; 1990). It should be said that not all philosophers find such examples convincing (see, e.g., Goldman 1979; Audi 1986).

2. See, for example, Burge (1986) who argues that the content of a perceptual belief is the usual or normal cause of that belief.

3. Note that Alston's account is not functional in our sense. He uses the term "function" in a mathematical sense.

4. I am using "reasons" here meaning "adequate reasons."
5. Sometimes Davidson's requirements are stronger demanding an interactive triangle. We do not need to go as far that stage here. For problems with Davidson's stronger versions of the triangulations thesis, see Pagin 2001.

7 Basic beliefs, easy knowledge and the problem of warrant transfer

1. In place of Wright's notion of positive entitlement, Davies (2004) proposes "negative entitlement" which merely amounts to not doubting the relevant background assumptions. But this does not seem to express more than the thought that in failing to uphold these assumptions, the agent has behaved reasonably and not contravened any epistemic obligations.
2. See Cohen (2002) for an early discussion and rejection of contextualism as a response to the problem of easy knowledge.
3. Wright emphasizes the internalist character of his position in (Wright 2004, p. 209).
4. Following Klein (1995), some philosophers, Silins (2005), have suggested that one's justification for believing a conclusion can be one's premise for the conclusion, rather than one's justification for the premise. See Brueckner (2000) for criticism.
5. Note these remarks do no apply to cases like **Zebra**. The main difference is that believing Zebra-II does not require believing Zebra-III. The two are not epistemically close which is why the question of whether one's evidence justifies Zebra-III, given that it justifies Zebra-II, is wide open.
6. This is not true of, say, Zebra-II and Zebra-III. There is nothing Moore-paradoxical about asserting "That animal is a Zebra but I have no reason to believe that it is not a cleverly disguised mule."

8 Belief, justification and fallibility

1. Is it really correct to describe Seth's mathematical belief under counterfactual circumstances as being *accidentally* true? It hardly makes sense to say of a necessarily true belief that it is accidentally true. What we should have said is that, in the counterfactual circumstances, Seth *arrives* at his true belief by accident – which is why if he had been unlucky he would have arrived at a *different* belief. Here there is an asymmetry with cases involving contingent beliefs. If, for example, in the barn scenario, our agent had been unlucky looking in the direction of a fake barn, he would have still ended up forming the same belief that he is seeing a barn.
2. Carrier (1993) also presents a similar definition of fallible knowledge though he does not provide the rationale behind it apart from its ability in accommodating knowledge of necessary truths. His real target in that article is skepticism and the principle of closure. Lehrer's and Kim's definition of "fallibility," on the other hand, is couched in terms of justification along the lines expressed in (II), although this is given an internalist bent in what, they call, the "fallibility principle" (Lehrer and Kim 1990). But their account does not

at all resemble what is proposed here. Their fallibility principle is merely an extension of the standard (generic) account of fallible justification to the case where justification is understood along the internalist lines.

3. A promising line of argument, I believe, can be set out along the following lines. If a cognizer is to be justified (in an internalist sense) in holding a belief B, she must know (by reflection alone) whether the ground of that belief (assuming it to be another belief) obtains. But if, as content externalism seems to imply, knowing the content of a belief requires empirical investigation, then it means that the justifiers of the cognizer's belief B are not internally (i.e., reflectively) available to her. So she will not be able to know (by reflection alone) whether the grounds of B obtain. Accordingly, content externalism (internalism) and justification internalism (externalism) are incompatible. The controversial premise in the above argument is, of course, the claim that justification internalism is incompatible with the time-honored thesis of privileged self-knowledge according to which we are able to know, without the benefit of empirical investigation, what the contents of our thoughts are in our own case (see Vahid 2003, for further elaboration).

9   Knowledge of our beliefs and privileged access

1. These two arguments are connected to one another in an interesting way other than the trivial reason that they both seek to establish the incompatibility thesis. See Section 9.5.

2. What is the status of Oscar's concepts in the interim, between the time he arrives on the planet and the time his concepts change? This is a general problem and I will not address it in this chapter. I just make two points. First, the points I make in this chapter should hold whatever account of this matter proves correct (so long as it is an external account). Secondly, as Ludlow has pointed out slow switching is altogether commonplace (Ludlow 1995). If content is socially determined and language groups are localized then there are many real world slow switching cases where individuals move across linguistic communities. Moreover, it is very common in the literature to suppose that, after a while, the concepts shift and that the only controversy is whether you end up with both sets or just with the new one. Burge now says that he always meant that you would end up with both sets, although it is nearer to the mark to say that it is not the way he thought of it in the original article.

3. (U) does not presuppose Closure, and so if the problem can be generated by principle (U), then one does not need to appeal to Closure to generate the problem. In fact, as we shall see later, I do not think that one needs to appeal to Closure to generate the skeptical problem.

4. What I tried to show in this section was that the standard strategy fails to refute the incompatibility thesis. This is not to defend the switching argument, but only to argue that the standard strategy fails to block it. The idea is simple enough. Knowledge involves justification, and one can have an infallible belief but not be justified in holding it (because it is obtained, say, in

an epistemically inappropriate way). (Note that the relevant alternatives theory is a theory of knowledge not justification. The inability to discriminate between relevant alternatives only undermines one's claim to knowledge. This is true, for example, of Goldman's discrimination account of knowledge which he then appends it with a justification clause, see Goldman 1986.) The switching argument will be criticized, however, in the next section on the ground that its moral can be acceptable, on a certain interpretation to a compatibilist.

5. So the problem is not really a Gettier problem, namely, whether a true justified belief counts as knowledge. The question is, rather, if we can know *a priori* what thoughts we are having. A priori knowledge, however, is characterized as knowledge whose justification-conferring grounds are obtained independently of experience. So what ultimately decided whether one's knowledge of one's thoughts is obtained in a privileged way is how the belief in question attains its justificatory status. This is where the question of positive versus negative dependence on experience of the justification-conferring grounds becomes important.

6. Note that what I am doing in this section is to argue that if, as the proponents of the switching argument claim, the moral of the argument is to show that "our knowledge of our own thoughts is more susceptible to empirical contingencies than we may have believed," then this is not sufficient to establish the incompatibility thesis. My claim here is that a compatibilist can, in principle, accept the moral of the switching argument but understand it as saying that introspective knowledge is only negatively dependent on the experience of the environment.

7. Note that the justification is question is only prima facie justification. One is prima facie justified in believing a proposition provided there are no sufficient defeaters for that belief. Suppose, looking an object in front of me. I take myself to be seeing a book. Here, I am prima facie justified in believing that there is a book before me. This justification can, however, be defeated by the larger epistemic context within which I am situated. So being based on adequate grounds (in the absence of defeaters) – as is the case here – is sufficient for prima facie justification.

8. Here I am alluding to the so-called EEG argument. Some philosophers seeking to cast doubt on the infallibility of introspective knowledge of our sensations have suggested the following argument (see, e.g., Armstrong 1963). It is possible, they say, that neurophysiology will advance to such a stage that EEG readings will provide an alternative and reliable source of evidence for our sensations and thoughts overriding introspective evidence in certain circumstances. I do not need to decide on the validity of this argument here. In fact, for my purpose of suggesting an example of a misleading evidence, I am assuming it to be invalid. Other examples of misleading evidence can be provided.

9. I am not therefore endorsing McGinn's account of knowledge. In fact, McGinn's dismissal of counterfactuals is problematic as he fails to specify exactly what the range of the relevance class must be. My aim is merely to highlight the fact that the switching argument makes its validity too dependent on the choice of its adopted theory of knowledge.

10. This comes very close to the second line of argument (due to McKinsey 1991), mentioned earlier in the chapter, for the incompatibility thesis. McKinsey-type arguments often proceed as follows.

(1) One knows a priori that one is thinking that, say, water is wet.

(2) If the concept of X is an atomic, natural kind concept, then it is metaphysically impossible to possess it unless one has causally interacted with instances of X.

Therefore,

(3) It is a priori knowable by one that one has causally interacted with instances of water.

((2) is a strong version of externalism due to McGinn 1989.)

References

Alston, W. 1971, "Varieties of Privileged Access," repr. in Alston 1989, *Epistemic Justification*, Ithaca, NY: Cornell University Press, pp. 249–85.

———. 1976, "Two Types of Foundationalism," repr. in Alston 1989, *Epistemic Justification*, Ithaca, NY: Cornell University Press, pp. 19–39.

———. 1988, "The Deontological Conception of Epistemic Justification," repr. in Alston 1989, *Epistemic Justification*, Ithaca, NY: Cornell University Press, pp. 115–53.

———. 1989, *Epistemic Justification*, Ithaca, NY: Cornell University Press.

———. 1995, "How to Think about Reliability," repr. in Sosa & Kim (eds), 2000, *Epistemology: An Anthology*, Malden, MA: Blackwell Publishers.

———. 2005, *Beyond "Justification": Dimensions of Epistemic Evaluation*, Ithaca, NY: Cornell University Press.

Armstrong, D. 1963, "Is Introspective Knowledge Incorrigible?" *Philosophical Review*, 77: 417–32.

Audi, R. 1988, *Belief, Justification and Knowledge*, Belmont, CA: Wadsworth Publishing Company.

———. 1986, "Belief, Reason and Inference," repr. in Audi, *The Structure of Justification*, Cambridge: Cambridge University Press.

———. 1993, *The Structure of Justification*, Cambridge: Cambridge University Press.

Ayer, A. J. 1956, *The Problem of Knowledge*, London: Macmillan.

Baldwin, T. 1990, *G. E. Moore*, London and New York: Routledge.

Benacerraf, P. 1973, "Mathematical Truth," *Journal of Philosophy*, 19: 661–79.

Bergmann, M. 2004, "Epistemic Circularity: Malignant and Benign," *Philosophy and Phenomenological Research*, 69: 709–27.

Block, N. 1986, "Advertisement for a Semantic for Psychology," *Midwest Studies in Philosophy X*, University of Minnesota Press.

Boghossian, P. 1989, "Content and Self-knowledge," *Philosophical Topics*, 27: 5–26.

BonJour, L. 1985, *The Structure of Empirical Knowledge*, Cambridge, MA: Harvard University Press.

———. 1998, *In Defense of Pure Reason*, Cambridge: Cambridge University press.

Bratman, M. 1999, "Practical Reasoning and Acceptance in a Context," in Bratman 1999, *Faces of Intention*, Cambridge: Cambridge University Press.

Brewer, B. 1999, *Perception and Reason*, Oxford: Oxford University Press.

———. 2001, "Replies," *Philosophy and Phenomenological Research*, LXIII (2): 449–64.

Brueckner, A. 1994, "Knowledge of Content and Knowledge of the World," *The Philosophical Review*, 103: 327–43.

———. 2000, "Klein on Closure and Skepticism," *Philosophical Studies*, 98: 139–51.

———. 2006, "Justification and Moore's Paradox," *Analysis*, 66 (3): 264–6.

Brueckner, A. and Oreste Fiocco, M. 2002, "Williamson's Anti-luminosity Argument," *Philosophical Studies*, 110: 285–93.

Burge, T. 1986, "Cartesian Error and the Objectivity of Perception," in Pettit and McDowell (eds), *Subject, Thought and Context*, Oxford: Oxford University Press.
——. 1988, "Individualism and Self-knowledge," *Journal of Philosophy*, 85 (11): 649–63.
——. 2003, "Perceptual Entitlement," *Philosophy and Phenomenological Research*, 67: 503–48.
Butler, K. 1997, "Externalism, Internalism, and Knowledge of Content," *Philosophy and Phenomenological Research*, LVII (4): 773–800.
Carrier, Leonard S. 1993, "How to Define Nonskeptical Fallibilism," *Philosophia*, 22: 361–72.
Casteñeda, H. 1963, " 'He': A Study in the Logic of Self-Consciousness," *Ratio*, 8: 130–57.
Chisholm, R. 1987, *Theory of Knowledge*, 2nd edn, New Jercy: Prentice Hall.
Cohen, S. 1988, "How to Be a Fallibilist," in Tomberlin (ed.), *Philosophical Perspectives*, vol. 2, Atascadero, CA: Ridgeview, pp. 91–123.
——. 1998, "Two Kinds of Skeptical Arguments," *Philosophy and Phenomenological Research*, LVIII: 143–59.
——. 2002, "Basic Knowledge and the Problem of Easy Knowledge," *Philosophy and Phenomenological Research*, 65: 309–29.
——. 2004, "Structure and Connection: Comments on Sosa's Epistemology" in Greco (ed.), *Sosa and His Critics*, Oxford: Blackwell Publishing.
——. 2005, "Why Basic Knowledge is Easy Knowledge," *Philosophy and Phenomenological Research*, 70: 309–29.
David, M. 2001, "Truth as the Epistemic Goal," in Steup (ed.) *Knowledge, Truth and Duty*, Oxford: Oxford University Press, pp. 151–70.
Davidson, D. 1963, "Actions, Reasons, and Causes," repr. in Davidson 1980, *Essays on Actions and Events*, Oxford: Oxford University Press.
——. 1976, "Reply to Foster," repr. in Davidson 1985, *Inquires into Truth and Interpretation*, Oxford: Clarendon Press.
——. 1984, *Inquires into Truth and Interpretation*, Oxford: Clarendon Press.
——. 1986, "A Coherence Theory of Truth and Knowledge," in LePore (ed.), *Truth and Interpretation*, Oxford: Basil Blackwell.
——. 2001, *Subjective, Intersubjective, Objective*, Oxford: Oxford University Press.
Davies, M. 2004, "Epistemic Entitlement, Warrant Transmission and Easy Knowledge," *Aristotelian Society Supplementary*, 78: 213–45.
de Almedia, C. 2001, "What Moore's Paradox is About," *Philosophy and Phenomenological Research*, 62: 33–58.
DeRose, K. 1995, "Solving the Skeptical Problem," repr. in DeRose and Warfield (eds), 1999, *Skepticism*, New York: Oxford University Press.
Dretske, F. 1971, "Conclusive Reasons," *Australasian Journal of Philosophy*, 49: 1–22.
Edidin, A. 1984, "A Priori Knowledge for Fallibilists," *Philosophical Studies* 46: 189–97.
Evans, G. 1982, *The Varieties of Reference*, New York: Oxford University Press.
Falvey, K. and Owens, J. 1994, "Externalism, Self-knowledge, and Skepticism," *The Philosophical Review*, 105: 327–43.
Feldman, R. 1985, "Reliability and Justification," *The Monist*, 68: 159–74.
Field, H. 1977, "Logic, Meaning and Conceptual Role," *Journal of Philosophy*, 74: 379–409.
——. 1989, *Realism, Mathematics and Modality*, Oxford: Basil Blackwell.

Fodor, J and LePore, E. 1991, "Why Meaning (Probably) Isn't Conceptual Role," *Mind and Language*, 6 (4): 328–43.

Fogelin, R. 1994, *Pyrrhonian Reflections on Knowledge and Justification*, Oxford: Oxford University Press.

Foley, R. 1987, *The theory of Epistemic Rationality*, Cambridge, MA: Harvard University Press.

Fumerton, R. 1995, *Metaepistemology and Skepticism*, Lanham, MD: Rowman and Littlefield.

Gibbard, A. 1994, "Meaning and Normativity," in Villanueva (ed.), *Philosophical Issues*, vol. 5, Ridgeview.

Gibbons, J. 1996, "Externalism and Knowledge of Content," *The Philosophical Review*, 105: 287–310.

Goldman, A. 1976, "Discrimination and Perceptual Knowledge," repr. in Goldman 1992, *Epistemic Liaisons*, Cambridge, MA: The MIT Press.

——. 1979, "What is Justified Belief," repr. in Goldman 1992, *Epistemic Liaisons*, Cambridge, MA: The MIT Press.

——. 1986, *Epistemology and Cognition*, Cambridge, MA: Harvard University Press.

——. 1988, "Strong and Weak Justification," repr. in Goldman 1992, *Epistemic Liaisons*, Cambridge, MA: The MIT Press.

——. 1992, *Epistemic Liaisons*, Cambridge, MA: The MIT Press.

——. 1999, "Internalism Exposed," *The Journal of Philosophy*, 96: 271–93.

Greco, J. (ed.) 2004, *Sosa and His Critics*, Oxford: Blackwell Publishing.

Hare, R. 1952, *The Language of Morals*, Oxford: Clarendon Press.

Harman, G. 1970, "Knowledge, Reasons and Causes," *The Journal of Philosophy*, LXVII (21): 841–55.

——. 1973, *Thought*, Princeton: Princeton University Press.

——. 1982, "Conceptual Role Semantics," *Notre Dame Journal of Formal Logic*, 23: 242–56.

——. 1986, *Change in View*, Cambridge, MA: The MIT Press.

Heal, J. 1994, "Moore's Paradox: A Wittgensteinian Solution," *Mind*, 103: 5–24.

Heck, R. 2000, "Nonconceptual Content and the 'Space of Reasons,'" *Philosophical Review*, 109 (4): 483–523.

Heil, J. 1992, *The Nature of True Minds*, Cambridge: Cambridge University Press.

Hempel, C. 1965, *Aspects of Scientific Explanation*, Free Press.

Hetherington, S. 1999, "Knowing Failably," *The Journal of Philosophy*, 96 (11): 565–87.

Hintikka, J. 1962, *Knowledge and Belief*, New York: Cornell University Press.

Horwich, P. 1998, *Meaning*, Oxford: Clarendon Press.

Kim, J. 1988, "What is Naturalized Epistemology," repr. in Kim 1993, *Supervenience and Mind*, Cambridge: Cambridge University Press.

——. 1990, "Supervenience as a Philosophical Concept," repr. in Kim 1993, *Supervenience and Mind*, Cambridge: Cambridge University Press.

——. 1993, *Supervenience and Mind*, Cambridge: Cambridge University Press.

Klagge, J. 1988, "Supervenience: Ontological and Ascriptive," *Australasian Journal of Philosophy*, 66: 461–9.

Klein, P. 1981, *Certainty*, University of Minnesota Press.

——. 1992, "Certainty," in Sosa and Dancy (eds), *A Companion to Epistemology*, Oxford: Blackwell, pp. 132–6.

——. 1995, "Skepticism and Closure: Why the Evil Genius Argument Fails," *Philosophical Topics*, 23: 213–36.

Korcz, K. 1997, "Recent Work on Basing Relation," *American Philosophical Quarterly*, 34: 171–91.

Kriegel, U. 2004, "Moore's Paradox and the Structure of Conscious Belief," *Erkenntnis*, 61: 99–121.

Kripke, S. 1982, *Wittgenstein on Rules and Private Language*, Oxford: Blackwell.

Kvanvig, J. 2004, "Nozickian Epistemology and the Value of Knowledge," *Philosophical Issues*, 14: 201–19.

Larkin, W. S. 1999, "Shoemaker on Moore's Paradox and Self-Knowledge," *Philosophical Studies*, 96: 239–52.

Lee, B. 2001, "Moore's Paradox and Self-ascribed Belief," *Erkenntnis*, 55: 359–70.

Lehrer, K. 1971, "How Reasons Give Us Knowledge, or the Case of Gypsy Lawyer," *Journal of Philosophy*, 68 (10): 311–13.

——. 1989, "Knowledge Reconsidered," in Clay and Lehrer (eds), *Knowledge and Skepticism*, Boulder: Westview.

——. 1990, *Knowledge*, London: Routledge.

——. 1995, "Supervenience, Coherence, and Trustworthiness," in Savellos (ed.), *Supervenience: New Essays*. Cambridge: Cambridge University Press.

——. 2000, "Sensitivity, Indiscernibility and Knowledge," *Philosophical Issues*, 10.

Lehrer, K. and Kim K. 1990, "The Fallibility Paradox," *Philosophy and Phenomenological Research*, 50 (Suppl): 99–107.

Leite, A. 2004, "On Justifying and Being Justified," *Epistemology. Philosophical Issues*, 14: 219–54.

LePore, E. (ed.) 1986, *Truth and Interpretation*, Oxford: Basil Blackwell.

Lewis, D. 1980, "Psychological and Theoretical Identifications," in Block (ed.), *Readings in Philosophical Psychology*, vol.1, pp. 207–16.

Ludlow, P. 1995, "Externalism, Self-knowledge and the Prevalence of Slow Switching," *Analysis*, 55: 45–9.

Markie, P. 2004, "Nondoxastic Perceptual Evidence," *Philosophy and Phenomenological Research*, LXVIII (3): 530–53.

——. 2005, "Easy Knowledge," *Philosophy and Phenomenological Research*, 70: 406–16.

——, 2006, "Epistemically Appropriate Perceptual Belief," *Nous*, 40:1.

Marr, D. 1982, *Vision*, San Francisco: W. H.Freeman.

McDowell, J. 1994, *Mind and World*, Cambridge, MA: Harvard University Press.

McGinn, C. 1982, "The Structure of Content," in Woodfield (ed.), *Thought and Object*, Oxford: Oxford University Press.

——.1984, "The Concept of Knowledge," in *Midwest Studies in Philosophy*, IX.

——. 1989, *Mental Content*, Oxford: Basil Blackwell.

McKinsey, M. 1991, "Anti-individualism and Privileged Access," *Analysis*, 51: 9–16.

McLaughlin, B. and Tye, M. 1998, "Externalism, Twin Earth, and Self-knowledge," in Wright *et al.* (eds), *Knowing Our Own Minds*, Oxford: Oxford University Press.

Millar, A. 1991, *Reason and Experience*, Oxford: Oxford University Press.

Moore, G. E. 1942, "A Reply to My Critics," in Schilpp (ed.), *The Philosophy of G. E. Moore*, pp. 543–667, Evanston: Tudor.

Moser, P. K. 1991, *Knowledge and Evidence*, New York: Cambridge University Press.

Neta, R. 2005, "A Contextualist Solution to the Problem of Easy Knowledge," *Grazer Philosophische Studien*, 69, 183–205.

Neta, R. and Bohrbaugh, G. 2004, "Luminosity and the Safety of Knowledge," *Pacific Philosophical Quarterly*, 85: 396–406.

Nozick, R. 1981, *Philosophical Explanations*, Cambridge, MA: Harvard University Press.

Owens, D. 2003, "Does Belief Have an Aim?" *Philosophical Studies* 115: 283–305.

Pagin, P. 2001, "Semantic Triangulation," in Kotakis *et al.* (eds), *Interpreting Davidson*, Stanford: CSLI, 199–212.

Pollock, J. 1986, *Contemporary Theories of Knowledge*, Lanham, MD: Rowman & Littlefield.

Pryor, J. 2000, "The Skeptic and the Dogmatist," *Nous*, 34: 517–49.

——. 2004, "What's Wrong with Moore's Argument?" *Philosophical Issues*, 14: 349–78.

——. Manuscript, "Is Moore's Argument and Example of Transmission Failure," http://www.jimpryor.net/research/papers/Moore2001.pdf

Putnam, H. 1975, "The Meaning of 'Meaning' " in *Mind, Language, and Reality: Philosophical Papers*, vol. 2, Cambridge: Cambridge University Press.

Reed, B. 2002, "How to Think of Fallibilism," *Philosophical Studies*, 107: 143–57.

Reynolds, S. 1991, "Knowing how to believe with justification," *Philosophical Studies*, 64: 273–92.

Rorty, R. 1980, *Philosophy and the Mirror of Nature*, Princeton: Princeton University Press.

Rosental, D. M. 1986, "Two Concepts of Consciousness," repr. in Block *et al.* (eds), 1997, *The Nature of Consciousness*, Cambridge, MA: The MIT Press.

Sainsbury, M. 1997, "Easy Possibilities," repr. in Sainsbury 2002, *Departing From Frege*, London: Routledge.

Sellars, W. 1963, "Some Reflections on Language Games" in *Science, Perception and Reality*, London: Routledge.

Shoemaker, S. 1963, *Self-knowledge and Self-Identity*, Ithaca: Cornell University Press.

——. 1996, "Moore's Paradox and Self-Knowledge," repr. in *The First Person Perspective and Other Essays*, pp. 74–97, Cambridge: Cambridge University Press, New York.

Silins, N. 2005, "Transmission Failure Failure," *Philosophical Studies*, 126: 71–102.

Sober, E. 1994, *From a biological point of view*, Cambridge: Cambridge University Press.

——. 2000, "Quine's Two Dogmas," *Proceedings of the Aristotelian Society*, Supplementary Volume 74.

Sorensen, R. 1988, *Blindspots*, New York: Oxford University Press.

Sosa, E. 1980, "The Foundations of Foundationalism," repr. in Sosa 1991, *Knowledge in Perspective*, Cambridge: Cambridge University Press.

——. 1991, *Knowledge in Perspective*, Cambridge: Cambridge University Press.

——. 2000, "Skepticsm and Contextualism," *Philosophical Issues*, 10: 108–16.

——. 2003, "The Place of Truth in Epistemology," in DePaul and Zagzebski (eds), *Intellectual Virtues: Perspectives From Ethics and Epistemology*, Oxford: Oxford University Press.

——. 2004, "Replies," in Greco (ed.), *Sosa and His Critics*, Oxford: Blackwell Publishing.

Stalnaker, R. 1984, *Inquiry*, Cambridge, MA: The MIT Press.

Sturgeon, S. 1993, "The Gettier Problem," *Analysis*, 53: 156–64.

Summerfield, D. 1991, "Modest A Priori Knowledge," *Philosophy and Phenomenological Research*, LI (1): 39–66.

Swain, M. 1979, "Justification and the Basis of Belief," in Pappas (ed.), 1981, *Reasons and Knowledge*. Ithaca: Cornell University Press.

Tolliver, J. 1981, "Basing Beliefs on Reasons," *Grazer Philosophische Studien*, 15: 149–61.

Tomberlin, J. 1980, "Critical Review of Carl Ginet's *Knowledge, Perception, and Memory*," *Nous*, 14: 157–70.

Vahid, H. 1999, "A Priori Knowledge, Experience and Defeasibility," *International Journal of Philosophical Studies*, 7 (2): 173–88.

———. 2001, "Realism and the Epistemological Significance of Inference to the Best Explanation," *Dialogue*, XL: 487–507.

———. 2003, "Content Externalism and the Internalism/Externalism Debate in Justification Theory," *European Journal of Philosophy*, 11 (1): 89–107.

———. 2005, "Moore's paradox and Evans's principle: a reply to Williams," *Analysis* 65: 337–41.

Van Cleve, J. 1985, "Epistemic Supervenience and the Circle of Belief," *The Monist*, 68: 90–104.

Velleman, D. 2000, "On the Aim of Belief," in *The Possibility of Practical Reason*, Oxford: Oxford University Press.

Vogel, J. 1987, "Tracking, Closure, and inductive Knowledge," in Luper-Foy (ed.), *The Possibility of Knowledge*, Rowman and Littlefield.

———. 2000, "Reliabilism Levelled," *Journal of Philosophy*, 97: 602–23.

Warfield, T. 1992, "Privileged Self-knowledge and Externalism are Compatible," *Analysis*, 52: 232–7.

Wedgwood, R. 2002, "The Aim of Belief," *Philosophical Perspectives*, 16: 267–97.

Williams, B. 1973, "Deciding to Believe" in Williams, *Problems of the Self*, Cambridge University Press.

Williams, J. N. 1994, "Moorean Absurdity and the Intentional 'Structure' of Assertion," *Analysis*, 54: 160–6.

———. 1998, "Wittgensteinian Accounts of Moorean Absurdity," *Philosophical Studies*, 92: 288–306.

———. 2004, "Moore's Paradox, Evans's Principle and Self-Knowledge," *Analysis*, 64 (4): 348–53.

———. 2006, "In Defence of an Argument for Evans's Principle: A Rejoinder to Vahid," *Analysis*, 66, 2: 167–71.

Williamson, T. 2000, *Knowledge and its Limits*, Oxford: Oxford University Press.

Wittgenstein, L. 1953, *Philosophical Investigations*, Basil Blackwell, Oxford.

Wright, C. 2002, "(Anti)-Sceptics Simple and Subtle: Moore and McDowell," *Philosophy and Phenomenological Research*, 65: 330–48.

———. 2003, "Some Reflections on the Acquisition of Warrant by Inference," in Nuccetelli (ed.), *New Essays on Semantic Externalism and Self-knowledge*," Cambridge, MA: The MIT Press.

———. 2004, "Warrant for Nothing (And Foundations for Free?)," *Aristotelian Society Supplementary Volume*, 78: 167–212.

Index

Notes are cited using the following format: *page number* (xx) *chapter number* (Ch.xx) *note number* (n.xx): Example. 300 Ch.10n.1.